The IDEOLOGIES of the
DEVELOPING NATIONS

The IDEOLOGIES of the DEVELOPING NATIONS

Edited and with an Introduction by
PAUL E. SIGMUND, Jr.

Foreword by
Reinhold Niebuhr

FREDERICK A. PRAEGER, *Publisher*

New York · London

Published in the United States of America in 1963
by Frederick A. Praeger, Inc., Publisher
64 University Place, New York 3, N.Y.

Published in the United Kingdom in 1963
by Frederick A. Praeger, Inc., Publisher
49 Great Ormond Street, London WC 1

© 1963 by Frederick A. Praeger, Inc.

Library of Congress Catalog Card Number: 63-10263

THE IDEOLOGIES OF THE DEVELOPING NATIONS
is published in two editions:

A paperback edition (U-529)
A clothbound edition

Printed in the United States of America

FOREWORD

Paul Sigmund has performed an invaluable service in providing for the students of current global politics an anthology of the political theories and ideologies of the leaders of the emerging nations of the world. These nations, located in such disparate regions and continents as Latin America, Africa, the Middle East, and Southeast Asia, are revealed in Mr. Sigmund's study to be animated by two similar passions, which they express in their dissimilar policies. They are interested in gaining or consolidating their integral nationhood against a background of previous subservience to a dominant power; and they are anxious to achieve technical competence and triumph over the poverty to which they were subjected in their either primitive or traditional economies.

It is important for the political observers of the Western world to note what attracts these nations to, and what repels them from, the democratic theories and practices of Western culture, and what affinities, if any, they have with the collectivism of the Communist world. The revelations of Mr. Sigmund's study about the differences among the conservative, moderate, and radical political leaders of these nations—differences that express themselves across the boundaries of their several regions—will be instructive to all students of the present contest between democracy and Communism.

It is important to know what motives prompt the general desire to remain neutral in the contest, why the new nations are more inclined to a one-party system than to a two-party or multiparty democracy as we know it in the West, why the leaders have invented various amendments to what we regard as pure democracy, and what promises and perils inhere in these adjustments. It is equally important to know how the principle of national federation—an issue in most of the emerging nations—may become, on the one hand, a safeguard against despotism and, on the other, a peril to national integrity.

In addition to its obvious usefulness, this study has the merit of being an extremely interesting display of the similarities and differences in the policies and moods of the leaders of the emerging nations. Their names appear daily in our public press. It is fascinating to learn how much an African leader may agree with one in Asia or Latin America, yet disagree with another leader in his own continent.

At a time when we are slowly—all too slowly—accustoming ourselves both to the extent of our power and responsibility in the world and to the undoubtedly long duration of our burdens, such a wise and perceptive analysis of the factors, forces, and personalities we encounter in the world will be invaluable to the American people.

—REINHOLD NIEBUHR

Stockbridge, Mass.
June, 1962

CONTENTS

ACKNOWLEDGMENTS

Permission to use copyrighted material has been acknowledged in footnotes at the beginning of each selection. My thanks are also due the following for providing me with relevant publications: The Embassy of the Republic of Tunisia, Washington, D.C.; The Supreme Council of Revolutionary Youth, Cairo, Egypt; *La Jeunesse du Rassemblement Démocratique Africain*, Conakry, Guinea; Chukumwa Azikiwe; The Delegation of Cuba to the United Nations; and Ramón Yllarramendy. My grateful appreciation also goes to Dr. Reinhold Niebuhr, for whose course at Harvard University many of these readings were collected; to Professor Rupert Emerson, for his constructive criticism of my Introduction; to my colleagues at Harvard, whose collective expertise supplied deficiencies in my own knowledge; to Mrs. Alfred G. Tottey, Jr., for her expert secretarial assistance; to Arnold Dolin, for his editorial work; and to the students and youth of the developing areas with whom I have been associated in various collective enterprises during the last decade—and to whom this book is dedicated.

—P. E. S.

Cambridge, Mass.
November, 1962

The IDEOLOGIES of the DEVELOPING NATIONS

do pol theorists have their problems imposed
upon them by

    c — Self-determination

a. Must we be convinced of the universality of
our own ideology?

INTRODUCTION

The dictionary defines "ideology" as "a systematic scheme or co-ordinated body of ideas about human life or culture"—a definition that seems to equate ideology with philosophy or social theory. In common usage, however, the word has additional connotations —of commitment (both emotional and intellectual), of action-orientation (the maintenance of the *status quo*, which may be the goal of conservative ideologies, is itself an action), and even of conscious or unconscious distortion of the facts to fit a pre-established doctrine.[1] The period from the seventeenth century to the nineteenth century in Europe has been described as the "age of ideology," for it saw an extraordinary outpouring of theories about the nature of man in relation to the present or future state of society. It was also a period of political, economic, and social revolution, in which the traditional order of medieval Europe gave way to a modern industrial society and men became conscious of the variety of alternative paths open to them in their own personal lives, in their religious, philosophical, and political creeds, and in the ordering of society.

This crisis of modernization has now affected large areas of Asia, Africa, the Middle East, and Latin America. What is often described as the "anticolonial revolution" is more than an attempt to assert political autonomy and to end European domination. It is also a social and economic revolution brought about by the attempt of the members of a Westernized elite to bring their countries into the modern world, to create modern states and industrialized economies where traditional cultures and subsistence production had predominated.

The fact that, in addition to its anticolonial character, this is a revolution of modernization makes it possible to consider Latin

[1] This is the sense in which it is used by Karl Mannheim when he defines ideologies as "more or less conscious disguises of the real nature of the situation." (*Ideology and Utopia* [New York: Harcourt, Brace & Co., 1954], p. 49.)

3

America, which has been politically independent for 130 years, in the same category as nations that have only recently received their independence. The leaders of the old nations of Latin America and of the new nations in other parts of the world are experiencing similar problems of economic development and social change, and are often developing similar solutions to them.

To explain to themselves and to others the nature and justification of the changes they wish to induce, the nationalist leaders have been compelled to give more specific content to the general goal of development to which they all subscribe. In doing this, they have been able to draw upon ideologies developed earlier in Europe. Especially in Latin America, the ideologies of the period of early industrialism in Europe have been adapted to fit an analogous situation in nations now experiencing the problems associated with modern development. Yet, if one takes a broader view of the developing areas as a whole, there is a notable absence of the conflict of ideologies that has characterized European political life during the last century. As recent debates in the United Nations have demonstrated, the leaders of the group of nations variously described as "new," "uncommitted," "emerging," or "developing" share many political, economic, and social ideas as to the type of society they are building. Although they may differ regarding the appropriate methods for reaching their goals, these leaders (with the exception of those in the most backward and tradition-bound areas) are united by a group of beliefs that give expression to common feelings about the past, present, and future.

These beliefs correspond to our definition of ideology in that they elicit an emotional commitment by the leadership and their followers and are directed toward action—the development of a new society in a certain direction, in conformity with certain goals. However, the doctrines of modernizing nationalism do not have the all-encompassing quality of the great ideological world-systems of Marxism, Christianity, or utilitarian liberalism, although they may coincide in some respects with one or another element in these ideologies. They are held by leaders with a wide variety of religious and philosophical outlooks, or with no particular metaphysical presuppositions. The particular problems of individual states also vary in accordance with their special situations. Yet, all the developing nations are undergoing the same general experience, and their reactions to it are similar in theoretical content and practical application. To determine whether these goals, aspirations, and doctrines—given their eclectic character and practical orientation—can be systematically organized in a way that would qualify them as an alternative ideology to current political creeds, it is necessary to give more detailed consideration to the specific content of the doctrines of modernizing nationalism.

National Independence and Freedom

A basic principle of the nationalist leaders has already been mentioned—the absolute primacy of the goal of national development. Since development takes place within the framework of the nation-state, whether it is in existence or in the process of being created, national independence is the first step on the road to development. As the inscription on Kwame Nkrumah's statue in Accra reads, "Seek ye first the political kingdom and all other things shall be added unto it." It is as a prerequisite to development that the nationalist leaders demand freedom. However, this freedom refers to *national* rather than individual liberty. It is the assertion of the right of the nation to self-direction and independence of foreign domination. Freedom is demanded for "the people," not for the individual.[2]

It is sometimes difficult to determine exactly what constitutes the nation that ought to be free. In Africa, and to some extent in the Middle East, where movements for regional unification are strong, there has been some ambivalence about national boundaries as they were imposed by the Europeans. However, on the whole, the existing divisions seem to be accepted as the basis from which to work. Except where the alteration of the frontier involves the elimination of a colonial enclave, as in Goa or Dutch New Guinea, the existing boundaries are accepted, and it is felt that they may only be changed by the free consent of the governments involved.

The meaning of the term "the people" is also in need of clarification. Independence, freedom, and development are asserted as goals in the name of the people. It is the authority of the people that gives legitimacy to anticolonial revolutions and post-independence governments. Yet, there is always a certain amount of

[2] "We have chosen the freedom, the right, the power, the sovereignty of the people, and not of the individual. Before this people you should have no individual personality. Our personality becomes part of the personality of the nation." (Sékou Touré, quoted in *West Africa*, July 22, 1961, p. 799.)

elitism mixed with the "populism" of the nationalist leadership.[3] Before independence, it was assumed without any need of proof that the people desired to be liberated from colonialism. Yet, after independence, a massive political education program often must be carried on to assure that the popular will actually corresponds to the conception of it in the theory of the nationalist leadership.

The Creation of Modern Nationalism

There are difficulties in determining what constitutes "the nation" or "the people" because in many cases neither entity really exists. A sense of nationhood and loyalty to the people as a collective entity must first be created to replace or supplement other allegiances based on traditional or hierarchical status differentiations. In Max Weber's terms, the transition must be made from a "traditional" to a "rational-legal" order.[4]

Westerners are familiar with the organic process by which European society was transformed from a largely traditional and agrarian, even tribal, social organization into the modern, rationalized, and institutionalized nation-state. European economic development, new organizational and scientific techniques, and the new political ideas drawn from the classical and Christian heritage of the late Middle Ages resulted in the radical change of ways of living and ways of thinking about life associated with the emergence of modern industrial civilization. Powerful ideological justifications for status differentiation, hereditary privilege, and hierarchical social organization were developed in Europe between the twelfth and the nineteenth century, and enclaves of traditionalism still remain. However, the overwhelming power of the nationalist and equalitarian ideology has either overcome other loyalties in the West or, alternatively, achieved a kind of coexistence with them which has permitted the integration of diverse ethnic, religious, and social groupings within a pluralistic consensus in the modern

[3] "He [the intellectual] looks up to the people and down on the masses." (Mary Matossian, "Ideologies of Delayed Industrialization," in John Kautsky [ed.], *Political Change in Underdeveloped Countries* [New York: John Wiley & Sons, 1962], p. 262.) On the "populism" of the nationalist leaders in relation to similar phenomena in Germany, Russia, and America, see the discussion by Edward Shils in the same collection (especially pp. 214–15).

[4] David Apter has used these categories in his analysis of the creation of a new nation, in *The Gold Coast in Transition* (Princeton, N.J.: Princeton University Press, 1955).

nation-state. In most Western countries, the organic development of national unity over the centuries has created a sense of common purpose and civic responsibility, and led to a rationalization and legalization of the structure of authority.[5]

The creation of loyalty to the nation and the emergence of the nation as a functional community is now under way in many of the new states. Differences of caste, tribe, clan, or religion must be integrated into the political process, and it is precisely because they loom so large as an obstacle to the creation of the modern nation-state that the leaders place great emphasis on the primacy of "the nation" and the elimination of traditional status differentiations.[6] In nationalist thinking, there is a recognition of the need for the creation of a broader community on a regional and international level, but the first requirement is the implementation of the common ideal of universal participation in the nation. The recent experience of the Congo, India's continuing problem with communalism, earlier difficulties with Ashanti regionalism in Ghana, and differences between the various regions of Nigeria are all examples of the fissiparous tendencies against which the new nation-builders must work.

In dealing with the problem of the creation of a new society and a new center of loyalty and faith, the leaders of Asia, Africa, Latin America, and the Middle East have taken three different positions. First, there remain the traditionalists or conservatives like King Saud of Saudi Arabia, the tribal leaders of Africa, or dictators like Stroessner of Paraguay. Such leaders try to preserve the existing oligarchic order, and view the disruptive forces of modernization as a threat to their maintenance of power (as indeed they are). Yet, they cannot avoid being drawn into the world-wide

[5] The divisions, traditional-modern or traditional-rational-legal, are not absolute. There are no completely "modern" systems, and, conversely, modern elements can be perceived in many traditional political cultures. (Cf. discussion in Gabriel Almond and James S. Coleman, *The Politics of the Developing Areas* [Princeton, N.J.: Princeton University Press, 1960], p. 11.)

[6] "In three or four years, no one will remember the tribal, ethnic, and religious differences which have caused so much difficulty to the country and people in the recent past. . . . We are for a united people, a unitary state at the service of an indivisible nation." (Sékou Touré, *La Lutte du Parti Démocratique de Guinée pour l'Emancipation Africaine* [Conakry: Imprimerie Nationale, 1959], pp. 58, 149.) Cf. Thomas Hodgkin, "A Note on the Language of African Nationalism," *African Affairs* (Carbondale, Ill.), No. 1 (1961), pp. 22–40.

technological revolution, with all its subversive social and political consequences. In order to justify their positions, these leaders may appeal to religious beliefs, custom, or the requirements of order and stability but the attraction of modernization to the educated elite makes it difficult for their regimes to compete for support. The second category of leaders comprises those who wish to strike a balance between the maintenance of traditional structures and the radical transformation of society as a whole. One thinks of such diverse figures as Gandhi, Ayub Khan, Léopold Senghor, or Joseph Kasavubu as typical of the reforming elite who wish to integrate and utilize the traditional loyalties and hierarchical groupings in the formation of a new nation, creating a synthesis of the old and the new. Finally, there is the third group, which, while not necessarily aiming at the destruction of traditional groups, wishes to eliminate them from political influence and power as obstacles to the process of social and political transformation.[7] The radical modernizers see no rational basis for status differentiations not based on political or economic function, and they are willing to use persuasion, propaganda, monolithic political parties, and sometimes force as well to bring about the new community.

While the first does no more than pay occasional lip service to the ideals of modernization, the other two types of ruling elite accept them completely. Neither the reformers nor the radicals wish to wait for organic development to bring their societies into the modern world. However, the two groups differ significantly on methods. And this particular difference has already made its impact in Africa in the Casablanca-Monrovia split; in Latin America in the profound division between Fidelist movements and reformist leaders like Betancourt, Figueres, and Haya de la Torre; and in Asia, where the Chinese revolution provides a Communist model of forced economic development that contrasts with the more gradual and democratic approach of India.

This is not to assert that there are not profound differences

[7] A similar but somewhat misleading distinction between "revolutionary" and "radical-reformist" Pan-Africanists is made by Colin Legum, in *Pan-Africanism* (New York: Frederick A. Praeger, 1962), pp. 62–64. Cf. also David Apter's distinction between "mobilization" and "consociational" regimes, in *The Political Kingdom of Uganda* (Princeton, N.J.: Princeton University Press, 1961), pp. 4–5; and the division into neotraditional, transitional, and actively modernizing oligarchies, in Max F. Millikan and Donald L. M. Blackmer, *The Emerging Nations* (Boston: Little, Brown & Co., 1961), pp. 79–88.

among the various representatives of both the radical and the reformist wings of the modernizing elite. To identify Sékou Touré's approach to social change with that of Fidel Castro, or Nehru's with that of Houphouet-Boigny or Haya de la Torre, is to ignore the diversity of national situations and of the solutions proposed. The division into traditionalists, reformers, and radicals is based on general similarities of attitude toward social, political, and economic change, within which there are considerable differences. However, it provides a more useful analytical tool than classifications reflecting European ideological categories or distinctions derived from the East-West conflict which are not related to the problems of modernization and development.

A National System of Education

Both the radicals and the reformers recognize the key role of education in nation-building. They criticize the unrealistic content and limited scope of the colonial educational systems, which reflected the standards and the needs of the metropoles and were often unrelated to local conditions and requirements. A system geared solely to the training of a few civil servants, teachers, and lawyers is not considered adequate for a nation undergoing an economic and social revolution. One of the first steps after independence, therefore, has been an increase in the number of primary and secondary schools and of universities and technical schools, as well as a reform of the content of education to meet the need for skilled and semiskilled personnel.

On a basic level, the problem of illiteracy is being attacked by massive programs of primary education, often with considerable political content. The literacy campaigns carried out by Fidel Castro in Cuba and by Sékou Touré in Guinea have demonstrated that an organized program can virtually eradicate this problem in a short time and can also be useful in building political loyalty. The illiterate masses who have had little or no relation to national politics are educated to read the party literature and to become aware of national and international problems from the party point of view.

It is not only the radical or revolutionary regimes that put a high priority on basic education and political indoctrination. All the modernizing nationalists recognize that the educational system can be used to develop loyalty to the nation—and to the party, often considered to be synonymous with the nation. The line between education for citizenship and political indoctrination is a thin one (as indeed it often is in the developed countries) but the modernizing nationalists universally accept the need for a high political content in education.

Because of both the political significance of education and its importance in developing the various levels of trained cadres required for economic development, the nationalist program usually calls for centrally planned control and development of the school system. Since education in many of the new nations had been carried out by missionary groups or under private auspices, there is a potential (and, in a few cases, actual) conflict between these groups and the nationalist leaders, who desire a "national" educational system. These tensions are aggravated by the accusation of radical nationalists (often themselves the products of mission schools) that missionary education is an instrument of colonial domination aimed at producing a subservient colonial mentality among the students. In some cases, this may lead to conflicts recalling the church-state struggles of Europe in the nineteenth and early twentieth centuries, while in others, a working adjustment may be worked out with a mutual recognition of the rights of private groups and the requirements of the new nations.

With national control of education, the curriculum is being altered to emphasize national history, culture, and politics. In Africa, where the Pan-African ideology is strong, there is also an increasing emphasis on the cultural heritage of the African peoples and their distinctive contributions to civilization (see discussion below of the "African personality").

Another aspect of the nationalist revolution as it affects education is the desire to develop a native teaching staff and reduce dependence on foreign teaching personnel. A number of African countries, for instance, are drawing up long-range programs of "Africanization" of education, but the expansion of education and the opening of other career opportunities for educated Africans make it likely that there will be a continued teacher shortage, despite the increase in teacher-training programs that has followed independence.

At the university level, a rapid development of educational facilities is also taking place, along with a shift of emphasis away from the humanistic bias of the colonial university and in the direction of technical subjects. The new University of Nsukka in Nigeria, sponsored by an American land-grant state university, is attempting to carry out this reorientation of the curriculum with emphasis on agriculture and technology rather than the classical subjects of the British university. In Guinea, a planned program for the development of technicians involves sending large numbers of students abroad to study technical subjects in both Eastern and Western countries. These efforts are aimed at producing native cadres who can carry out programs of national development, for education is a means to nation-building, not only in the sense of the creation of nationhood but also as a prerequisite of economic progress.

Economic Development Through "Socialist" Methods

When the nationalist leaders speak of the "development" of the nation, they are speaking primarily of *economic* development. The leadership and members of nationalist movements are acutely aware of the galling contrast between the poverty, illiteracy, and disease of their own countries and the affluence of the economically developed areas. For them, the crucial division in the world is not between the rival political faiths of Communism and liberal democracy, but between the rich and the poor, the economically developed and the underdeveloped, the technically competent and the technologically "backward" areas of the world. The key to the eradication of this difference in living standards lies in economic development, and more particularly in industrialization. With development and industrialization, it will be possible to achieve social equality, educational opportunity, and minimum standards of health and sanitation—in short, the modern welfare state. Without it, population growth and the "revolution of rising expectations" will bring about increasing suffering, political frustration, and social discontent.

Nationalist thinking has given less attention to the need for agricultural development than to the requirements of industrialization, although the present agricultural difficulties of the Soviet Union and China are an indication of the importance of the balanced development of the agricultural sector of the economy. A steel mill is a more dramatic symbol of economic development and national prestige than is a bag of fertilizer, and it seems to promise a much more immediate effect on economic growth. Moreover, agriculture is involved too closely with their former colonial status as a source of primary products to engender much enthusiasm among nationalist leaders.

In their drive toward industrialization, the modernizing nationalists are not prepared to follow the model of the United States, the European nations, or Japan, each of which achieved economic development under private auspices. The nationalist leaders, with the exception of some Latin Americans, are in agreement in rejecting the capitalist method of development as slow, inefficient, and unsuited to their conditions. It is their view that rapid economic growth can only be attained by "socialist" methods, although the precise meaning of this socialism is rarely defined in detail.

Capitalism is rejected and socialism preferred for moral as well as economic reasons. The socialism of the developing nations is said to be directed at the establishment of a society based on justice rather than profit, rational planning rather than the blind operation of the market, and forced economic growth and industrialization as opposed to the orientation of the economy to the production of raw materials for the profit of foreign enterprises. These goals are accepted by nearly all the leaders of Asia, Africa, Latin America, and the Middle East, although their implementation is not as commonly agreed upon or even understood.

Since the Soviet bloc describes itself as the "camp of socialism" or the "socialist countries,"[8] there is the appearance of similarity between Communist goals and methods and those of the emerging nations. Yet, while there is no denying the appeal of the Soviet example of economic development, to equate the two positions is to ignore a fundamental and recurring feature in the ideology of modernizing nationalism—its attempt to establish a separate identity in an intermediate position between East and West. The nationalist leaders insist that they are forging a new approach to economic development that avoids the errors of both capitalism and Communism. Whether it is the "democratic collectivism" of Nehru, the "African socialism" of Senghor, the "communitarianism" of Nyerere, the "communocracy" of Sékou Touré, or the "democratic, socialist, cooperative democracy" of Nasser, there is a common commitment to a new form of development that will allow planning and central control of the economy while continuing to permit some measure of private initiative. At the same time that these theories denounce a stereotyped

[8] Even Julius Nyerere speaks of the Communist countries as the "socialist bloc" in "Nationalism and Pan-Africanism" (see below, p. 206).

capitalism for its excessive individualism, its lack of concern with human and social values, and its fostering of the spirit of ruthless competition, they also criticize a stereotyped Communism for its excessive collectivism, its suppression of the individual, its materialism, and its narrow commitment to the national interest of a single country or group of countries.

Because of the intimate involvement of capitalism in the colonial enterprise, the criticisms of capitalism often seem considerably harsher than those of Communism. Even native capitalists are linked to the colonial rulers in nationalist theory. Capitalists are concerned only with profit, the argument goes, and they are willing to collaborate with those who have financial control—in the case of the colonial countries, with the foreign rulers. They are not concerned with the welfare of the people, with national independence, or with economic development—but only with the maximization of their profits (usually lodged in foreign banks).

This is an accurate description of the conduct of certain business leaders in the underdeveloped countries, but it ignores the contributions—financial, intellectual, and political—that others have made to the nationalist cause. In addition, even if the businessman is acting merely out of his own economic interest, independence may be more to his immediate benefit than foreign rule. It can give him a protected market, a government subsidy, and restrictions against foreign competition. Some of the strongest support for economic nationalism and "anti-imperialism" in Latin America, for instance, comes from the domestic business interests, and the Congress Party in India received heavy financial assistance from Indian business leaders throughout its long struggle with the British. In Africa as well, native businessmen have been deeply involved with nationalist parties.

Capitalism also suffers from its association with the evils of colonialism, described in the Leninist theory of imperialism. The theory of imperialism that has achieved the status of "conventional wisdom" among the nationalist leaders does not emphasize, as did Lenin, the importance of finance monopoly and finance capital in generating the need for overseas investment opportunities. The nationalists accept the more general Marxist theory that, because of increased production costs and their inability to dispose of consumption goods, the colonial countries seek a cheap source of raw materials and a market for their products.[9] It is the nature of capitalism to seek to maximize profits, the argument goes, and colonial domination assures the capitalists of a protected market from which all competition is excluded, and it maintains the colony in a permanent state of underdevelopment, so that wages will remain low and raw materials cheap.[10]

The part of the Leninist theory with the greatest appeal to nationalist thinking is Lenin's argument that the continued success of capitalism in advanced countries is based on capitalist bribes to the workers from the fruits of colonial exploitation. In nationalist thinking, Lenin's theory is transformed from an ideological justification of Marxist predictions into a burning indictment of the evils of colonial oppression. If the prosperity of the advanced nations is grounded on the exploitation of colonies, then foreign aid, for instance, is not an act of generosity or of mutual interest. It is either an attempt to maintain continued economic control or, alternatively, a meager effort to restore to Africa (or Latin America or the Middle East) the riches stolen during centuries of imperialist exploitation.[11] (The fact that countries such as Sweden have attained a high level of prosperity without colonies—demonstrating that the prosperity of the advanced nations depends on something more than colonies and cheap raw materials—is not considered, for the theory is not so much an argument as a rationalization or ideological justification for needed economic assistance from the West.)

The nationalists' suspicion of the economic influence of the

[9] The Senegalese nationalist leader Abdoulaye Ly attributes this theory to Rosa Luxemburg; quoted in Hodgkin, *op. cit.*, p. 32. However, the link between overproduction and the need for foreign markets is a commonplace of Marxist theory.

[10] "The economy of European nations consists fundamentally of selling manufactured products at high prices and buying raw materials from them at the lowest possible cost." (Léopold Sédar Senghor, *African Socialism*; see below, p. 242.)

"Human greed . . . stimulated a search for territories from which raw materials could be obtained cheaply and plentifully. After the raw materials had been processed into manufactured goods, it became necessary again to look for markets which would be under their control, so that the manufactured goods could be sold at prices to suit them." (U Nu, *Toward a Socialist State*; see below, p. 64.)

[11] "The states with a colonialist past are, more than others, compelled to offer to other nations aspiring to development part of the national wealth they sapped when that wealth was booty for all looters." (Nasser, "Arab Socialism"; see below, p. 135.)

West is expressed in their theory of "neocolonialism." As developed by the radical nationalists, but also given wide credence among the more moderate group, this theory asserts that although political independence has been achieved, there are still links of economic dependence that vitiate the apparent autonomy of the new nations. The wealthy nations wish to exploit the proletarian nations in order to keep them poor and underdeveloped, as well as politically favorable to the policies of the "neocolonialist" powers. Proponents of the theory cite the powerful influence of the United States in Latin America, politically independent since the early nineteenth century, demonstrated by the unanimity with which (before the rise of Castro) the Latin American nations followed U.S. policy in the United Nations. They note that the new states of French-speaking Africa that are most dependent economically on France consistently supported the French position on the Algerian question in the United Nations, despite the unanimity of African support for the rebel nationalists. The division of Africa into two general groupings—and more particularly into many small and economically nonviable states (described as "Balkanization")—is seen as an effort both to maintain political influence and to assure economic domination and the maintenance of profits.[12] Above all, the events following the independence of the Congo, the secession of Katanga and the murder of Lumumba, have appeared to confirm the belief in the sinister machinations of international capitalist interests.

The extent to which these events are attributed exclusively to economic factors is a measure of the impact of Marxist theories of causation on the thinking of many of the leaders of emergent nationalism. To explain colonialism and the politics of the postcolonial era solely in terms of economic domination is simple and intellectually satisfying; moreover, it often seems to fit the facts. On this basis, colonial domination and imperialism are the result of capitalism, and the Western "capitalist" nations are necessarily imperialistic, while the Communist states, lacking an economic motive for imperialist expansion, are exempt from this criticism.[13]

[12] See, for example, the resolutions on neocolonialism adopted at the All-African Peoples' Conference, Cairo, March 23–31, 1961, in Legum, *op. cit.*, pp. 254–57.
[13] "Imperialism and its twin sister, capitalism, are by their very nature and content the main causes of wars." (Kofi Baako, "Nkrumaism—Its Theory and Practice"; see below, p. 191.)

Yet, many nationalist leaders recognize that the Leninist theory is inadequate. They perceive that colonial domination and post-colonial attempts to retain control and influence are the products of the rivalries of powerful nations, which will inevitably attempt to draw weak nations into their spheres of influence.[14] While the economic motive is a factor in the assessment of the conduct of the "capitalist" West, *all* powerful nations, whatever their economic system, are regarded as potentially imperialistic. This alternative theory of imperialism is quite compatible with the neutralist orientation of the nationalists. It applies to the Soviet Union as much as to the West—and, taking into account the lack of restraints on power in the U.S.S.R., with an even greater validity. Yet, those who give greater emphasis to power politics as an explanation of imperialism have experienced only Western imperialism and hence are likely to continue to direct their criticisms principally at the West. Imperialism usually means Western "capitalist" imperialism, and Soviet imperialism is only rarely criticized.[15]

In the stereotype of the nationalist ideology, both the domestic capitalists and the "international imperialists" are associated in their common desire to control the political process so as to assure that it does not interfere with their economic interests. The domestic capitalists are the "stooges" of the international exploiters. Together with the feudal aristocracy and traditional ruling classes, they form the controlling "oligarchy" whose power, supported by foreign interests, must be broken by the nationalist leaders.[16]

[14] Nyerere speaks of the two "power blocs" using the slogans of anti-Communism and anti-imperialism in a "second scramble for Africa." ("Nationalism and Pan-Africanism"; see below, p. 209.) Nasser also warns that both sides in the Cold War are trying to draw the U.A.R. into a "zone of influence." ("The National Union Party"; see below, p. 128.) See also Reinhold Niebuhr, "The Relation of Strength to Weakness in the World Community," in Laurence W. Martin (ed.), *Neutralism and Nonalignment* (New York: Frederick A. Praeger, 1962), pp. 196–98.

[15] Archbishop Makarios of Cyprus was the only leader at the Belgrade Conference in September, 1961, to take a strong stand on Berlin and on the Soviet resumption of nuclear tests.

[16] Cf. Nasser, "Principles of Socialist, Cooperative Democracy," *Egyptian Economic and Political Review*, September–October, 1961, p. 23, in which he denounces "the inherited social system dominated by the imperialists and their stooges, feudalists, and capitalists." On the role of the "oligarchy" in Latin America, see Romulo Betancourt, "Democracy in Venezuela" (below, p. 301). In Africa, the terms "Uncle Tom" and "Quisling" are used to the same effect. (Cf. Hodgkin, *op. cit.*, p. 29.)

Here economic and political objectives join with the equalitari-
anism of nationalist social thought in the demand for the elimination of economic differences in the new "socialist" society being
built. The prejudice against both domestic and foreign capitalism
is not only based on the narrow concern of the capitalists with the
maximization of profits and their supposed opposition to economic
development in the emerging nations. It is also derived from a
view of capitalist society as one that is essentially based on social
and economic inequality. Contrasted with the passionate concern
of the nationalist leaders to eliminate inequality and to develop
economically, the wealthy nations are seen as conspiring with the
wealthy classes in the poor nations to maintain poverty, illiteracy,
and underdevelopment.

The "socialism" of the new nations is thus fed by antiforeign
feelings, by a passion for social equality, and by a desire for rapid
economic development. It is influenced by the Marxist analysis
of capitalism and the Leninist description of imperialism, but it
does not accept the entire Marxist-Leninist theory as the basis of
action. It is a *nationalist* socialism, and therefore it rejects the
Marxist-Leninist theory of the class struggle, at least as applied
to internal economic relations. The working men (and, more important, the peasants) *do* have a country—despite Marx's assertion to the contrary—and the unity of the people in building the
nation requires that the nationalist leader play down the special
interests of any one class, including the proletariat. The African
leaders who are most influenced by Marxism assert that Africa is
now a classless society and therefore is not subject to the contradictions of the Marxist class struggle.[17]

In addition, it is a *humanist* socialism and therefore opposed to
Marxist materialism. The nationalist leaders—whether Nasser,
Nkrumah, or Senghor—insist that there is no opposition between
their socialism and spiritual or religious values.[18] In fact, they

[17] "[The African] rejects the class struggle because of African social groups'
identity of living conditions and lack of differentiation into antagonistic
classes." (Sékou Touré, quoted in Legum, *op. cit.*, pp. 128–29.) Nasser, in his
speech to the National Congress of Popular Forces, on May 21, 1962, specifically ruled out the class struggle as part of "Arab socialism" (see below,
p. 131).

[18] "Islam in its early days was the first socialist state." (Nasser, "Principles
of Socialist, Cooperative Democracy," p. 27.)

"Today I am a nondenominational Christian and a Marxist socialist, and assert that their socialism is more in accord with religious and moral norms than the *laissez-faire* capitalism they reject.

It is also a socialism *planned by an elite*. If socialism means participation by the worker in the process of economic planning, there seems to be little evidence of thinking in this direction in the writings or speeches of these nationalists. Although Nasser speaks of his socialism as "cooperative," and although there may be admiration and imitation of the Yugoslav system of workers' councils, there does not seem to be any real intention in the new nations (any more than there is in Yugoslavia) of allowing important economic decisions to be made democratically or as the result of any but the most superficial public discussion. Even in the developed countries, only the general lines of economic policy are decided on by popular consultation. Still more in the case of the developing nations, economists of a wide variety of political and economic beliefs accept the need for a rationalized development through expert planning.[19] When the Kennedy Administration reorganized the U.S. foreign-aid program in the Agency for International Development (AID) in 1961, it indicated that greater U.S. assistance would be forthcoming to those countries presenting an integrated program or plan of economic development. It recognized that in countries where the per capita income is under $100 a year (and this applies to areas containing 50 per cent of the world's population),[20] the transition from traditional and subsistence economies to an expanding and developing dynamic economic system must be made by government planning, whether it is described as socialism or not.

The socialism of the modernizing nationalists often involves

I have not found any contradiction between the two." (Nkrumah, *Ghana: The Autobiography of Kwame Nkrumah* [New York: Thomas Nelson and Sons, 1957], p. 13.)

"We stand for a middle course, for a *democratic socialism* which goes so far as to integrate spiritual values, a socialism which ties in with the old ethical current of the French socialists." (Senghor, *African Socialism*; see below, p. 244.)

[19] Latin American criticisms of development through state planning are the exception. (Summarized in Albert O. Hirschman, "Ideologies of Economic Development in Latin America," in Albert O. Hirschman [ed.], *Latin American Issues, Essays and Comments* [New York: The Twentieth Century Fund, 1961], pp. 23 ff.)

[20] See Millikan and Blackmer, *op. cit.*, pp. 149–59.

some measure of nationalization. The ideology of the nationalist leaders leads them to regard nationalization as a preferred means of assuring national control and direction of economic development. In addition—as was made clear in Nasser's speech of July 22, 1961, when he nationalized major industries and confiscated the holdings of the wealthiest Egyptians—nationalization is considered useful as a measure to bring about social equality and eliminate hostile foreign influences (the alliance of domestic capitalists with former colonial rulers or foreign capitalist interests). Problems may be created, however, if ideological preconceptions interfere with a realistic assessment of the best method to achieve the goal of maximum economic growth. Guinea, for instance, has already been forced to dismantle its State Trading Commission, through which it attempted to nationalize all import and export activity and to control most of the distribution of goods. The Guineans learned that it was difficult, if not impossible, to centralize in a government bureau in Conakry all the countless decisions involved in distribution; while retaining a centralized development plan, they have now substantially decentralized decision-making in this area.

The difficulty with the nationalist ideology of economic development is that it does not distinguish between the new-style economically productive business innovators and the old-style nonproductive absentee landlords and moneylenders. There is still a lingering suspicion of the businessman's role as essentially exploitative and a hesitancy to recognize his contribution to national development.

Yet, recently, the doctrinaire espousal of nationalization has given way to a search for new forms of economic life, combining over-all government promotion and direction of economic development with a measure of individual initiative and private ownership. Nasser followed his large-scale nationalizations with measures to promote private ownership of land (up to 100 acres) and of small enterprises. Fourteen years of economic planning in India have also shown that nationalization is not always the appropriate way to economic development. Despite his espousal of socialism, Prime Minister Nehru has been frank to admit that nationalization will not assure the rationalized development of the economy that India seeks. The Indian experience seems to demonstrate that as an economy expands, an entrepreneurial class of "innovators" emerges which can invest and utilize the new surpluses more efficiently than government planners.[21]

In Africa, there is little evidence of impending large-scale nationalization even among the more radical Casablanca nations. Both the radicals and the more moderate governments agree that controls on private business are needed, and both recognize that it has a place in the national economy. However, the radicals tend to prefer a mixture that leans more heavily in the direction of state control.

The same pattern emerges in attitudes toward investment by foreign private capital. The moderate reformers are more eager to encourage private companies and investors to engage in economic development, but they are also aware of the need for appropriate government regulation to assure that this investment is directed toward the development of the country. The radicals, while eager to have foreign capital, often prefer to secure it through direct government-to-government relations, and the restrictions they place on foreign private investment may discourage the additional flow of such capital in their direction, particularly when there are other countries that can offer better terms.[22]

This does not mean, however, as the Marxist analysis would have it, that the individual nation (like the individual worker in the days before the advent of trade unionism) is always at the mercy of international monopoly capitalism because of its weak competitive bargaining position. Larger nations and federal group-

21 See Nasser's speech on "Arab Socialism" (below, pp. 133–34), delivered on May 21, 1962. Nehru discusses nationalization in "Indian Socialism" (see below, pp. 102–3). On the role of entrepreneurs in the economies of the developing nations, see Barbara Ward, *India and the West* (New York: W. W. Norton & Company, 1961), Chap. xv; Millikan and Blackmer, *op. cit.*, Chap. v; W. W. Rostow, *The Stages of Economic Growth* (New York: Cambridge University Press, 1960), pp. 50 ff.; Edward Shils, "The Concentration and Dispersion of Charisma," *World Politics*, XI, No. 1 (October, 1958), 1–19.

22 Examples of the two approaches would include the moderate policies toward foreign and domestic capital adopted by Nigeria and Senegal, and the more stringent controls by the governments of Guinea, Ceylon, and Indonesia. Ghana invites foreign investment, but its official position favors government loans as a preferable method of development. (Cf. Kofi Baako, "Nkrumaism— Its Theory and Practice" [below, p. 193]: "The Nkrumaist prefers loan capital to investment capital. . . . Loan capital allows the receiver . . . say, the government—to use its loan to set up any state enterprises within the framework of its socioeconomic plan.")

ings are often in a better position to assert control over economic activity by foreign investors (and this is one of the numerous reasons for the movements for a common market in Latin America, and for regional federation in Africa and the Middle East), but even the smaller nations, if they are politically independent, can gain certain advantages from the current competition by foreign investors for investment opportunities in developing countries. The recent increase in the percentage of profits allocated to Iran and other countries by an Italian oil company from the standard 50–50 arrangement to a 75–25 division is an example of the possibilities to be derived from such competition.

That similar advantages can also come from competition among the governmental sources of capital is clear to all the leaders of the developing nations. The reformists and radicals among the modernizing elite agree on the virtues of "aid without strings" from both East and West. The examples of Nasser's success in playing off the rival blocs in the Cold War and of the construction of steel mills in India by rival teams from the Soviet Union and West Germany have not been lost on other nationalist leaders. It should not be surprising, therefore, if increasing numbers of nations in Asia, Africa, Latin America, and the Middle East turn to the Soviet Union, Eastern Europe, and China for economic assistance, since this policy would conform both to their own urgent need for additional foreign capital and to their ideological position of neutralism or nonalignment in international affairs.

If the developing nations are internally strong, if by maintaining economic links with the West as well as the East they avoid becoming dependent on the Soviet bloc, and if they are themselves committed to democratic methods, aid from the East may strengthen democracy and weaken internal pressures for the more drastic methods of totalitarian control. This is the case already in India, where aid from the Soviet bloc has helped the Congress Party in its struggle to develop the country in the face of both the external example of China and the internal threat of the Indian Communist Party.[23]

When it is a question of *military* aid from the Soviet Union, the situation becomes more complicated. Nasser does not seem to

[23] See Paul Sigmund, "The Uses of Neutralism," *Commonweal*, LXXIII, No. 21 (February 17, 1961), 523–26.

have compromised his independent policy by accepting Soviet and
Czech weapons, but it would appear that, if only because of the
need for ammunition and replacement parts, a certain dependence
may result. In addition, the military advisers who accompany this
aid may also influence government policy. In apparent recognition
of the difference between the two types of aid, the nations of the
uncommitted world have so far been much less eager to secure
military assistance than economic aid from the Soviet bloc, although India, Indonesia, Guinea, and Mali, in addition to Egypt,
have received such military assistance.

Strong Government Under a Single or Dominant Party

All the nationalist leaders see the need for a strong government
to achieve the goals of modernization and development. To carry
out a social and economic revolution in addition to a political
transfer of power requires a government that can act vigorously to
educate the people in the new nationalism and to initiate a program of forced economic development. Development requires foreign assistance, whether private or governmental, and a strong
government is also considered necessary to direct and control the
use of this capital in accordance with national objectives.

The failure of parliamentary regimes to provide this type of
effective leadership has meant that a reforming military elite has
taken control in a number of the new states. Unlike the old military oligarchies of Latin America and the Iberian peninsula, these
new military rulers are committed to the goals of modernization
and development. They reject as inapplicable and even fraudulent
the party systems borrowed from European parliamentary practice. However, they may retain, in an altered form, the representative assembly and periodic elections by universal suffrage, which
are needed to demonstrate that political power comes from the
people, the sole source of legitimacy in the modern state.[24]

The modernizing military oligarchies usually justify their authoritarianism as temporary in character, preparing for the introduction of democracy when economic and social progress permit. In
the past, the model for this type of transitional authoritarianism

[24] Nasser is currently attempting to establish a modified parliamentarism
after ten years of military rule. For a defense of army rule without deference
to democratic forms, see Abdul Karim Kassem, "The Army and the Parties"
(below, pp. 117–20).

has been the modernizing rule of Kemal Atatürk in Turkey, which prepared the way for what appeared to be an orderly transition to democracy (although recent events in Turkey have called into question the success of that transition).

A similar transitional role may be played by the popular leader with quasi-charismatic qualities derived from his part in the nationalist effort to gain independence. This is the case in Africa, where there is no significant military elite, and in countries like India, where the tradition of subordination of the military to the civilian authority is strong. The nationalist leaders have developed an effective instrument of modernization in the single or dominant nationalist party reaching down into every level of national life. Military reformers like Nasser have recognized its effectiveness and have attempted to develop their own nationalist parties to organize the people, to control and to respond to public opinion, and to give legitimacy to the government.

Both the moderate and radical wings of the nationalist elite favor the single or dominant national party, and such parties exist in many of the new nations of Africa, in several countries in Asia, and, in the case of Mexico, in Latin America as well.[25] However, the structure of a dominant moderate or reformist party is usually different from that of a radical one. Where the radicals create an entirely new structure from the basic unit (or "cell") to the leadership, the reformists often make use of existing groups and traditional loyalties to build their parties. In the latter instance, the dynamic of social change is considerably diminished since groups with an interest in the present arrangement of society often form an important segment of the party.[26]

Similarly, the more moderate parties are less eager to mobilize and control the various voluntary groups in the society as auxiliaries of the party. The radical leaders argue that the task of nation-building requires that student, youth, labor, and women's groups

[25] Senghor has defended the existence of an opposition party (see below, p. 247), but Senegal now has, in effect, a one-party system. Nigeria, because of its federal structure, is an exception to the one-party rule in Africa.

[26] This distinction based on attitudes toward other groups in the society differs from the mass-party, elite-party dichotomy based on internal structure, which is utilized by Thomas Hodgkins, in *African Political Parties* (Baltimore, Md.: Penguin Books, 1961), pp. 68–75, and by Ruth Schachter, in "Single Party Systems in West Africa," *American Political Science Review*, LV, No. 2 (June, 1961), 294–307. Houphouet-Boigny's PDCI, for example, is a mass party with a moderate reformist program.

be organized and directed toward national goals by the party, rather than being left to their own parochial concerns. In the more extreme versions of this theory, every such group organized in the colonial period is viewed as an instrument of colonialist and imperialist attempts to influence the thinking of the colonized peoples. Whether it is the Boy Scouts or the Young Men's Christian Association, or international affiliation with groups like the World Assembly of Youth or the International Confederation of Free Trade Unions, all are suspect as organizations that either divert the energies of the interest group in question from the task of nation-building or are actively used by an external enemy to subvert national independence. (In Africa, some of the more moderate regimes have also borrowed the radicals' techniques and decreed the dissolution of student, youth, and labor groups or their integration into the party, particularly when they are opposed to the government.)

The nationalist leaders admit to a degree of elitism in their views on the relation of party and government to the people. Whether in the "guided democracy" of Sukarno, the "basic democracy" of Ayub Khan, or the "democratic dictatorship" of Sékou Touré, the popular will from which a government or ruling party must derive its legitimacy in a democratic age seems to consist as much in what the people *should* desire as in what they *do* desire. That there should be some confusion on this point is not surprising since democratic theory has always been ambiguous in this respect. The classical democratic assumption of the automatic coincidence of the subjective will of the majority and the objective standard of natural law or the greatest good of the greatest number has not always been realized in fact. Rousseau himself admitted that a "legislator" was required to prepare the people to exercise their responsibilities as participants in the general will.[27] In a sense, the nationalist leaders see themselves as the "lawgivers" of the new dispensation, involving the entire population, and imposing modernization, economic development, and "democracy."

As in the case of the reformist military regimes, the single party is defended as a transitional stage necessary to establish the essential preconditions of liberal democracy. The new nations are

[27] Jean Jacques Rousseau, *The Social Contract*, Chap. VII. The "legislator" also appears in Greek thought and in Machiavelli's *Discourses*.

said to lack a minimum national unity and consensus on basic values, the economic basis for a middle class to give stability to the system, a sufficiently high literacy rate to make political discussion and choice meaningful, and a tradition of self-restraint on the part of both majority and minority necessary for the give and take between those in power and the loyal opposition that is characteristic of a democratic system.[28] Yet, despite the admitted authoritarian elements, the single party is said to be democratic in structure and purpose. It is a mass organization open to all the citizenry—and this is an important difference from the Leninist conception of the party as an elite group.[29] It is the energizing force that carries out the program of development, but it is also in touch with the people and communicates their feelings to the leadership. In some defenses of the single party by leaders of Africa, Asia, and the Middle East (and by Cuba's Castro as well), it is even argued that a new and superior form of democracy is being developed in the single party.

The single or dominant party system is said to be more democratic than a system of two or more parties, since the Western parties usually represent narrow class, religious, or ethnic interests rather than the nation as a whole. Even in the two-party system, rule is exercised by a majority that may be as small as 50 per cent plus one, instead of by the whole people.[30] Those most influenced by the Marxist analysis argue that in the case of the United States, for instance, both parties are under the control of the same oligarchy of wealthy business interests. To an even greater extent, the multiparty systems of the colonial or semicolonial period are viewed as a façade for control by foreign or capitalist interests. Outside influences use the divisions and rivalries of the multiparty system and play upon the selfishness of petty politicians who are concerned only with playing the parliamentary game,

[28] For a typical expression of the view that under present conditions there is no alternative to one-party rule in Africa, see Immanuel Wallerstein, *Africa, The Politics of Independence* (New York: Random House, 1961), p. 163. An opposing view, which denounces the Western paternalism implied in this attitude, appears in Obafemi Awolowo's autobiography, *Awo* (see below, pp. 223–28).

[29] Fidel Castro has now adopted a Leninist conception of the party as an elite "vanguard of the proletariat." (See below, p. 275.)

[30] Sukarno criticizes "free-fight liberalism, where half plus one is always right" (see below, p. 62). Cf. Julius Nyerere, "One-Party Rule" (below, pp. 197–202).

rather than working for reform and development. In a new nation where, except for "the agents of imperialism," there is no sharp differentiation of economic interest, the single party is more appropriate to the economic and social development of society, and more necessary in order to resist outside pressures and pursue the interest of the nation as a whole.[31] The requirements of democracy are observed, say the defenders of the single-party system, *within* the parties rather than between them. There is no need for more than one party if there is freedom of discussion, democratic election of party leaders, and responsiveness of those in power to a mass membership that is broadly representative of the whole population. Multipartyism encourages disunity and factionalism, even subversion, at a time when there is the greatest need for national unity.

If this argument sounds suspiciously like the Soviet defense of "democratic centralism," this is no accident. Sékou Touré, the leading apologist for the single party, is frank to acknowledge the influence of the Leninist theory. However, while not ignoring Lenin's insistence on rigid party discipline, Touré emphasizes the importance of the maintenance of democratic procedures within the party and sees it as a mass movement rather than a conspiratorial elite.[32] Not only the Marxists defend the single party for nations undergoing the revolution of modernization. Leaders as diverse as Julius Nyerere of Tanganyika and President Sukarno of Indonesia assert that it is in keeping with the traditional methods of decision-making in their societies, which tend to operate on the basis of consensus rather than dialectical opposition. Democracy is "talking until you agree," says Nyerere, not opposition for opposition's sake.[33]

The analogy in the one-party theory is more with Rousseau than with Lenin. The single party is "democratic" not because it is a vanguard that has an insight into the real meaning of economics and history, but because all participate and there is a continual

[31] See Sékou Touré on Africa as a classless society (p. 17, n. 17); Nasser's defense of the National Union Party (below, pp. 127–29); and Castro's description of the bourgeois party as "a gang of politicians, a conglomeration of individuals who defend class interests" (below, p. 275).
[32] See below, p. 167. Use of the term "democratic centralism" to describe the party structure is characteristic of the radical wing of African nationalism, but it is not used by other nationalist parties.
[33] "One-Party Rule" (below, p. 197).

dialogue among leader, leading party, and the masses. The ambiguity in Rousseau's "general will" and its potential for tyranny, whether by the leader or by the majority, is shared by the theory of the single party, which often tends to minimize the possibility of a conflict between the individual and the group, party, or nation.

Yet, in his classic defense of the single party, Madeira Keita, now Minister of the Interior of the Republic of Mali, recognizes that there are real dangers in this system. Keita emphasizes the great demands that the absence of an organized opposition places upon the leadership of the single party. (Keita also notes that he prefers the term "unified party," emphasizing the variety of tendencies within the movement.) Perhaps in anticipation of subsequent developments, the French-speaking African intellectual Cheikh Anta Diop, commenting on Keita's speech, expressed the fear that unless the African territories formed a larger federation, the single-party systems in each country would become the instrumentalities of "petty ephemeral dictatorships" of the Latin American type.[34]

In the absence of institutional safeguards for the expression of dissenting opinions, there is a danger that the charismatic leader, convinced of his mission to reform society, may suppress even legitimate criticism of those in power. Some observers see in the auxiliary organizations of youths, students, labor, etc., the means of institutional expression of criticism, but Roberto Michels' "iron law of oligarchy," a sociological generalization from the experience of the concentration of power at the top of any institutional hierarchy, suggests that this might not often take place.[35] Particularly when nationalist leaders are enjoying the perquisites of power after a revolt against existing laws, it may be difficult to develop respect for the sharing of power in accordance with legal and institutional norms.

The danger is all the more real, since the single-party ideology, while allowing and encouraging mass affiliation and freedom of

[34] See Madeira Keita, "The Single Party in Africa" (below, pp. 176, 181).

[35] Michels, *Political Parties, A Sociological Study of Oligarchical Tendencies of Modern Democracy* (Glencoe, Ill.: The Free Press, 1958). The argument concerning auxiliary organizations is made by Clement Moore, in "The National Party: A Tentative Model," in C. J. Friedrich and Seymour Harris (eds.), *Public Policy*, X (1960), 262 ff. See also Douglas Ashford, "Labor Politics in a New Nation," *Western Political Quarterly*, XIII, No. 2 (June, 1960), 312–31.

discussion for differing points of view, is often unwilling to accord these rights to the representatives of the traditional order, the "feudal classes," or to those who are considered to be or to have been collaborators with foreigners. Loose charges of "reactionary feudalist" or "imperialist stooge" can be used to stifle legitimate dissent, and the prisons can contain both loyal and disloyal oppositionists. The theory of the single party can result in the revolutionary transformation of society by means of persuasion and democratic discussion, or it can be used to justify the imposition of the will of an oligarchic elite by coercion, propaganda, and Rousseauan mysticism about the will of the people.

An optimistic view is that once the single party has initiated economic development and succeeded in replacing local, tribal, caste, and religious loyalties with a sense of involvement in the nation, it will develop a healthy pluralism of parties or interest groups. Within the national consensus, there will thus be an institutionalized opportunity for the expression of differences as to the method or pace of social change, or even simply of the opposition of the "outs" to the "ins."[36] The Congress Party of India, for instance, once contained within its ranks the leaders of the present Communist and Praja Socialist parties, and recently the supporters of the right-wing Swatantra (Freedom) Party have split off from it.

On the other hand, a more pessimistic critic might doubt whether those who hold power are not more likely to label legitimate economic and social grievances as the product of foreign intrigue and domestic reaction, and thus to step up the pace of repressive measures as the opposition becomes less able to pose a threat to those in control.

Regional Cooperation or Federation

As the example of Nigeria seems to indicate, there is also the possibility that movements toward federation may promote politi-

---

[36] Tom Mboya has said that opposition parties will develop "in ten or more years . . . as a normal and natural process of the individual freedom of speech and freedom to criticize the government." (Quoted in Legum, *op. cit.*, p. 123.) Characteristically, Sékou Touré links the existence of the opposition party to the state of economic development. In developed countries, he says, political opposition "by its presence and action, increases the dynamism of the party in power." (Quoted in Immanuel Wallerstein, "Political Theory in an African Context," paper presented to the African Studies Association, September, 1960, p. 13.)

cal pluralism. States of differing political persuasion in geographical proximity may hesitate to suppress political groups in a position
to retaliate in a neighboring state of the same federal grouping.
Yet, thus far, the two unsuccessful examples of such federation—
the union of Syria and Egypt in the United Arab Republic, and
that of Senegal and the Sudan (now the Mali Republic) in the
Federation of Mali—seem to indicate that organic federation between states of differing ideologies and social systems is very difficult.

The movement toward regional federation or confederation is
not an important one in Asia (although the Bandung Conference
of 1955 gave a symbolic expression to the solidarity of Asians and
Africans). But in Africa, the Middle East, and Latin America, the
desire to create regional structures is strong enough to be a major
factor in the ideological appeal of certain nationalist leaders, such
as Nasser and Nkrumah, both within and outside their own territorial limits. Nasser has used Pan-Arab feeling to increase Egyptian
influence elsewhere in the Middle East; and at one point after the
Suez crisis, he seemed close to realizing the dream of Arab unity.
In Africa, the movement toward closer cooperation on a Pan-
African level receives the support of all groups, but there is disagreement as to the methods and rate by which the goal of a
united African continent is to be attained. The Casablanca powers
take a more radical stance, calling for political union and taking
measures such as the establishment of an African Military High
Command, while the more moderate Monrovia group supports the
establishment of functional links (customs, a common currency,
etc.) that can form the basis of closer cooperation in the future.
The Monrovia group accuses the Casablanca powers of fomenting
subversion and attempting to alter existing national boundaries,
while the Casablanca group views the Monrovia nations as tools of
"neocolonialism."[37] Yet, both groups agree on the danger of the
Balkanization of the continent, and both urge a Pan-African regional grouping. Despite the schism in Africa, the appeal of the
Pan-African ideal is so great that the present divisions may only

[37] The differences between the two conceptions are described in the speech
by Nnamdi Azikiwe to the opening session of the Lagos Conference of Heads
of African States, on January 25, 1962 (see below, pp. 216–22). (It should be
noted that Morocco, although a member of the Casablanca group, does not
take a radical approach to internal development.)

be temporary, and a broader form of Pan-African cooperation may be developed in the future.

In Latin America and the Middle East, efforts at regional co-operation have had little success. The mystique of regional coopera-tion or unification is not enough, it seems, to overcome personal antagonisms and nationalistic rivalries. Territorial expansion by a strong power is one classic way in which unification has taken place, but the new nations thus far lack the military power to engage in this form of unification, and the great powers, their rela-tionship delicately stabilized in a balance of mutual terror, seem reluctant to involve themselves in a major way in the rivalries of the new nations.

Another possible means to union is a joint effort against a com-mon enemy. The African threat of a crusade to liberate Angola and the Republic of South Africa may someday result in the realization of the projected African army repeatedly discussed during the Congo crisis.[38] Fidel Castro has attempted to use hostil-ity to "Yankee imperialism" in a similar way in Latin America, and the Suez crisis was one of the few occasions in which the Arab world was united.

The remaining alternative, that of a gradual evolution of regional cooperation, is not an appealing one to the impatient nationalists, but it is possible that closer ties will come about through the de-velopment of further economic and cultural links rather than by political means. The United Nations Economic Commission for Latin America (ECLA), with headquarters in Santiago de Chile, has already influenced Latin American economic thinking along regional lines, and preliminary efforts have been made to create common organs of regional economic cooperation in Latin Amer-ica. The Economic Commission for Africa is also exerting a simi-lar influence, and the obvious mutual interdependence of many of the African states has already led to the lowering of some of the economic barriers raised at the time of national independence. The African states continue to meet together, and the tentative gropings of youth, student, and trade-union organizations in Latin America and Africa for regional cooperation either within or out-

[38] An African army was proposed by President Nkrumah in his speech to the United Nations on September 23, 1960, and by Julius Nyerere speaking to the Pan-African Seminar of the World Assembly of Youth (WAY) at Dar-es-Salaam on August 6, 1961. The Casablanca group has recently decided to establish an African High Command in Accra.

side existing international organizations are a further reassertion
of the federalist ideal.[39]

The Revival of Traditional Culture

Part of the impetus to regional cooperation comes from the
awareness of a common heritage of values. Again, this is not true
of Asia as a whole, although the consciousness of an underlying
unity among the diverse cultures of India is an important element
in Indian nationalism. However, the common background of
Islamic culture and Arab language in the Middle East, Latin
America's belief in a community of values derived from the Iberian peninsula but given a different content by its fusion with
Indian and Negro elements, and (especially) the rediscovery or
creation of an African culture symbolized by Senghor's Negritude
and Nkrumah's "African personality"—all serve in varying degrees
to strengthen the common bonds in their respective regions.

Despite their desire for modernization, the nationalist leaders
feel a need to maintain elements of their traditional cultures and
the moral values they represent. Nehru has alluded to the "spiritual loneliness" of the Westernized elite, which both needs and
rejects the values of traditional civilization. The description in
Nasser's *Philosophy of the Revolution* of an Egyptian family in

[39] The relation of the voluntary organizations of students, youth, labor
unions, etc., to the movements for regional federation lies outside the scope
of this book. Relevant regional groups include the All-African Trade Union
Federation formed in Casablanca in May, 1961, the African Trade Union
Conference established in Lagos in 1962, the recently established Pan-
African Youth Movement (MJP), the Latin American Student Congress,
the Organisacion Interamericana de Trabajadores (ORIT), and the African
Regional Organization (AFRO). Only the last two groups are associated with
an international organization, the International Confederation of Free Trade
Unions. In recent years, both the Communist front organizations (e.g., the
World Federation of Democratic Youth, the International Union of Students,
the World Federation of Trade Unions, and the International Federation
of Teachers' Unions) and the non-Communist groupings (e.g., the International Student Conference, the World Assembly of Youth, the International Confederation of Free Trade Unions, and the World Confederation of
Organizations of the Teaching Profession) have greatly increased their regional
programing in Asia, Africa, the Middle East, and Latin America. For examples on the Communist side, see Robert H. Bass, "Communist Fronts,"
Problems of Communism, IX, No. 5 (September–October, 1960), 8–17. A
detailed account of the political struggle over the establishment of the All-
African Trade Union Federation appears in Legum, *op. cit.*, pp. 81–91.

which one son is English-educated, a daughter French-educated, the father comes from an Egyptian peasant family, and the mother has a Turkish background is typical of the cultural confusion produced by the disorganizing impact of the West.

The reassertion of certain features of traditional culture is psychologically necessary to balance the overwhelming technical, economic, and military superiority of the West. Characteristically, the nationalist leaders stress the moral, religious, or spiritual superiority of their culture in contrast to the materialism, utilitarianism, and technocracy of the West (and not only of the West, since these qualities can be attributed with even greater validity to the Communist world).[40] They hail the distinctive contributions of native music, literature, art, and poetry, and warn against the "mental colonialism" that has separated the intellectuals from their cultural heritage and subjected them to the alien values of the dominant European civilization.[41] The cultural renaissance in the developing nations is thus a partial rejection of the Western culture, which was held up previously as a model. It is an effort to establish national pride and self-respect—integral factors in the building of new nations.

Indian nationalism had a rich culture to draw on, but the interest in African culture and history that now forms an important part of the ideology of African nationalism stemmed from the work of English anthropologists and French-speaking African in-

[40] "Among Indian and African civilizations, which are essentially spiritualistic, the idea of economic utility is appreciated otherwise than in the old or young materialistic civilizations, or civilizations issuing from formative processes where, in spite of spiritual factors, the materialistic element dominates." (Mamadou Dia, The African Nations and World Solidarity; see below, p. 237.)

"The tendency of Indian civilization is to elevate the moral being, that of the Western civilization is to propagate immorality." (Gandhi, Indian Home Rule; see below, p. 78.)

"Between the ideology of Communism and the materialist conceptions of the West, Islam is the only point of view that can prevent the spirit of humanity from being destroyed." (Ayub Khan, "Islam in Pakistan"; see below, p. 110.)

"A third revolution is taking place, as a reaction against capitalistic and Communistic materialism—one that will integrate moral, if not religious, values with the political and economic contributions of the two great revolutions [French and Russian]." (Senghor, African Socialism; see below, p. 245.)

[41] The term "mental colonialism" is used by Haya de la Torre, (see below, p. 289). See also Sékou Touré's discussion of the French attempt to "depersonalize and Westernize" the African intellectual elite (below, p. 156).

tellectuals in Paris. The very names Ghana and Mali are a conscious attempt to recall the glories of the medieval empires under those names, and the governments of Senegal, Mali, Guinea, and Ghana have subsidized and popularized the work of African and European scholars on these subjects. To the charge that there is a racist element in the glorification of the past accomplishment of the African, Léopold Senghor replies that a period of self-assertion of African values is necessary to correct the distortions of African culture and history produced by the inevitable bias of European historians. In righting the balance to emphasize the positive achievements and values of the "African personality," a dialogue between the two views will be created that can contribute to universal culture. A national and regional cultural revival thus precedes a higher and truer internationalism that will include African culture and civilization on an equal basis with that of other parts of the world.[42]

Nonalignment in International Affairs

With some exceptions dictated by special circumstances, most of the new nations in Asia, Africa, and the Middle East (but not in Latin America) have adopted a policy of nonalignment with either East or West in the Cold War. While remaining outside alliances and power groupings, they have not hesitated to pass judgment on the actions of the great powers, seeing themselves as specially fitted for this role because of their nonaligned position. Since each of the new nations has a vote in the U.N. General Assembly, they have an international forum in which, particularly in recent years, they exert a voting strength far out of proportion to their power in international affairs. They are thus encouraged, if not compelled, to take positions on a wide range of problems and to pursue an active international policy.

Since the General Assembly is dominated by their votes, the representatives of the developing nations view it as an instrument to defend the small and weak nations against the large and powerful. Conscious of their own weakness in physical power, they have resisted attempts to dilute the effectiveness of the U.N., since it

[42] Senghor, "What Is 'Negritude'?" (see below, pp. 248–50). See also the interview with Ayo Ogunshaye in Melvin Lasky, "Africa for Beginners," *Encounter*, XVII, No. 1 (July, 1961), 44–46.

remains the best forum for the exercise of moral pressure by them upon the great powers.

To Western critics, the nationalist leaders seem to overemphasize the virtues of moral suasion and to underestimate the importance of a military balance in maintaining the present uneasy peace—and even in maintaining their own national independence. Yet, the nonaligned nations are not willing to leave to the stronger nations the problems of international war and peace because their entire effort to develop would be destroyed by a war between the great powers.

At the same time, they also insist that they be left to regulate their internal and regional affairs among themselves. As the example of the Congo demonstrates, the major powers may not be willing to comply with this demand, particularly when it is put forward by countries with ambitions of their own in the area. Moreover, the nationalists' principle of nonintervention is not an absolute. The Latin Americans condemn the United States for not taking action against authoritarian dictatorships in Central and South America, and the Africans have pressed us to take drastic action against our allies who still hold colonial territories. Nonintervention is a doctrine to be applied to legitimate regimes, but not to colonial or reactionary governments.

The claim of the uncommitted nations to represent the "unbiased conscience of humanity,"[43] is somewhat tarnished by what appears to Western eyes to be a greater readiness to condemn Western misdeeds than those of the Soviet Union, as well as by the neutrals' support of the use of violence in the case of Goa. Examples like India's attitude on Kashmir or Morocco's claim to Mauritania indicate that on questions affecting what are considered to be their vital interests, the uncommitted nations are no more likely to defer to international morality and opinion than do the more powerful nations whom they upbraid for their immoral behavior. Yet, despite the fact that no nation is ready to abjure the use or threat of violence, the very military weakness of the new nations which leads them to adopt a moralistic attitude also makes armed conflict among them less likely, provided the great powers

[43] Statement by Premier Saeb Salaan of Lebanon to the United Nations General Assembly; quoted by Ernest W. Lefever, in "Nehru, Nasser, and Nkrumah on Neutralism," in Martin, *op. cit.*, p. 103.

restrain themselves or are restrained from becoming deeply involved in their rivalries.

In addition to their role as the moral conscience of humanity, the uncommitted nations also view themselves as a balance or intermediary between the two power blocs. Nationalist thinking has added the theory of the "third area" countries to the older bipolar view of world politics. Like the bipolar theory, this view of international relations overlooks the pluralistic elements in the West and (especially since the recent Sino-Soviet ideological division) in the East as well, but it serves the purpose of establishing a separate identity and special role in international affairs for the new nations. Yet, the two roles—that of the independent moral conscience exercising an unbiased judgment on each case, and that of the balance wheel located precisely midway between the positions of East and West—need not lead to the same conclusions. The conception of themselves as the mean between the extremes, typical of the thinking of emergent nationalists, leads to an automatic assumption of a middle ground on East-West questions, with quite different results from the attempt to make an independent assessment of the moral worth of the claims of the two antagonists.[44]

However, one might question whether the third area can also be described as a third bloc. Many of the speakers at the Belgrade Conference denied that it was their intention to act as a bloc, and the divisions among the nations of Asia, Africa, and Latin America are such that the probability is slight that they will be able to act together on any regular basis. Moreover, with the exception of Cuba, Latin America has so far not been considered a member of the uncommitted group. However, a common concern with development, a similar suspicion of strong and wealthy nations, and parallel problems of social and economic reform make it likely that closer links will be developed among the developing nations,

[44] "Neither side has won us and we are determined that neither side will." (Statement by an African diplomat at the United Nations; quoted by Henry Kissinger, in *The Necessity for Choice* [New York: Harper & Brothers, 1961], p. 330.) This should be compared with Modibo Keita's statement: "[Nonalignment] must not be compared with *equilibrisme*, with a balancing act which takes up no fundamental position and which aligns itself now with one, now with the other of the two blocs." (Quoted in Legum, *op. cit.*, pp. 112–13.) Neutralism is criticized by Chief Awolowo (see below, pp. 228–31) and (in certain forms) by Mamadou Dia (see below, pp. 234–35).

particularly on issues such as colonialism and underdevelopment, on which there is a large measure of agreement.[45]

The most powerful motivating force determining the policy of the uncommitted nations is neither neutralism nor the urge to sit in judgment upon their fellows, but nationalism and the desire for national independence and prestige. A neutral or nonaligned position, meetings of the uncommitted nations, and a moralistic attitude toward world politics help to create an international climate in which the weak nations can better defend and develop themselves economically and politically. The East-West question and the ideological conflict surrounding it, while they may indirectly benefit the new nations, are more often viewed as obstacles to the goal of national independence, economic development, and social change. To divide the new nations into pro-Western and pro-Eastern is to be ignorant of this primary concern and of the frequently expressed disinterest of the new nations in becoming involved in the ideological struggles of the great powers.

Modernizing Nationalism and Communism

If, as the preceding discussion seems to indicate, there is a belief system that can be classified as the ideology of modernizing nationalism, if what the French call the *Tiers-Monde* has a world view of its own, then a terminology of international politics derived from the Cold War is inadequate. Different questions must be asked and a different classification utilized. At the outset, the question was posed as to whether the common ideas of modernizing nationalism could be described as an ideology, similar to but different from the ideological systems of Europe. This review of the ideas of the nationalist leaders has suggested that, if we omit the leaders of traditional and conservative oligarchies, the two other general types of nationalist leaders, the radicals and the reformers, share a body of political and economic theory, distinct from both Western liberalism and Soviet collectivism. It is a suffi-

[45] The denials by Nasser, Nkrumah, and others at the Belgrade Conference are quoted in Legum, *op. cit.*, p. 115. A typical expression of the three-bloc conception appears in Sukarno's "Lecture to the Students of Hasanuddin University": "These three groupings I regard as a phenomenon of the twentieth century: the group of Thomas Jefferson, the group adhering to the Communist Manifesto, and the group of Asian and African nationalism." (See below, p. 58.) Note that Sukarno appears to consider Latin America as part of the Western group.

what is it?

ciently coherent body of ideas to be called an ideology—the ideology of modernizing nationalism. The goal of national development elicits an emotional response and commitment on the part of the members of the nationalist movement. It is accompanied by a set of doctrines about the proper methods to attain economic progress, the nature of world politics, and the special contribution of the new nations to world culture and world peace. The ideology has a function—to carry the nation through the period of modernization of traditional society and to justify the ensuing sacrifices and dislocations. For its content, it draws upon the political ideas of both East and West.

This is not to ignore the real dangers in the appeals of Communism to the developing nations. The examples of China, of Cuba since late 1959, or even of Russia itself demonstrate that the ideology of Marxism-Leninism has a particular appeal for a nation undergoing the upheavals and dislocations associated with modernization and development.[46] It is only to assert that Marxism-Leninism is not the only ideology appropriate to this process, and that, in fact, the modernizing nationalists have developed an alternative set of ideological assumptions and propositions that shares some elements of the Marxist-Leninist model, but differs significantly from it in other respects. Moreover, this ideology is in many ways superior to Marxism-Leninism, since it is more pragmatic and more related to the problem of modernization than are the simplistic dogmas derived from the experience of nineteenth- and early twentieth-century Europe which comprise the Marxist-Leninist solution.[47]

From the Marxist analysis, the modernizing nationalists have accepted certain elements and rejected others. While recognizing the central importance of economic motivation, they do not accept

[46] Cf. Adam B. Ulam, "The Historical Role of Marxism and the Soviet System," *World Politics*, VIII, No. 1 (October, 1955), 20–45.

[47] The inapplicability of classical Marxism to the problems of an agrarian society was recognized by Mao Tse-tung in his *On New Democracy* (see below, pp. 44–50), which describes "the joint dictatorship of several revolutionary classes," including the peasants and intelligentsia. The European derivation of Marxism-Leninism is also the basis of the criticism of Communism by Haya de la Torre of Peru (see below, p. 290), and by a group of African Marxists who, at the Second Conference of Negro Writers and Artists in Rome, March 25–April 1, 1959, adopted a resolution calling for a revision of Marxism to make it less Western and more universal in its application. (The resolution is printed in Legum, *op. cit.*, p. 220.)

Marxist economic determinism. In nationalist thinking, political forces are capable of subduing and controlling economic forces, and the state is not destined to wither away. Moreover, Marxist materialism is specifically rejected in favor of the recognition of the importance of the spiritual aspects of life. Marxist class analysis is also regarded as inadequate. History involves more than the struggle of the proletariat and bourgeoisie. Other groups in society are also significant, among them the rural elements, the intellectuals, and perhaps the military men as well. The nation as a whole is the primary unit of loyalty, not the class, and in the case of the African nationalists, it is denied that class divisions even exist in the new nations.[48]

In the case of Lenin's additions to Marxist theory, there is the same pattern of partial incorporation and partial rejection. On the one hand, the Leninist theory of imperialism is widely accepted, but on the other, the Leninist association of Western capitalism with imperialism does not prevent the developing nations from inviting Western investment and accepting Western aid. In addition, there remains a healthy suspicion of Soviet intentions which, while perhaps not as strong as the suspicion of the West, demonstrates the nationalists' assumption that tendencies toward domination are not a capitalist monopoly. The Leninist conception of the role of the party and auxiliary organizations in mobilizing the society has been accepted by the radical wing of modernizing nationalism, but thus far even the radical parties have been more open and less rigidly authoritarian in character than was Lenin's elite "vanguard of the proletariat." The same regimes also use Leninist vocabulary—"democratic centralism," "Young Pioneers," "Politbureau," etc.—but this does not necessarily mean that the centralized totalitarianism of the Soviet Party is reproduced wherever the same terms are used.

Undoubtedly, there are strong authoritarian tendencies in the desire of the nationalist leaders to remold their societies by government action, but thus far there is little evidence of the characteristic totalitarian attempts at thought control, absolute unanimity, and the establishment of the infallibility of leader and party. The

[48] Soviet writers have criticized African leaders for their refusal to apply the Marxist class analysis to the West African scene. See David L. Morison, "Communism in Africa: Moscow's First Steps," *Problems of Communism*, X, 6 (November–December, 1961), 8–15.

emphasis is on persuasion, negotiation, and conciliation, while the threat or use of violence that has typically accompanied the totalitarian attempts to transform society is largely absent.[49] Moreover, with the exception perhaps of Ghana's version of Pan-Africanism, the ideology itself is limited in its goals to national independence and development and does not have the universality or inherent expansionism of the totalitarian doctrines.

Marxism-Leninism also provides a model of forced economic development by state action—a goal that the modernizing nationalists share. However, the lack of success of the Soviet and Chinese regimes in developing the agricultural sector of the economy should be a warning that their method is not without failings. The nationalists are not willing, thus far, to carry out a ruthless program of collectivization of rural producers, although the establishment of rural cooperatives is often part of their program. Similarly, except in Cuba and the U.A.R., there has been little actual large-scale nationalization or confiscation of private business and native industry, as called for by Marxist-Leninist dogma.

With the exception of Cuba, even the nationalists most heavily influenced by Marxism have criticized Soviet policy and taken measures against domestic Communist subversion. Sékou Touré, who has borrowed Soviet organizational techniques and accepted considerable amounts of Soviet aid, has twice publicly indicated his opposition to Soviet interference in the affairs of other countries—in his 1960 speech to the United Nations and during the "teachers' plot" in 1961, which led to the departure of the Soviet Ambassador from Guinea. While they are willing to use the Soviet Union for their own purposes, as Nasser did in 1955 in order to reduce his dependence on the West for military and economic aid, the nationalist leaders have no desire to substitute one form of domination for another, or to adopt what is to them an alien ideology.

The modernizing regimes need an ideology because they are engaged in a social and economic revolution and they must dramatize the changes they wish to bring about. But it is an ideology resembling that of Atatürk more than that of Marx—an ideology of development and industrialization based in national culture

[49] The lack of violence in African politics is emphasized in Herbert J. Spiro, *Politics in Africa, Prospects South of the Sahara* (Englewood Cliffs, N.J.: Prentice-Hall, 1962).

goals

and tradition and related to local conditions.[50] As the Cuban example demonstrates, it is necessary to have an organization as well as a specific program; if not, the local Communist Party's superior organizational techniques and tactical skill may enable it to take over the social and economic revolution that the nationalist leader is attempting to bring about. But with a strong party organization, a popular leader, and some progress in meeting the desire for modernization and development, a nation can pursue its own course without resort to Communist ideology or affiliation with the Soviet bloc.

These are the goals of modernizing nationalism: national independence; rapid economic development; the creation of a nation-state governed by a regime based on a populist identification of leader, party, and people; regional federation; and nonalignment in international affairs. There is no mention of liberal pluralistic democracy in the Western sense, because—except for countries like Nigeria and India, where the leadership, experience, and internal balance of forces favor political development along Western lines—the theory and practice of constitutional democracy as it is known in Europe or North America is not much in evidence. What has emerged in the developing nations is a reasonably coherent set of ideas about society and government which constitutes the ideology of modernizing nationalism. It is in the hope of achieving a better understanding of these ideas that the selections from the speeches and writings of a wide range of nationalist leaders are presented in this volume.

—P. E. S.

[50] For an earlier version of modernizing nationalism, see the program of "Kemalism," published by Atatürk's party in 1935. (Printed as Appendix E to Donald E. Webster, *The Turkey of Atatürk* [Philadelphia: The American Academy of Political and Social Science, 1939], pp. 307–18; note particularly the economic and cultural sections.) The Turkish example poses the question of the capacity of modernizing nationalism to maintain its dynamism when it is in power for an extended period.

PART I

ASIA

It is far more difficult to generalize about ideology and politics in an area as vast and diverse as Asia than in the case of the other areas under consideration. Asians have much less in common with one another, and national traditions and cultures are stronger than in Africa, the Middle East, and Latin America. Moreover, the travail of securing and consolidating national independence is largely past in most Asian countries. Reasonably stable and permanent regimes to which the populace is loyal are in control in most Asian countries, making ideological appeals less necessary. In one instance, Japan, the rate of economic development has progressed to such a point that the nation can no longer be considered underdeveloped.

Yet, there are some common elements in Asian political psychology and ideology. Asian philosophy and political practice emphasize conciliation in the resolution of conflict, and this is expressed in the speeches and writings of Asian political leaders by the attempt to stress common elements in conflicting views and to achieve a consensus as a basis for policy.* This consensus is often to be found or typified in a single leader, endowed with quasi-religious charismatic qualities.

The attempt to find agreement and to gloss over differences also characterizes the approach of Asian leaders to the East-West conflict. It is no accident that the philosophy of neutralism was first formulated by Nehru and Sukarno, although it should be noted that this philosophy is not operative in Asian countries where there is an immediate Communist threat to national integrity.

In economic development, a mixed economy predominates in

* See the selections by Sukarno and U Nu.

practice, although Marxist anticapitalism has strongly influenced the theories of the intellectuals and the speeches of political leaders.* Today, two models of economic and political development, those of China and of India, are in competition for Asian allegiance, symbolizing the choice between democratic planning in an open society and forced growth under a totalitarian regime.

This competition is also one of cultural influence. India and China have old and deeply rooted cultural traditions, and both have been subjected to heavy Western influence, but they have reacted in different ways. The urbane and civilized synthesis of East and West typified by the character and personality of Nehru contrasts with the crusading aggressiveness of the Chinese transformation of an ancient culture into a modern nation, following the Soviet example, but making its own alterations and innovations.

Since the Bandung Conference in 1955, China has attempted to develop its relations with other underdeveloped countries. More recently, it has embarked upon a program of trade, aid, and propaganda in Asia and Africa that has capitalized on the desire of the new nations to establish new contacts and learn from all national experiences. Yet, thus far, the uncommitted nations, while accepting Chinese assistance, have been careful to maintain their neutrality, and they continue to view China as a committed member of one of the two world blocs. India, on the other hand, plays a leading role in the councils of the uncommitted world, and the writings of Gandhi and Nehru have considerable influence on the attitudes and opinions of the leaders of Asia, Africa, and, more recently, Latin America.

* See the selections by Nehru and U Nu.

1. Mao Tse-tung

Mao Tse-tung, the Chairman of the Politbureau of the Chinese Communist Party, was born in 1893 in a village in northern China. The son of a peasant landowner, Mao wished to become a scholar. After his mother's death in 1918, he went to Peking University, where he worked as assistant librarian and came under the influence of two professors who were among the founders of the Chinese Communist Party. In 1921, he attended the first Congress of the Chinese Communist Party and was elected to its Central Committee. After the split between Chiang Kai-shek and the Communists, he established himself as political commissar of the Red Army, and by 1935 he had achieved supremacy in the Party. At this time, he led the Long March of the Communists from southeast to northwest China. Starting from a base in Yenan and gaining peasant support through a program of agrarian reform, he expanded his control of China. Finally, in 1949, Chiang Kai-shek was driven off the Chinese mainland. From then until 1959, Mao Tse-tung was President of the Chinese People's Republic. He resigned from this post, but continues to serve as Party Chairman. In his On New Democracy, written in 1940, Mao saw the significance of the anticolonial revolution and tried to identify Communism with the desires of traditional societies for national independence and economic development. He also developed a theory of "joint dictatorship of all anti-imperialist classes" that departs from the classical Marxist belief in the dictatorship of the proletariat as the stage that follows capitalism.

ON NEW DEMOCRACY*

The Chinese Revolution as Part of the World Revolution

The historical feature of the Chinese revolution consists in two steps, democracy and socialism; the first step is no longer democracy in a general sense, but democracy of the Chinese type, a new and special type—New Democracy. How, then, has this historical feature come into existence? Has it been in existence for the past hundred years, or is it of only recent birth?

If we make a study of the development of China and of the world, we shall see that this historical feature did not emerge as a consequence of the Opium War, but began to take shape only after the first imperialist world war and the October Revolution in Russia. Let us now study the process of its formation.

Evidently, the colonial, semicolonial, and semifeudal character of present-day Chinese society requires two steps in the Chinese revolution. The first step is to change a colonial, semicolonial, and semifeudal society into an independent, democratic society. The second is to push the revolution further and build a socialist society. The Chinese revolution at present is taking the first step. . . .

The Revolution of 1911 was the beginning of that revolution in a fuller sense. In its social character that revolution is bourgeois-democratic and not proletarian-socialist. It is not yet completed, and great efforts are still required because its enemies remain very powerful. When Dr. Sun Yat-sen said, "The revolution is not yet completed; all my comrades must strive on," he was referring to the bourgeois-democratic revolution.

A change, however, occurred in the Chinese bourgeois-democratic revolution after the outbreak of the first imperialist World War in 1914 and the founding of a socialist state on one-sixth of the globe in consequence of the October Revolution in Russia in 1917. Before these events, the Chinese bourgeois-democratic revolution belonged to the category of the old bourgeois-democratic world revolution, and was part of it. After these events, the Chinese bourgeois-democratic revolution changes its character and

* Excerpts from Mao Tse-tung, *On New Democracy* (Peking: Foreign Languages Press, 1960).

comes within the category of the new bourgeois-democratic revolution and, so far as the revolutionary front is concerned, forms part of the proletarian-socialist world revolution.

Why? Because the first imperialist World War and the first victorious socialist revolution, the October Revolution, have changed the course of world history and marked a new historical era. This is an era in which the capitalist front has collapsed in one part—one-sixth—of the world and fully revealed its decadence in other parts; those parts still under capitalism cannot get along without depending more than ever on the colonies and semicolonies; a socialist state has come into being and has declared itself willing to help the liberation movement of all colonies and semicolonies; the proletariat of the capitalist countries is increasingly freeing itself from the social-imperialist influence of the social-democratic parties and has also declared itself in support of the liberation movement of the colonies and semicolonies. In this era, any revolution that takes place in a colony or semicolony against imperialism—that is, against the international bourgeoisie and international capitalism—belongs no longer to the old category of bourgeois-democratic world revolution. . . . Such revolutionary colonies and semicolonies should no longer be regarded as allies of the counterrevolutionary front of world capitalism: They have become allies of the revolutionary front of world socialism.

Although in its social character the first stage or step of such a revolution in a colonial and semicolonial country is still basically bourgeois-democratic, and although the task imposed on it by objective conditions is to clear the path for the development of capitalism, it is no longer a revolution of the old type led by the bourgeoisie and aimed at establishing a capitalist society and a state under bourgeois dictatorship, but one of the new type led by the proletariat and aimed at establishing in the first stage a New Democratic society and a state under the joint dictatorship of all revolutionary classes. Thus, this revolution will clear an even wider path for the development of socialism. In the course of its progress, such a revolution, owing to changes in the situation of its enemies and to changes of alignment within its own front, passes through several further stages; but its basic character remains unchanged.

This revolution attacks the very foundation of imperialism, and for this reason is disapproved and opposed by imperialism. But it is approved by socialism and supported by a socialist state and the international socialist proletariat. Therefore, such a revolution inevitably becomes part of the proletarian-socialist world revolution.

The correct formulation that the Chinese revolution is part of the world revolution was made as long ago as 1924–27, during China's first great revolution. It was made by the Chinese Communists and approved by all those taking part in the anti-imperialist and antifeudal struggle of the time. However, the theoretical implication of this formulation was not then fully expounded, and consequently the whole question was only vaguely understood.

The "world revolution" referred to here is no longer the old world revolution or the old bourgeois world revolution, for that ended long ago, but a new world revolution, the socialist world revolution. Similarly, the "part" is not a part of the old bourgeois revolution but of the new socialist revolution. This is a tremendous change unparalleled in the history of China and of the world.

This correct formulation made by the Chinese Communists is based on Stalin's theory. As early as 1918, Stalin wrote in an article commemorating the first anniversary of the October Revolution:

The great world-wide significance of the October Revolution chiefly consists in the fact that:

1. It has widened the scope of the national question and converted it from the particular question of combating national oppression in Europe into the general question of emancipating the oppressed peoples, colonies, and semicolonies from imperialism.

2. It has opened up wide possibilities for their emancipation and the right paths toward it, has thereby greatly facilitated the cause of the emancipation of the oppressed peoples of the West and the East, and has drawn them into the common current of the victorious struggle against imperialism.

3. It has thereby erected a bridge between the socialist West and the enslaved East, having created a new front of revolutions against world imperialism, extending from the proletarians of the West, through the Russian Revolution, to the oppressed peoples of the East.*

Thus it can be seen that there are two kinds of world revolution, the first belonging to the bourgeois and capitalist category. The

* Stalin, *Works* (Eng. ed.; Moscow, 1953), IV, 169–70.

era of this kind of world revolution is long past, having come to
an end as early as 1914, when the first imperialist World War
broke out, and especially in 1917, when the October Revolution
occurred in Russia. Since then, the second kind—namely, the proletarian-socialist world revolution—has started. The main force in
this revolution is the proletariat of the capitalist countries, and it
has as its allies the oppressed peoples of the colonies and semicolonies. No matter what classes, parties, or individuals in the oppressed nations join the revolution, and no matter whether or not
they are conscious of this fact and fully understand it, so long as
they oppose imperialism, their revolution becomes part of the
proletarian-socialist world revolution, and they themselves become
allies of this revolution.

Today, the Chinese revolution assumes an even greater significance. This is a time when the world is being plunged more and
more deeply into the Second World War by the economic and
political crises of capitalism; when the Soviet Union has reached
the period of transition from socialism to Communism and is now
capable of leading and helping the proletariat and oppressed nations of the world in their fight against imperialist war and capitalist reaction; when the proletariat of the capitalist countries is
preparing to overthrow capitalism and establish socialism; and
when China's proletariat, peasantry, intelligentsia, and other sections of the petty bourgeoisie have become a mighty independent political force under the leadership of the Chinese Communist Party. At such a juncture, are we not right in claiming that
the Chinese revolution has assumed a greater significance in the
world? I think we are. . . .

The first stage of the Chinese revolution, which contains many
subdivisions, belongs, so far as its social character is concerned, to
a new type of bourgeois-democratic revolution which is not yet a
proletarian-socialist revolution in itself, but it has long been part
of the proletarian-socialist world revolution and is now even an
important part of it and a powerful ally. The first step or stage of
this revolution is certainly not, and cannot be, the establishment
of a capitalist society under the dictatorship of the Chinese bourgeoisie, but will be the establishment of a New Democratic society under the joint dictatorship of all Chinese revolutionary classes
headed by the Chinese proletariat. Then the revolution will
develop into the second stage to establish a socialist society in
China. . . .

New Democratic Politics

The Chinese national bourgeoisie, because it belongs to a colonial and semicolonial country and lives under imperialist oppression, retains, even in the era of imperialism, at certain periods and to a certain degree, a revolutionary quality as expressed in its opposition to foreign imperialism and the home governments of bureaucrats and war lords (instances of the latter can be found in the Revolution of 1911 and in the Northern Expedition), and can ally itself with the proletariat and the petty bourgeoisie to oppose those enemies whom it wants to oppose. This is the difference between the Chinese bourgeoisie and the bourgeoisie of old Czarist Russia. Since Czarist Russia was already a militarist and feudalist imperialist power which carried on aggression against other countries, her bourgeoisie was in no way revolutionary. In Czarist Russia, the task of the proletariat was to oppose the bourgeoisie, not to unite with it. On the other hand, because China is a colony and a semicolony suffering from aggression by others, her national bourgeoisie has at certain periods and to a certain degree a revolutionary quality. Thus, in China, the task of the proletariat is to take into account the revolutionary quality of the national bourgeoisie and form with it a united front against imperialism and the bureaucratic and war-lord regime. . . .

It is quite evident that whoever in China can lead the people to overthrow the imperialist and feudal forces will win the people's confidence, because these forces, especially imperialism, are the mortal enemies of the people. Today, whoever can lead the people to drive out Japanese imperialism and carry out democratic policies will be the savior of the people. History has proved that the Chinese bourgeoisie is incapable of fulfilling this responsibility, which consequently falls upon the shoulders of the proletariat.

Therefore, in all circumstances, the proletariat, the peasantry, the intelligentsia, and other sections of the petty bourgeoisie in China are the basic forces which decide China's fate. These classes, some already awakened and others on the point of awakening, will necessarily become the basic components of the state structure. The democratic republic of China, which we now want to establish, can only be a democratic republic under the joint dictatorship of all anti-imperialist and antifeudal people, led by the proletariat—that is, a New Democratic republic. . . .

While different from the old European-American form of capitalist republic under bourgeois dictatorship, which is now out of date, this New Democratic republic is also different from the socialist republic of the type of the U.S.S.R., the republic of the dictatorship of the proletariat. The socialist republic is already flourishing in the Soviet Union, and will be established in all the capitalist countries and undoubtedly become the dominant form in the structure of state and political power in all industrially advanced countries, but, during a given historical period, it is not yet suitable for revolutions in colonial and semicolonial countries. Therefore, a third form of state must be adopted . . . namely, the New Democratic republic. This is the form for a given historical period and therefore a transitional form, but it is the necessary form to which there is no alternative.

The multifarious types of state system in the world can be reduced to three basic kinds, according to the class character of their political power: (1) republics under bourgeois dictatorships; (2) republics under the dictatorship of the proletariat; and (3) republics under the joint dictatorship of several revolutionary classes.

The first kind includes the old democratic states. Today, after the outbreak of the second imperialist war, there is no longer even a trace of democracy in many of the capitalist countries, which have come under, or are coming under, the bloody militarist dictatorship of the bourgeoisie. Certain countries under the joint dictatorship of the landlords and the bourgeoisie can be classed with this kind.

The second kind exists in the Soviet Union, and conditions for its birth are ripening in all capitalist countries. In the future, it will become the dominant form throughout the world for a certain period.

The third kind is the transitional form of state to be adopted in revolutions in colonial and semicolonial countries. Of course, revolutions in different colonial and semicolonial countries necessarily have certain different characteristics, but these are only minor differences within a general framework of uniformity. So long as they are revolutions in colonies or semicolonies, the form of state and political power will of necessity be basically the same, a New Democratic state under the joint dictatorship of several anti-imperialist classes. . . .

As to the question of political structure, it concerns the structural form of political power, the form adopted by certain social classes in organizing their political power to protect themselves against their enemies. Without a suitable organ of political power, there would be nothing to represent the state. In China, we can adopt a system of people's congresses—the national people's congress, the provincial people's congress, the county people's congress, the district people's congress, down to the township people's congress, and let these congresses at various levels elect the organs of government. But a system of really universal and equal suffrage—irrespective of sex, creed, property, or education—must be introduced so that each revolutionary class can be equitably represented according to its status in the state, the people's will properly expressed, the revolutionary struggles properly directed, and the spirit of New Democracy properly embodied. This is the system of democratic centralism. Only a government of democratic centralism can fully express the will of all the revolutionary people and most effectively fight the enemies of the revolution. The spirit of the phrase "not to be monopolized by a few" must be embodied in the government and the army apparatus; without a genuinely democratic system, this aim can never be attained, and there will be a discrepancy between the political structure and the state system.

The state system—joint dictatorship of all revolutionary classes. The political structure—democratic centralism. This is New Democratic government; this is a republic of New Democracy. . . .

2. Chou En-lai

Chou En-lai was born in 1898 of a scholarly Mandarin family. He studied in Nankai University in Tientsin, where he edited a radical student newspaper and was arrested for leading an antigovernment demonstration. Continuing his studies in Paris and Germany between 1920 and 1923, he organized Communist groups among overseas Chinese students. On his return to China, he became one of the early members of the Chinese Communist Party. In 1927, after an unsuccessful coup d'état in Shanghai led to a rupture of

*the Nationalist-Communist coalition, he was one of the founders
of the Chinese Red Army. In 1931, he was political director of the
Army, and in 1934 he participated in the Long March to Yenan
in the northwest. Chou En-lai headed the Communist delegation
in the diplomatic negotiations with the Marshall mission after
World War II. Then, when the Communists came to power in
1949, he became Premier and Foreign Minister. His speech at the
Bandung Conference (April, 1955) represented an attempt to
break out of China's isolation and establish contact even with anti-
Communist nations such as Thailand and the Philippines. In it,
Chou tried to identify China with the anticolonial revolution and
to suggest that the Chinese model of economic development should
be followed by other underdeveloped nations.*

SPEECH TO THE BANDUNG
CONFERENCE*

The Asian-African Conference, on which the whole world is focus-
ing its attention, has begun its session. . . .

It is the first time in history that so many countries of Asia and
Africa have gathered together to hold a conference. On these two
continents live more than half of the world population. The people of Asia and Africa created brilliant ancient civilizations and
made tremendous contributions to mankind. But ever since modern times, most of the countries of Asia and Africa in varying degrees have been subjected to colonial plunder and oppression, and
have thus been forced to remain in a stagnant state of poverty and
backwardness. Our voices have been suppressed, our aspirations
shattered, and our destiny placed in the hands of others. Thus,
we have no choice but to rise against colonialism. Suffering from
the same cause and struggling for the same aim, we the Asian and
African peoples have found it easier to understand each other and
have long had deep sympathy and concern for one another.

Now the face of the Asian-African region has undergone a radical change. More and more countries have cast off or are casting

* From *China and the Asian-African Conference* (*Documents*) (Peking:
Foreign Languages Press, 1955).

off the shackles of colonialism. The colonial powers can no longer use the methods of the past to continue their plunder and oppression. The Asia and Africa of today are no longer the Asia and Africa of yesterday. Many countries of this region have taken their destiny into their own hands after long years of endeavors. Our conference itself reflects this profound historical change.

However, the rule of colonialism in this region has not yet come to an end, and new colonialists are attempting to take the place of the old ones. Not a few of the Asian and African peoples are still leading a life of colonial slavery. Not a few of the Asian and African peoples are still subjected to racial discrimination and deprived of human rights. The courses which we peoples of the Asian and African countries have taken in striving for freedom and independence may vary, but our will to win and preserve our freedom and independence is the same. However different the specific conditions in each of our countries may be, it is equally necessary for most of us to eliminate the state of backwardness caused by the rule of colonialism. We need to develop our countries independently with no outside interference and in accordance with the will of the people.

The peoples of Asia and Africa have long suffered from aggression and war. Many of them have been forced by the colonialists to serve as cannon fodder in aggressive wars. Therefore, the peoples of these two continents can have nothing but strong detestation of aggressive war. They know that new threats of war will not only endanger the independent development of their countries, but also intensify the enslavement by colonialism. That is why the Asian and African peoples all the more hold dear world peace and national independence.

In view of the foregoing, the common desire of the peoples of the Asian and African countries cannot be anything other than to safeguard world peace, to win and to preserve national independence, and, accordingly, to promote friendly cooperation among nations. . . .

The overwhelming majority of the people throughout the world, regardless of what social system they live under, want peace and are opposed to war. The peace movement of the people in different countries has become more extensive and intensive. They demand the end of the armament race and preparations for war. They demand that first of all the big powers should reach agreement on the reduction of armaments. They demand the prohibition of atomic weapons and all other weapons of mass destruction. They demand that atomic energy be used for peaceful purposes in order to bring welfare to mankind. Their voices can no longer be ignored. The policy of aggression and war is becoming more and more repugnant to the people. The plotters of war are resorting even more frequently to threats of war as an instrument of their aggressive policy. However, threats of war can frighten into submission no one who is determined to resist. They can only place the threat-makers in a more isolated and confused position. We believe that if only we are determined to preserve peace together with all the peace-loving nations and peoples of the world, peace can be preserved.

The majority of our Asian and African countries, including China, are still very backward economically, owing to the long period of colonial domination. That is why we demand not only political independence but economic independence as well. Of course, our demand for political independence does not mean a policy of exclusion toward countries outside of the Asian-African region. However, the days when the Western powers controlled our destiny are already past. The destiny of Asian and African countries should be taken into the hands of the peoples themselves. We strive to realize our own economic independence, but this does not mean the rejection of economic cooperation with any country outside of the Asian-African region. However, we want to do away with the exploitation of backward countries in the East by colonial powers in the West and to develop the independent and sovereign economy of our own countries. Complete independence is an objective for which the great majority of Asian and African countries have to struggle for a long time.

In China, ever since the people became masters of their own country, all their efforts have been directed to the elimination of backwardness left behind by the prolonged semicolonial society and the building of their country into an industrialized one. In the last five years, we have rehabilitated the national economy ruined by long years of war, and have since 1953 started the First Five-Year Plan of economic construction. As a result of these efforts, production in all the main fields, such as iron and steel, cotton cloth, and grains, has exceeded the level of any period in the history of China. But these achievements are still very small as compared with the highly industrialized ones. Like other countries in Asia and Africa, we are in urgent need of a peaceful international environment for the development of our independent and sovereign economy. . . .

We Asian and African countries need to cooperate in the economic and cultural fields in order to facilitate the elimination of the economic and cultural backwardness caused by the long period of colonial exploitation and oppression. This cooperation should be based on equality and mutual benefit, with no conditions for privilege attached. The trade relations and economic cooperation between us should have for its purpose the promotion of the independent economic development in each country, and not to convert any country into a sole producer of raw materials and a market for consumer goods. Our cultural exchange should have respect for the development of the national culture of each country, and not ignore the characteristics and special merits of the culture of any country so that we may learn and benefit from each other.

Today, when the peoples of Asia and Africa are increasingly taking their destiny into their own hands, even though the present economic and cultural cooperation among ourselves cannot yet be of a very large scale, it can be definitely said that this cooperation based on equality and mutual benefit will have a great future. We are convinced that with the advancement of industrialization of our countries and the raising of our peoples' standards of living, and with the elimination of artificial trade barriers placed between us from without, trade intercourse and economic cooperation among the Asian and African countries will become ever closer, and cultural interflow will be ever more frequent.

If we follow the principles of mutual respect for sovereignty and territorial integrity, nonaggression, noninterference in each other's internal affairs, equality, and mutual benefit, the peaceful coexistence of countries with different social systems can be realized. When these principles are ensured of implementation, there is no reason why international disputes cannot be settled through negotiation.

In the interest of defending world peace, we Asian and African countries, which are more or less under similar circumstances, should be the first to cooperate with one another in a friendly manner and put peaceful coexistence into practice. The discord and estrangement created among the Asian and African countries by colonial rule in the past should no longer be there. We Asian and

African countries should respect one another and eliminate any suspicion and fear which may exist between us.

The Government of the People's Republic of China fully agrees to the aims of the Asian-African Conference as defined by the prime ministers of the five South Asian countries in the Joint Communiqué of the Bogor Conference. We hold that in order to promote world peace and cooperation, the countries of Asia and Africa should first of all, in line with their common interest, seek good will and cooperation among themselves and establish friendly and neighborly relations. India, Burma, and China have affirmed the five principles of peaceful coexistence as the guiding principles in their mutual relations. These principles have received support from more and more countries. Following these principles, China and Indonesia have already achieved good results in their preliminary talks on the question of the nationality of the citizens of one country residing in the other. During the Geneva Conference, China also expressed its readiness to develop friendly relations with the Indochinese states on the basis of these five principles. There is no reason why the relations between China and Thailand, the Philippines, and other neighboring countries cannot be improved on the basis of these five principles. China is ready to establish normal relations with other Asian and African countries on the basis of the strict adherence to these principles, and is willing to promote the normalization of the relations between China and Japan. In order to promote mutual understanding and cooperation among us, we propose that the governments, parliaments, and people's organizations of the Asian and African countries make friendly visits to each other's countries.

Gone forever are the days when the destiny of the Asian and African peoples was manipulated at will by others. We believe that if we are determined to preserve world peace, no one can drag us into war; if we are determined to strive for and safeguard our national independence, no one can continue to enslave us; if we are determined to enter into a friendly cooperation, no one can split us.

What we Asian and African countries want are peace and independence. It is not our intention to make Asian and African countries antagonistic to countries in other regions. We want just as well the establishment of peaceful and cooperative relations with countries in other regions.

This meeting of ours was not easily brought about. Though there are among us many different views, they should not influence the common desires that we all hold. Our conference ought to give expression to our common desires and thus make itself a treasured page in the history of Asia and Africa. At the same time, the contact that has been established by us through this conference should be maintained in order that we may make a greater contribution to world peace.

As His Excellency President Sukarno of the Republic of Indonesia has rightly said, we Asians and Africans must be united.

Let us greet in advance the success of our conference.

3. Sukarno

Sukarno, President of Indonesia, was born in 1901 at Surabaya, the son of a village teacher. At the age of twelve, he entered a Dutch elementary school, and later was sent to secondary school by a nationalist friend of his father. He joined a nationalist organization, and entered the Engineering School at Bandung, where he received his degree in 1925. Subsequently, Sukarno helped form the Indonesian National Party (PNI). He was imprisoned by the Dutch in 1929, and again in 1933, when he was exiled to a remote part of Indonesia. He was freed by the Japanese in 1942. On August 17, 1946, before the return of the Dutch, Sukarno declared his country's independence. In 1949, after several years of fighting, sovereignty was finally transferred by the Dutch.

In 1959, Sukarno dissolved parliament and outlawed several of the political parties. He now rules according to "guided democracy"—through leadership by an elite, consultation with an advisory parliament that represents social and economic groups, and decision-making by discussion and consensus rather than by voting.

In the following selection—taken from a lecture given by Sukarno on October 31, 1958, to students of the Hasanuddin University—Sukarno describes his view of the contemporary world as divided into three groups of nations, and recommends an eclectic

*approach to national development. In addition, he defends
"guided democracy" as superior to what he calls "free-fight liberalism."*

LECTURE TO THE STUDENTS OF
HASANUDDIN UNIVERSITY*

Jefferson and Marx

. . . The British philosopher Bertrand Russell divides mankind at
present into two groups, following two different philosophies. One
group has faith in the Declaration of Independence of Thomas
Jefferson, while the other group believes in the Communist Manifesto of Karl Marx. . . .

Bertrand Russell is not partial to one or the other group. He
only hopes that the competition between the followers of these
two philosophies would not be determined on the battlefield. It
should not be solved through the destruction of men by men,
because of the signs we see now and which have also been observed by themselves, but at the end they want to prove their
stand by fighting one another, destroying one another in war.

Bertrand Russell said: Compete with each other, but do not try
to reach a solution on the battlefield. Compete in a field that
brings prosperity to mankind. Please compete and try to achieve
prosperity of mankind by applying your respective ideas. Followers of Thomas Jefferson, please try to establish the prosperity of
men according to your world of thought, and followers of Karl
Marx, please try to bring prosperity to mankind. Those who will
bring the greatest prosperity to men will prove to be the victors in
this competition. . . .

I do not agree with Bertrand Russell when he said that humanity
only consists of these two groups. There is a third group, which
numbers more than a billion, maybe even more than one and a
half billion people—namely, the people who live under the flags
of nationalism in Asia and Africa.

Those are the people whose hearts throb eagerly, who are very

* Translated and published by the Ministry of Information, Djakarta, Indonesia, 1959.

anxious to realize their national independence by establishing a just and prosperous society without getting involved in any way with the two ways of thought mentioned by Bertrand Russell. These three groupings I regard as a phenomenon of the twentieth century: the group of Thomas Jefferson, the group adhering to the Communist Manifesto, and the group of Asian and African nationalism. . . . We not only advocate the coexistence of what is known as the Western bloc and the Communist bloc—the bloc of the United States and that of the Soviet Union, we not only want coexistence between these two blocs, but we also suggest that these two blocs should coexist with Asian-African nationalism. I suggest this because I have seen that Asian-African nationalism, the third group, is always disturbed and attacked by people from outside. It is not respected by people from outside. People even try to suppress and destroy it.

It is my sincere hope, and this hope I put on all the Indonesian students, that we should not, as a nation that has just been established as a state, that is eager to establish a just and prosperous society, a nation that is eager to build up, a nation that thus needs to look at the experiences of the outside world, indulge in too many theories and look for the small mistakes in other people's ideas, so that at the end we only see these mistakes. This attitude is useless. . . . We do not have to look deliberately for errors in the Declaration of Independence, concentrate and pounce on it when we have found one. Neither do we look only for the mistakes of Karl Marx and Friedrich Engels and doggedly criticize and analyze them. It is of no use for the community we are building. We are looking for the experience of other nations outside of Indonesia, especially in these later periods; we use their good experiences to build up our community and country, and cast away the bad experiences.

That is why it is so important to send our scientists, cadres, and youth to other parts of the world. If our government had enough money, I would ask Pak Prijono, the Minister of Education, to send as many students as possible to the United States, to the Soviet Union, to Canada, to the People's Republic of China—everywhere—to get experience.

Do not say first, I do not want to go to the United States, as it follows the world of thought of Thomas Jefferson. Or do not say, I do not want to go to the People's Republic of China, as it is within the world of thought of Karl Marx. This kind of opinion is wrong. I have mentioned earlier that the world of thought of Thomas Jefferson has a great number of followers. It is impossible for human beings not to be rational, not to see some good things in the world of thought of Thomas Jefferson. Because of the existence of some good points in the world of thought of Thomas Jefferson, that world of thought has tens of millions, hundreds of millions of followers, because human beings have sound minds. The same applies to Karl Marx. . . .

The problem our country faces now is in the first place to provide our people with a good living. Therefore, the present is no time for us for too much theorizing. We had better be practical and pick out whatever is good from the ideas of Thomas Jefferson as well as those from Karl Marx—without, however, taking sides. In politics, this attitude is known as our independent and active policy. But I would like this attitude to be taken in the field of science, too. . . .

Guided Democracy

For reconstruction, three basic requirements are needed:

Firstly, capital. It is clear that one cannot build up without capital. Furthermore, capital, if possible, should be our own capital—national capital—owned and raised by the Indonesian people themselves. If our own capital is not sufficient, we can contract loans from abroad. If we cannot obtain enough loans, then only can we invite foreign capital to invest here, but remember, my friends, I mention capital investment as number three here. Firstly, we have to get our own capital. Whenever it is not enough, there is nothing we can do except to borrow, to borrow capital which we will repay in terms. Only when it is necessary, foreign capital has to be imported.

Secondly, managerial know-how. One cannot build without the knowledge of how to organize. That is the reason why we make a blueprint, that is the reason why we established this university, to train and educate cadres—as many as possible. . . . We are grateful that at present we have 30,000 students in the whole of Indonesia. But that is not enough yet. I think that we need more than 150,000 students whose spirits are alert and whose minds are filled with practical, managerial, and applied sciences.

Thirdly, a political atmosphere which is conducive to reconstruction. Even though we possess capital (the first requirement), although we possess managerial know-how (the second requirement), if the political atmosphere is not conducive to reconstruction, development cannot be carried out smoothly. How is our political atmosphere at present? I have said over and over again, our political atmosphere is an unhealthy one, a liberal political atmosphere, an atmosphere of "free-fight liberalism." An atmosphere in which we continuously fight and quarrel, each claiming to be right, looking for mistakes of one another. It is a situation where there is no order and no unity, no one yielding to the other. One is eager to destroy the other. We must abandon this free-fight liberalism completely, if we want to develop and build up in the right way.

Indeed, the delegations which I sent have come back with an answer from the people of the countries they visited. Indonesia is richer than those countries. The Indonesians do not lack intelligence or brains. We also know that the Indonesian people have enough spirit. But why do we not build up speedily, why are we lagging behind? That is why, on the 17th of August, 1957, I said that the political atmosphere in Indonesia had to be changed. That is why I suggested that the free-fight liberalism which gives us this unhealthy atmosphere has to be abandoned. In order to draw up a blueprint, I suggested what is called democracy with leadership.

The day before yesterday, in Bogor, I was visited by a large delegation of 260, representing cooperative bodies of the whole of Indonesia. Their spokesman said the following: "Mr. President, with our cooperatives we have been able to raise the standard of living of the people a little. And for your knowledge, we would like to inform you that in the world of cooperatives, democracy with leadership or guided democracy is applied. In the world of cooperatives . . . we have a clear aim, a clear-cut way of working and distribution of profit—everything is clearly under leadership."

Within the world of cooperatives, then, guided democracy is applied. If the blueprint of the National Planning Council is finished, the execution thereof could not be carried out smoothly without guided democracy, without leadership. The number-one leader is the blueprint itself. One cannot carry out a blueprint and at the same time debate about it, after it has been approved by parliament. This blueprint becomes the property of the Indonesian people, becomes national property. . . . This blueprint has to be carried out, and its principles cannot be debated again.

I am myself a qualified engineer. Very often, when I was in the construction business, I received blueprints of things to be built. I carried out those blueprints as they were. I did not argue why, for instance, certain lines went a certain way, why a certain thing should be made of concrete and not of wood, why its stories were that high when they were not lower. It was a blueprint entrusted to me, for me to carry out, and I would carry it out. The blueprint was my guide, and I myself guided and led the employees. As a qualified engineer, I had under me superintendents and foremen. I was their leader, and I had conferences with them. But my conferences with them were not of that type of free-fight liberalism. I conferred with them about the execution of the blueprint. I asked the superintendents: These things have to be made out of concrete; what would be the best way to get them done? One superintendent would suggest: Pak, I think this is the best way; get stones, gravel, sand, and cement, call a lot of people—twenty, a hundred—and have everything mixed by hand. I then asked another superintendent what his opinion was. He answered: No, do not work by hand, Bung, this building is too large for that; buy a concrete mixer at once; with that we can mix concrete for this building and others. I conferred with my foremen—I practiced democracy with them—I asked for their opinion. I also discussed the choice of the materials; I conferred with my men. On all aspects of the execution of the blueprint, I held discussions, but these discussions were under guidance—the guidance of the blueprint, my guidance, the constructor of the building.

That is why it is wrong when people say that guided democracy is a false democracy, that it is a form of dictatorship. I even said in my statement of October 28, 1958, that democracy with leadership is a true Indonesian democracy. This is the danger you are facing, the danger that many of you become copyists. You have heard of the word "democracy"; democracy is indeed good. What does America say about democracy? It is to be found in certain American books. What does England say, France, the Netherlands, Germany? They each have their own reference books. Well, one of them must be the genuine democracy. Thus, you then try to apply in Indonesia democracy as it is practiced in America, Germany, France, England, the Netherlands, the U.S.S.R., or in other countries? You are only trying to copy!

No, as I have said before, we have to return to our own personality; we want to return to our own identity. Do not let us become a carbon-copy nation. We have had a democracy since olden times. I do not imply that we should remain as we were then. But the things of former times are good material for us today to refer to, because we are going to establish democracy in our own country.

How was democracy of former times in Indonesia? It still is practiced today in the villages in Java, Minangkabau, Sulawesi, Lombok, Bali, and other places—namely, in their laws and their system of *musjawarah* and *mufakat* (discussion and agreement). Every village practices democracy. But do they in these village meetings apply the practice of voting? Of free-fight liberalism, where half plus one is always right? No, the *musjawarah* is held under the guidance of Lurah, the Chief of the Elders, of Nini Mamak, the guidance of whoever is leader. Everybody says something different until at one time a compromise is achieved out of all these different opinions, without voting. This is what is called *mufakat* (agreement)—that by *musjawarah* (discussion) without voting, a joint compromise is achieved. There is no dictatorship in *musjawarah* and *mufakat*. That is why democracy with leadership is a true, original Indonesian democracy. This is one of the most important sources for us from which we can draw material to find a new, clear democracy—not American democracy, Dutch, French, British, German, or Soviet, or anybody else's democracy. Let us find a democracy which is suitable for our own identity. And use sources and material which are to be found in our own country.

Regarding our own democracy, I initiated the idea, calling on the people to join to fight the diseases that were the results of free-fight liberalism. I called on the people to destroy free-fight liberalism completely, and to change it into Indonesian democracy, guided democracy, or democracy with leadership. If people asked me to explain in detail what it means, I would not be able to give a proper answer. No, I want this guided democracy to become the property of the Indonesian people again. That is why I suggest to the people, especially the experts, scientists, students, to think. Please think and rethink, make and remake. Think, carry it out so that as a joint result we can achieve a new democratic system which I call democracy with leadership, or guided democracy, which is suitable for conditions in Indonesia. . . .

4. U Nu

U Nu was born in 1907, the son of a small trader. He went to a secondary school established by Burmese nationalists in Rangoon, and later attended Rangoon University, where he was President of the Student Union when it staged a violent strike against British rule. Afterward, he wrote nationalist books and pamphlets, and led the underground resistance movement. During World War II, he first served as Foreign Minister in the puppet government set up by the Japanese, but then, in 1944, joined in the establishment of the Anti-Fascist People's Freedom League (AFPFL), which opposed the Japanese. After the war, U Nu became Vice-President of the AFPFL and, in 1947, was unanimously elected President of the Burmese Constituent Assembly. When Prime Minister Aung San was assassinated in 1947, U Nu succeeded him, leading Burma to independence on October 17, 1947. Although he had continual difficulty with separatist minority groups and with the Communists, U Nu retained power until 1958. At that time, he turned over the government to General Ne Win, calling upon him to stabilize conditions and root out corruption. In 1960, U Nu's party won an overwhelming electoral victory, and he returned to office, only to resign once again in favor of General Ne Win in early 1962.

U Nu is a devout Buddhist. He has also been strongly influenced by Marxism, but maintains a critical attitude toward both capitalism and Communism. The following selection demonstrates U Nu's belief in democracy, socialism, and neutralism.

TOWARD A SOCIALIST STATE*

Actually, socialism is a doctrine or political philosophy which arose because of capitalism. I will explain this further:

1. The capitalists, under capitalism, want profits.
2. Because of this profit motive, there is exploitation.
3. From the time exploitation came into existence, two classes of people came into being—namely, the exploiting class and the exploited class.
4. Because of this fact of exploitation, and in spite of the fact that this world has a sufficiency of natural resources, there arose such problems as poverty and starvation, social insecurity, ill health on a large scale, and as a consequence of economic insufficiency, immorality.
5. Human greed led the capitalists, who were making profits, to want to make ever larger and better profits. This, in turn, stimulated a search for territories from which raw materials could be obtained cheaply and plentifully. After the raw materials had been processed into manufactured goods, it became necessary again to look for markets which would be under their control, so that the manufactured goods could be sold at prices to suit them. This search for territories, for raw materials and controlled markets, led to imperialistic expansion, and to wars between imperialist powers.

Men of good will felt unhappy at the sight of so much poverty and starvation in the world—in spite of the world having such great natural resources—and at the sight of so much ill health, immorality, and bloodshed and destruction through wars of imperialistic expansion all over the world. The unhappiness led the men of good will to seek ways and means by which the world might be free of its troubles. This search led to the discovery that the main cause of the troubles of the world was the desire for making profits. It was seen that so long as people were actuated by the profit motive, there would be exploitation of human beings

* Excerpts from a speech delivered by U Nu to the Third All-Burma Congress of the AFPFL on January 28, 1958; translated and published by the Ministry of Information, Rangoon, Burma, 1958.

by other human beings, and so long as there was exploitation, there would be the aforesaid troubles of the world: poverty, starvation, immorality, and imperialistic wars. Therefore, if these troubles of the world . . . were to disappear, the root cause of all, the profit motive, must be tackled. This was realized by the men of good will. Then they cast about for ways and means by which commodities, instead of being produced for profit, were to be produced for the use of people. They found the answer. I would like to give the answer in simple words.

If the production of commodities for profit was to be replaced by the production of commodities for use by people, the means of production must be transferred from the capitalists to the workers. This was not an easy task. About the time that men of good will were looking for a solution to their problems, the powers that be in their countries were either capitalists themselves or allies of capitalists. Because of this, the administrative apparatus and the legal provisions worked to the advantage of the capitalists. Since this was so, let alone endeavoring to transfer actually the means of production from the capitalists to the workers, even an attempt at this would have been met by oppressive measures from the capitalists, who would use their administrative and legal apparatus freely to squash this attempt. Therefore, if production of commodities for profit was to be replaced by production for use, there remained no other means but to take over the political control of the country by the workers themselves. This was how the men of good will reasoned. These men of good will became socialists, and their convictions became socialism. In trying to gain political control, two methods became clear: One was to gain political control by armed revolution; the other was to gain political control through an elected parliament, by democratic means. Some of the socialists preferred the first method, and other socialists preferred the second method. I will state fully, later on, which method the AFPFL has chosen and accepted, and why. . . .

If the socialist state that we are building can merely guarantee the full exercise of all the fundamental rights, but is not able to provide a minimum standard of living for the citizens, so that there is insufficiency in food, shelter, and clothing, then this so-called "socialist state" will also be just a gilded façade with a worthless interior.

But there is something worse than all this. We declare and proclaim that we will build a socialist state. But if, instead of working for the welfare and the interest of the people, we seek selfish advantages and act only in self-interest, with laws defied and broken not by the ordinary citizens but by the very people who are supposed to be building the socialist state, then the state we build will not be a socialist state. It will be an utterly rotten state which will not even have a gilded façade to cover up a worthless interior. . . .

The socialist state that we are creating must not be imposed on the people from above, against their will and desire. Such an imposition on the people of the Union of Burma can never be made, so long as we are convinced that the fundamental political right of free election of a government by the people, in accordance with law, should be maintained, so long as we accept and practice this right, and so long as we defend the continued existence of this right. Since it would be possible to create a socialist state only on the basis of a mandate freely and willingly given by the electorate—that is, the people—those individuals who aim to create the socialist state will not dare to ignore or set aside the temperament, the heritage, the traditions, the culture, and the religious beliefs of the people. These elements of tradition, culture, and religion will have to be accepted as component elements of the socialist state. And this acceptance will ensure the cooperation and ardent support of the entire people of the country in the task of building the socialist state. This cooperation and fervent support will in turn imply that the socialist state we are creating will not be a socialist state of a group of individuals, but the socialist state of the entire mass of people in the country. If we can build a socialist state like that, not belonging to a few individuals, but belonging to all the people of the country, then our socialist state will endure longer, and more firmly, than any other socialist state. Therefore, I earnestly urge that we should take particular care to create a socialist state that belongs to the entire people of the country, and not to a group of individuals or to a party.

Attitude to Marxism

We find that there are two kinds of people in relation to their attitudes to Marxism. The first kind believe and accept without reservation all the three parts of Marxism—namely, dialectical materialism, historical materialism, and economic determinism—as infallible and utterly correct. These people are Communists.

They are also called Marxists. The other kind accept Marxism as one of the guides to political action. These people do not believe unreservedly in Marxism as an infallible and utterly correct doctrine, as the Communists do. They accept only such portions of Marxism as they think fit. Such people cannot be called Marxists.

The Marxists or Communists, who belong to the first category, cannot believe in or accept any other faith or religion. Thus, for these people, Marxism is the sole faith, the sole bible, the sole religion. Therefore, those who wish to be Marxists or Communists must first of all study Marxism in relation to the religion they believe in. Only after such study, if they come to believe in Marxism, they will have to give up their religion.

If they retain their belief in their religion, they will have to give up Marxism. It is entirely impossible to take the attitude that both Marxism and religion are in the right, and that, therefore, both can be accepted.

When we were younger, we had not yet studied Marxism in detail and in all its aspects. Neither did we know Buddhism in detail or with any exactness. At that time, more or less on hearsay and cursory reading, we impetuously and loudly claimed that Marxism was the same as Buddhism. We are very remorseful for having made, at one time, such ill-considered and unfounded claims.

I do not approve, in principle, of dragging religion into a political discussion. The reason for dragging religion into the present discussion of Marxism is simply because Marxism itself is a religion for the Marxists, and also because those who believe in and accept Marxism can neither believe in nor accept any other religion. If Marxism would not imply any interference with or abandonment of belief in or acceptance of any other religion, then there would be no necessity at all for dragging religion into this discussion. . . .

I will now consider the concept of the dictatorship of the proletariat. We cannot accept the idea of the dictatorship of the proletariat, which means the dictatorship of one party. It has been laid down that after the workers destroy capitalist society, they are to establish a socialist state through the dictatorship of the proletariat. To us, the dictatorship of the proletariat is a terrible and dangerous means. I do not think that I need to enlarge on the reasons why it is terrible and dangerous, since you know the reasons already.

A group of individuals has to be given the power to govern and run a country. But it can never be possible to entrust any group with political power unconditionally and without restraints. While, on the one hand, political power has to be entrusted in the hands of a group of individuals, on the other hand, there will have to be checks and counteracting factors to prevent abuse of such power. These checks and counteracting factors are no other than: (1) the right of free speech; (2) the right of free expression; (3) the right of free organization; (4) the independence of the judiciary; and (5) the right of the people to elect the government they prefer, according to due law and process.

My listeners must have heard of the saying "Power corrupts; absolute power corrupts absolutely." This throws light on what is liable to happen to human nature when it can indulge in power. Those who are entrusted with power are at first quite good people. But after a time, they begin to love the taste of power. As soon as they have that love for power, they will use all means to ensure that power remains in their hands. And when they resort to all means of retaining power, the people of the country will lose their fundamental rights, and the country will become a police state. This is not the end. From that will develop struggles for power. These struggles for power mean that those in power will try to eliminate by any means their opponents or those who might become their opponents. But it will not end with these struggles for power among those who hold power. In the struggles, the armed forces will have to take sides. This will lead to a disintegration of discipline. And when discipline is gone, the armed forces will begin to think that it is better to seize power for themselves, rather than be stooges of ambitious politicians. When this idea grows strong enough, ambitious leaders of the armed forces will push out the politicians whose stooges they have been and will seize power for themselves. The day that a country's armed forces enter the sphere of politics will mark the beginning of the end of the country. The reason is that once it is realized that it is possible to seize power through force, other ambitious leaders in the armed forces will gather a following and will depose the people above them from power. Thus, in a vicious circle of one ambitious man after another seizing power, the country is bound to be ruined. . . .

As the AFPFL does not believe that Marxism is a doctrine that is infallible, the AFPFL approves of only some parts of the economic doctrine of Marxism, and rejects Marxism as the ideology of the AFPFL.

We accept some parts of the economic doctrine of Marx. It is our belief that commodities should not be produced for profit, but for use. The production of goods for profit and not for use is one of the main causes of poverty and starvation in the midst of plenty, and one of the main causes of ill health and disease, of immorality, and of destructive and bloody wars.

It is not an easy task to establish a system in which goods are produced not for profit but for use. In attempting to establish such a system, the most difficult part would be to overcome human greed. If greed can be overcome successfully, to that extent will the establishment of such a system be successful. However, difficult as it may be to overcome human greed, as socialists, we must make it our goal to establish a system in which goods are produced not for profit but for use. There will be plenty for all if we are successful in establishing that system.

In endeavoring to establish this system, we would wish to avoid doing it through a wrong ideology. That is why we have categorically stated in our declaration "Our Goal" that "in endeavoring to establish this socialist state, we must never lose sight of the fact that the socialism that we will put into practice implies neither Communism nor state capitalism."

I have explained at length and in detail why our ideology cannot be Communism or Marxism, and I hope I have made the reasons clear to you. I now want to explain why the socialism that we will put into practice will not be state capitalism.

State capitalism, I believe, has as its basis Hegelianism. I have already explained earlier what Hegelianism is, but I will summarize it again, so that my listeners can remember the essential points. According to Hegelianism, the citizens or individuals exist for the state. They must live and die for the state. In the state, there should be no opposition to the government. Thus, Hegelianism clearly supports autocracy. As state capitalism is autocratic, exploitation of workers under state capitalism can be much worse than under ordinary capitalism.

That is why we have definitely declared, in . . . "Our Goal," that "we must take particular care not to allow the exploitation, the tyranny, and the oppression that are inherent evils in Communism and in state capitalism to become any part of the socialist state that we wish to create." . . .

The Two Blocs

As regards world peace, I am very hopeful and optimistic. Among the reasons for my optimism, the more important are as follows:

1. The two opposing power blocs very well realize that if there were a third world war, there would be no victors or vanquished, but only a universal holocaust.

2. The two opposing power blocs are more or less even in their strength.

3. The leaders of the two blocs—President Eisenhower, Prime Minister Macmillan, Khrushchev, Premier Bulganin, Chairman Mao Tse-tung, and Premier Chou En-lai—do not desire war and are leaders who really want world peace.

4. All the peoples of the world really long for the maintenance of peace.

However, although world peace is within reach, it seems to elude our grasp, for suspicion and doubt on both sides are deeply rooted. Therefore, the first essential task for getting world peace is to clear away these deep-rooted suspicions and doubts. And for this purpose, summit conferences are very helpful. Therefore, we support emphatically the principle of holding summit conferences and urge that they be held as soon as possible.

Further, neutral countries like Burma play an important part in dispelling doubts and suspicions on either side. As both the power blocs have accepted the fact that Burma is nobody's stooge, that Burma is not afraid to do what is right and just, and that Burma is genuinely and disinterestedly desirous of world peace, it is my belief that Burma can do a lot to lessen suspicion between the two blocs and to work for greater understanding between them.

I would like you to know that we are putting forth our best endeavors on this question of world peace. I hereby declare on behalf of both the government and the AFPFL that we pledge ourselves to continue to work with ever greater endeavor for world peace.

The Defense of Democracy

After speaking on world peace, I would like to talk about democracy. I have related earlier how we defended democracy. It cannot be said that by being merely defended, democracy becomes enduring and firm. There is a lot to do in the future to make democracy firm and stable. If we study the history of Spain and Germany, we will find that it was due to an indulgent attitude toward activities of the Fascist Franco and the Nazi Hitler that democracy disappeared in those countries. Therefore, every true son of the Union of Burma who loves democracy must join with us in keeping watch and ward on the enemies of democracy. We must not be slow in dealing effectively with any threat to democracy. I admit that we have been rather laggard in some cases. This has made some people impatient with us. I admit that we must learn not to waver at critical moments. . . .

However, the mere use of the label and the name of democracy does not guarantee that a particular system of government is a real democracy. Just as in many walks of life, there are imitations and forgeries of good and valuable things, there are such things as "imitation democracy," "forged democracy," and "gold-plated democracy." Therefore, I warn you, do not accept as true democracy all governments which go under the name of democracy. Just as one has to test a lump of seeming gold to find out whether it is really gold or merely brass coated with gold, one has to test whether it is a true democracy. There are five tests:

1. Is there a right of free assembly and association in that state? Are there political parties founded in exercise of this right of free assembly and association, which freely act as the opposition to the government?

2. Is there a right of free speech in that state? Can you find or hear people in that state who exercise this right of free speech and freely criticize and condemn the government?

3. Is there a right of free expression in that state? Can you find people (or read their writings) who exercise this right of free expression, write, draw, print, or publish articles, letters, and cartoons which freely criticize and condemn the government?

4. Can the courts in that state freely administer justice according to law? Can you find, or hear judgments of courts, which the courts (in exercise of their right to administer justice freely according to law) have passed without considering whether the government will be pleased or displeased with their decisions, and endeavoring only to be correct and just according to law?

5. Can the people of that state elect, according to the procedure laid down in their constitution, the government that they like and want? Do you find that once in every three years, or four years,

or five years the people, in exercise of this right, do elect according to the procedure laid down in the constitution, the government that they want? . . .

Every member of AFPFL must follow the five cardinal rules of conduct:

1. We must practice the moral precepts. Even if all the moral precepts cannot be followed, a member of the AFPFL at least should not drink, should not gamble, should not have illicit sexual relations, should not seek wealth by unjust and illegal means. If the members merely follow these four simple moral rules, the good name and the good conduct of AFPFL as a whole are assured. Even if it is found that all the members of the AFPFL cannot follow these precepts, at least the leaders of the AFPFL should follow them. Leaders are chosen by the people because of their character and ability, and if those leaders drink, gamble, have illicit sexual relations, and get rich by unjust and illegal means, how can their followers respect them? They will watch with folded arms, only because they cannot do anything else. In their minds, the followers would lose respect for their leaders and would call them "immoral fools." One thing we must always bear in mind: If you do not conduct yourselves according to morality . . . you will never do well in life. Drunkards, gamblers, seducers, and thieves can never build a socialist state, however much they argue and shout that they will build such a state, because a socialist state is founded on morality. . . . Therefore, at least, leaders of all degrees at the various AFPFL headquarters, starting from the central headquarters at Rangoon down to ward headquarters, must keep these precepts.

2. We must not be conceited. We must not have an exaggerated opinion of ourselves. I think this rule of conduct to be of greater importance to members of AFPFL than to others. I will explain to you why I think so.

After I had been Prime Minister for a considerable length of time, I found that the dreaded disease of conceit had gradually but surely taken hold of me. From the day the disease developed, I began to think, "I am the most courageous member of AFPFL, I am the most able, I am the most industrious, I am the most honest." "I" became the subject of my thoughts. The moment I became conceited in that way, I began to look down upon my own colleagues, and wanted to treat them with contempt. I admit that the present lack of harmony in the AFPFL has its roots partly in that conceit. When a person is attacked by this disease, the patient thinks highly of his own virtues and less of his faults, and thinks highly of other people's faults and less of their virtues. When this disease becomes an epidemic in any party, order and unity and harmony will disappear. I will illustrate this with a little story.

Once, in a village, there were two households. In the first household, every day, the sound of quarrels and fights rang through the neighborhood. From the second household, however, no sound whatsoever was heard. So a neighbor went to the second household and praised the head of the household. The latter replied, "In the other house, they are all good people, so they quarrel. In this house, however, we are all wicked, so there is no quarrel. I will explain this. In the first household, when anything goes wrong, the husband blames the wife, because he is good, and the wife blames the husband, for she is good, too. The result is a quarrel. But in my house, if anything goes wrong, I blame myself, for I am bad, and my wife blames herself, for she is bad, too. So there is no argument and no quarrel."

Let us be like the people in the second household. In the past, we have looked only at our virtues and at others' faults. Let us in the future look also at our own faults and others' virtues. Let us learn to think less of our own ability and more of others' ability. Let us endeavor to develop this noble trait of character a thousand-fold. I myself hereby promise that I shall endeavor to avoid in the future the mistakes to which I have admitted.

3. We must not gather strength, in the form of followers and supporters, for ourselves individually. We must gather strength for the AFPFL as a whole. If every leader tries to gather around him a body of followers and supporters in his self-interest, the AFPFL will be broken up into as many little factions as there are leaders. If the leaders gather strength for the whole AFPFL organization, instead of each one for himself, then each one also will find himself in a position of strength. Therefore, I urge the leaders to gather strength for the entire organization, and not for themselves individually.

4. In our relations with the public, we must practice the two principles of respectfulness and humility that are enjoyed by the Lord Buddha as beatitudes. AFPFL members are liable to lose

their sense of proportion and their balance when they have been long in power. This is an insidious process. One does not know oneself that one has lost a sense of balance. The unpopularity of people in power with the public is caused by the people in power behaving rudely to members of the public, exercising their power unduly and unfairly, and assuming a haughty attitude toward others. The people are the source of our power. We are in their debt. They are our benefactors. One must not turn against one's benefactors. Therefore, in our relations with our benefactors, we must endeavor particularly to show respect in the manner that is proper, and we must endeavor particularly to be humble. If we find that anyone from among ourselves conducts himself rudely, insultingly, or haughtily toward the public, we should at least go and apologize to these members of the public. If possible, we should go and pay respect to them according to Burmese custom. A man's courage and nobility can be judged from his ability to humble himself. Therefore, we must not hesitate or feel shy to apologize for our mistakes, and must go and pay respect to the injured party in the Burmese customary manner. We must be brave enough to do this. The advantages of doing that will be innumerable, both in a worldly and a religious sense. Therefore, I emphatically urge you to exercise respectfulness and humility in your relations with the public.

5. We must not depend on force and arms for our organizational tasks. We must rely only on correct ideology, sound policy and program, and leadership ability. . . .

If a politician collects arms, recruits criminals, and subverts members of the armed forces for his own purpose, then this politician is not one who believes in democracy. He must be a politician who believes in dictatorship. This kind of politician does not have a correct ideology or program. Such a politician has no qualities of leadership. Such a politician has no integrity. If we say that we believe in democracy, it is not enough to pay lip service to it. We must show by our deeds that we really believe in democracy. If we shout about our belief in democracy from the roof tops and then in practice do undemocratic deeds, we will be hypocrites. Therefore, no member of the AFPFL must rely on force. We must rely on our own ideology, our own policy and program, our own ability, and our own integrity. . . .

5. *Mohandas K. Gandhi*

Mohandas K. Gandhi was born in 1869 in western India, a member of the merchant caste. He studied law in London, was admitted to the bar in 1891, and then returned to India to practice law. Two years later, he went to South Africa, where he organized his first passive-resistance campaign against racial discrimination. On his return to India in 1915, he became one of the most influential members of the Indian Congress Party. After World War I, he organized campaigns of passive resistance calling for an end to British rule over India. Between 1922 and 1942, Gandhi was repeatedly imprisoned, but gained a vast following both in India and abroad. In 1948, after Indian independence had been established, Gandhi was assassinated by a Hindu fanatic—thus becoming a martyr to his belief in tolerance for all religions.

The Indian Congress Party still accepts Gandhi's philosophy as the basis of its ideology, although under Nehru it has taken a more favorable attitude toward industrialization. Kwame Nkrumah also mentions Gandhi as one of the important influences upon his thinking.

The following selections are from a pamphlet Gandhi wrote in 1909. They include his explanation of passive resistance, and his defense of village and home industries as a more appropriate economic system than the machine civilization of the West.

INDIAN HOME RULE*

True Civilization

Reader: You have denounced railways, lawyers, and doctors. I can see that you will discard all machinery. What, then, is civilization?

* Excerpts from *Indian Home Rule* (Ahmedabad: Navajivan Trust, 1946); reprinted by permission.

Editor: The answer to that question is not difficult. I believe that the civilization India has evolved is not to be beaten in the world. Nothing can equal the seeds sown by our ancestors. Rome went; Greece shared the same fate; the might of the Pharaohs was broken; Japan has become Westernized; of China, nothing can be said; but India is still, somehow or other, sound at the foundation. The people of Europe learn their lessons from the writings of the men of Greece or Rome, which exist no longer in their former glory. In trying to learn from them, the Europeans imagine that they will avoid the mistakes of Greece and Rome. Such is their pitiable condition. In the midst of all this, India remains immovable, and that is her glory. It is a charge against India that her people are so uncivilized, ignorant, and stolid that it is not possible to induce them to adopt any changes. It is a charge really against our merit. What we have tested and found true on the anvil of experience we dare not change. Many thrust their advice upon India, and she remains steady. This is her beauty; it is the sheet anchor of our hope.

Civilization is that mode of conduct which points out to man the path of duty. Performance of duty and observance of morality are convertible terms. To observe morality is to attain mastery over our mind and our passions. So doing, we know ourselves. The Gujarati equivalent for civilization means "good conduct."

If this definition be correct, then India, as so many writers have shown, has nothing to learn from anybody else, and this is as it should be. We notice that the mind is a restless bird; the more it gets the more it wants, and still remains unsatisfied. The more we indulge our passions, the more unbridled they become. Our ancestors, therefore, set a limit to our indulgences. They saw that happiness was largely a mental condition. A man is not necessarily happy because he is rich, or unhappy because he is poor. The rich are often seen to be unhappy, the poor to be happy. Millions will always remain poor. Observing all this, our ancestors dissuaded us from luxuries and pleasures. We have managed with the same kind of plough as it existed thousands of years ago. We have retained the same kind of cottages that we had in former times, and our indigenous education remains the same as before. We have had no system of life-corroding competition. Each followed his own occupation or trade, and charged a regulation wage. It was not that we did not know how to invent machinery; but our forefathers knew that, if we set our hearts after such things, we would become slaves and lose our moral fiber. They therefore, after due deliberation, decided that we should only do what we could with our hands and feet. They saw that our real happiness and health consisted in a proper use of our hands and feet. They further reasoned that large cities were a snare and a useless encumbrance and that people would not be happy in them, that there would be gangs of thieves and robbers, prostitution, and vice flourishing in them, and that poor men would be robbed by rich men. They were, therefore, satisfied with small villages. They saw that kings and their swords were inferior to the sword of ethics, and they, therefore, held the sovereigns of the earth to be inferior to the rishis and the fakirs.* A nation with a constitution like this is more fit to teach others than to learn from others. This nation had courts, lawyers, and doctors, but they were all within bounds. Everybody knew that these professions were not particularly superior; moreover, they did not rob people; they were considered people's dependants, not their masters. Justice was tolerably fair. The ordinary rule was to avoid courts. There were not touts to lure people into them. This evil, too, was noticeable only in and around capitals. The common people lived independently and followed their agricultural occupation. They enjoyed true home rule.

And where this cursed modern civilization has not reached, India remains as it was before. The inhabitants of that part of India will very properly laugh at your newfangled notions. The English do not rule over them, nor will you ever rule over them. Those whose name we speak we do not know, nor do they know us. I would certainly advise you and those like you who love the motherland to go into the interior that has not yet been polluted by the railways, and to live there for six months; you might then be patriotic and speak of home rule.

Now you see what I consider to be real civilization. Those who want to change conditions such as I have described are enemies of the country and are sinners.

Reader: It would be all right if India were exactly as you described it, but it is also India where there are hundreds of child widows, where two-year-old babies are married, where twelve-year-old girls are mothers and housewives, where women practice poly-

---

* A rishi is an ancient sage of the Hindu religion; a fakir is a religious ascetic.—ED.

andry, where the practice of *niyog** obtains, where, in the name of religion, girls dedicate themselves to prostitution, and where, in the name of religion, sheep and goats are killed. Do you consider these also symbols of the civilization that you have described?

Editor: You make a mistake. The defects that you have shown are defects. Nobody mistakes them for ancient civilization. They remain in spite of it. Attempts have always been made, and will be made, to remove them. We may utilize the new spirit that is born in us for purging ourselves of these evils. But what I have described to you as emblems of modern civilization are accepted as such by its votaries. The Indian civilization, as described by me, has been so described by its votaries. In no part of the world, and under no civilization, have all men attained perfection. The tendency of Indian civilization is to elevate the moral being, that of the Western civilization is to propagate immorality. The latter is godless, the former is based on a belief in God. So understanding and so believing, it behooves every lover of India to cling to the old Indian civilization even as a child clings to its mother's breast. . . .

Passive Resistance

Reader: Is there any historical evidence as to the success of what you have called soul-force or truth-force? No instance seems to have happened of any nation having risen through soul-force. I still think that the evildoers will not cease doing evil without physical punishment.

Editor: The poet Tulsidas has said: "Of religion, pity or love is the root, as egotism of the body. Therefore, we should not abandon pity so long as we are alive." This appears to me to be a scientific truth; I believe in it as much as I believe in two and two being four. The force of love is the same as the force of the soul or truth. We would disappear without the existence of that force. But you ask for historical evidence. It is therefore necessary to know what history means. The Gujarati equivalent means: "It so happened." If that is the meaning of history, it is possible to give copious evidence. But if it means the doings of kings and emperors, there can be no evidence of soul-force or passive resistance in such history. You cannot expect silver ore in a tin mine.

* *Niyog* is a practice that permits the husband to have sexual intercourse with others when his wife is ill or pregnant.—ED.

History, as we know it, is a record of the wars of the world, and so there is a proverb among Englishmen that a nation which has no history—that is, no wars—is a happy nation. How kings played, how they became enemies of one another, and how they murdered one another is found accurately recorded in history; and, if this were all that had happened in the world, it would have been ended long ago. If the story of the universe had commenced with wars, not a man would have been found alive today. Those people who have been warred against have disappeared—as, for instance, the natives of Australia, of whom hardly a man was left alive by the intruders. Mark, please, that these natives did not use soul-force in self-defense, and it does not require much foresight to know that the Australians will share the same fate as their victims. "Those who wield the sword shall perish by the sword." With us, the proverb is that professional swimmers will find a watery grave.

The fact that there are so many men still alive in the world shows that it is based not on the force of arms, but on the force of truth or love. Therefore, the greatest and most unimpeachable evidence of the success of this force is to be found in the fact that, in spite of the wars of the world, it still lives on.

Thousands—indeed, tens of thousands—depend for their existence on a very active working of this force. Little quarrels of millions of families in their daily lives disappear before the exercise of this force. Hundreds of nations live in peace. History does not, and cannot, take note of this fact. History is really a record of every interruption of the even working of the force of love or of the soul. Two brothers quarrel; one of them repents and reawakens the love that was lying dormant in him; the two again begin to live in peace; nobody takes note of this. But if the two brothers, through the intervention of solicitors or some other reason, take up arms or go to law—which is another form of the exhibition of brute force—their doings would be immediately noticed in the press; they would be the talk of their neighbors, and would probably go down in history. And what is true of families and communities is true of nations. There is no reason to believe that there is one law for families, and another for nations. History, then, is a record of an interruption of the course of nature. Soul-force, being natural, is not noted in history.

Reader: According to what you say, it is plain that instances of this kind of passive resistance are not to be found in history. It is necessary to understand this passive resistance more fully. It will be better, therefore, if you enlarge upon it.

Editor: Passive resistance is a method of securing rights by personal suffering; it is the reverse of resistance by arms. When I refuse to do a thing that is repugnant to my conscience, I use soul-force. For instance, the government of the day has passed a law which is applicable to me. I do not like it. If, by using violence, I force the government to repeal the law, I am employing what may be termed body-force. If I do not obey the law, and accept the penalty for its breach, I use soul-force. It involves sacrifice of self.

Everybody admits that sacrifice of self is infinitely superior to sacrifice of others. Moreover, if this kind of force is used in a cause that is unjust, only the person using it suffers. He does not make others suffer for his mistakes. Men have before now done many things which were subsequently found to have been wrong. No man can claim to be absolutely in the right, or that a particular thing is wrong, because he thinks so, but it is wrong for him so long as that is his deliberate judgment. It is, therefore, meet that he should not do that which he knows to be wrong, and suffer the consequence whatever it may be. This is the key to the use of soul-force.

Reader: You would then disregard laws; this is rank disloyalty. We have always been considered a law-abiding nation. You seem to be going even beyond the extremists. They say that we must obey the laws that have been passed, but that, if the laws be bad, we must drive out the lawgivers even by force.

Editor: Whether I go beyond them or whether I do not is a matter of no consequence to either of us. We simply want to find out what is right, and to act accordingly. The real meaning of the statement that we are a law-abiding nation is that we are passive resisters. When we do not like certain laws, we do not break the heads of lawgivers, but we suffer and do not submit to the laws. That we should obey laws, whether good or bad, is a newfangled notion. There was no such thing in former days. The people disregarded those laws they did not like, and suffered the penalties for their breach. It is contrary to our manhood if we obey laws repugnant to our conscience. Such teaching is opposed to religion and means slavery. If the government were to ask us to go about without any clothing, should we do so? If I were a passive resister, I would say to them that I would have nothing to do with their law. But we have so forgotten ourselves and become so compliant, that we do not mind any degrading law.

A man who has realized his manhood, who fears only God, will fear no one else. Man-made laws are not necessarily binding on him. Even the government do not expect any such things from us. They do not say: "You must do such and such a thing," but they say: "If you do not do it, we will punish you." We are sunk so low that we fancy that it is our duty and our religion to do what the law lays down. If man will only realize that it is unmanly to obey laws that are unjust, no man's tyranny will enslave him. This is the key to self-rule or home rule.

It is a superstition and an ungodly thing to believe that an act of a majority binds a minority. Many examples can be given in which acts of majorities will be found to have been wrong, and those of minorities to have been right. All reforms owe their origin to the initiation of minorities in opposition to majorities. If, among a band of robbers, a knowledge of robbing is obligatory, is a pious man to accept the obligation? So long as the superstition that men should obey unjust laws exists, so long will their slavery exist. And a passive resister alone can remove such a superstition.

To use brute force, to use gunpowder, is contrary to passive resistance, for it means that we want 'our opponent to do by force that which we desire but he does not. If such a use of force is justifiable, surely he is entitled to do likewise by us. And so we should never come to an agreement. We may simply fancy, like the blind horse moving in a circle around a mill, that we are making progress. Those who believe that they are not bound to obey laws which are repugnant to their conscience have only the remedy of passive resistance open to them. Any other must lead to disaster.

Reader: From what you say, I deduce that passive resistance is a splendid weapon of the weak, but that when they are strong, they may take up arms.

Editor: This is gross ignorance. Passive resistance—that is, soul-force—is matchless. It is superior to the force of arms. How, then, can it be considered only a weapon of the weak? Physical-force men are strangers to the courage that is requisite in a passive resister. Do you believe that a coward can ever disobey a law that he dislikes? Extremists are considered to be advocates of brute force. Why do they, then, talk about obeying laws? I do not blame them. They can say nothing else. When they succeed in driving out the English and they themselves become governors, they will want you and me to obey their laws. And that is a fitting thing for their constitutions. But a passive resister will say he will not obey a law that is against his conscience, even though he may be blown to pieces at the mouth of a cannon.

What do you think? Wherein is courage required—in blowing others to pieces from behind a cannon, or with a smiling face to approach a cannon and to be blown to pieces? Who is the true warrior—he who keeps death always as a bosom-friend, or he who controls the death of others? Believe me that a man devoid of courage and manhood can never be a passive resister.

This, however, I will admit: that even a man weak in body is capable of offering this resistance. One man can offer it just as well as millions. Both men and women can indulge in it. It does not require the training of an army; it needs no jujitsu. Control over the mind is alone necessary, and when that is attained, man is free like the king of the forest, and his very glance withers the enemy.

Passive resistance is an all-sided sword; it can be used any way; it blesses him who uses it and him against whom it is used. Without drawing a drop of blood, it produces far-reaching results. It never rusts and cannot be stolen. Competition between passive resisters does not exhaust. The sword of passive resistance does not require a scabbard. It is strange indeed that you should consider such a weapon to be a weapon merely of the weak.

Reader: You have said that passive resistance is a specialty of India. Have cannons never been used in India?

Editor: Evidently, in your opinion, India means its few princes. To me, it means its teeming millions, on whom depends the existence of the princes and our own.

Kings will always use their kingly weapons. To use force is bred in them. They want to command; but those who have to obey commands do not want guns, and these are in a majority throughout the world. They have to learn either body-force or soul-force. Where they learn the former, both the rulers and the ruled become like so many madmen, but where they learn soul-force, the commands of the rulers do not go beyond the point of their swords, for true men disregard unjust commands. Peasants have never been subdued by the sword, and never will be. They do not know the use of the sword, and they are not frightened by the use of it by others. That nation is great which rests its head upon death as its pillow. Those who defy death are free from all fear. For those who are laboring under the delusive charms of brute force, this picture is not overdrawn. The fact is that, in India, the nation at large has generally used passive resistance in all departments of life. We cease to cooperate with our rulers when they displease us. This is passive resistance.

I remember an instance when, in a small principality, the villagers were offended by some command issued by the prince. The former immediately began vacating the village. The prince became nervous, apologized to his subjects, and withdrew his command. Many such instances can be found in India. Real home rule is possible only where passive resistance is the guiding force of the people. Any other rule is foreign rule. . . .

Machinery

Reader: When you speak of driving out Western civilization, I suppose you will also say that we want no machinery.

Editor: By raising this question, you have opened the wound I had received. When I read Mr. Dutt's *Economic History of India,* I wept; and, as I think of it again, my heart sickens. It is machinery that has impoverished India. It is difficult to measure the harm that Manchester has done to us. It is due to Manchester that Indian handicraft has all but disappeared. . . .

Machinery has begun to desolate Europe. Ruination is now knocking at the English gates. Machinery is the chief symbol of modern civilization; it represents a great sin. The workers in the mills of Bombay have become slaves. The condition of the women working in the mills is shocking. When there were no mills, these women were not starving. If the machinery craze grows in our country, it will become an unhappy land. It may be considered a heresy, but I am bound to say that it were better for us to send money to Manchester and to use flimsy Manchester cloth, than to multiply mills in India. By using Manchester cloth, we would only waste our money, but by reproducing Manchester in India, we shall keep our money at the price of our blood, because our very moral being will be sapped, and I call in support of my statement the very mill hands as witnesses. And those who have amassed wealth out of factories are not likely to be better than other rich men. It would be folly to assume that an Indian Rockefeller would be better than the American Rockefeller. Impoverished India can become free, but it will be hard for any India made rich through immorality to regain its freedom. I fear we will have to admit that moneyed men support British rule; their interest is bound up with its stability. Money renders a man helpless. The other thing as harmful is sexual vice. Both are poison. A snake bite is a lesser poison than these two, because the former merely destroys the body, but the latter destroys body, mind, and soul. We need not, therefore, be pleased with the prospect of the growth of the mill industry.

Reader: Are the mills, then, to be closed down?

Editor: That is difficult. It is no easy task to do away with a thing that is established. We therefore say that the nonbeginning of a thing is supreme wisdom. We cannot condemn millowners; we can but pity them. It would be too much to expect them to give up their mills, but we may implore them not to increase them. If they would be good, they would gradually contract their business. They can establish in thousands of households the ancient and sacred hand looms, and they can buy out the cloth that may be thus woven. Whether the millowners do this or not, people can cease to use machine-made goods.

Reader: You have so far spoken about machine-made cloth, but there are innumerable machine-made things. We have either to import them or to introduce machinery into our country.

Editor: Indeed, our gods even are made in Germany. What need, then, to speak of matches, pins, and glassware? My answer can be only one. What did India do before these articles were introduced? Precisely the same should be done today. As long as we cannot make pins without machinery, so long we will do without them. The tinsel splendor of glassware we will have nothing to do with, and we will make wicks, as of old, with home-grown cotton, and use handmade earthen saucers for lamps. So doing, we shall have our eyes and money, and will support Swadeshi,* and so shall we attain home rule. It is not to be conceived that all men will do all these things at one time, or that some men will give up all machine-made things at once. But if the thought is sound, we will always find out what we can give up, and will gradually cease to use this. What a few may do, others will copy, and the move-

* Swadeshi is a program of the Indian nationalists to boycott British goods and to buy only Indian-made products.—ED.

ment will grow like the coconut of the mathematical problem. What the leaders do, the populace will gladly follow. The matter is neither complicated nor difficult. You and I shall not wait until we can carry others with us. Those will be the losers who will not do it, and those who will not do it—although they appreciate the truth—will deserve to be called cowards.

Reader: What, then, of the tramcars and electricity?

Editor: This question is now too late. It signifies nothing. If we are to do without the railways, we shall have to do without the tramcars. Machinery is like a snake hole which may contain from one to a hundred snakes. Where there is machinery, there are large cities; and where there are large cities, there are tramcars and railways; and there only does one see electric light. English villages do not boast of any of these things. Honest physicians will tell you that where means of artificial locomotion have increased, the health of the people has suffered. I remember that when, in a European town, there was a scarcity of money, the receipts of the tramway company, of the lawyers, and of the doctors went down, and the people were less unhealthy. I cannot recall a single good point in connection with machinery. Books can be written to demonstrate its evils.

Reader: Is it a good point or a bad one that all you are saying will be printed through machinery?

Editor: This is one of those instances which demonstrate that sometimes poison is used to kill poison. This, then, will not be a good point regarding machinery. As it expires, the machinery, as it were, says to us: "Beware and avoid me. You will derive no benefit from me, and the benefit that may accrue from printing will avail only those who are infected with the machinery craze." Do not, therefore, forget the main thing. It is necessary to realize that machinery is bad. We shall then be able gradually to do away with it. Nature has not provided any way whereby we may reach a desired goal all of a sudden. If, instead of welcoming machinery as a boon, we would look upon it as an evil, it would ultimately go.

6. Jawaharlal Nehru

Jawaharlal Nehru, the Prime Minister of India, was born in Al-
lahabad in 1889, the only son of a Kashmiri Brahmin. His father
was a wealthy and successful lawyer, and he was sent to Britain
for his schooling. He attended Harrow and then Cambridge, where
he was graduated with honors in science in 1910. For the next
two years, he studied law in London. When he returned to India,
he met Gandhi at the annual conference of the Indian National
Congress in 1916, and became his lifelong disciple. He became
General Secretary of the Congress in 1923, and was repeatedly
imprisoned by the British for passive-resistance activities. He was
elected President of the Congress several times. During World
War II, Nehru began the negotiations with Britain that culminated in Indian independence on August 15, 1947. Since that
time, he has continued as Indian Prime Minister and Minister of
Foreign Affairs, supported by a large Congress majority in the Indian parliament. Although he has asserted a major role for India
in international relations, he has been equally concerned with the
problem of economic development, and despite the socialism he
adopted in his early days in England, Nehru now takes a more
pragmatic view, favoring a mixed economy as more effective in development.

The first group of selections below is taken from The Discovery
of India, a book that was written by Nehru in 1944 but is still
valid today as the expression of his personal philosophy and political and social ideas. The contrast between his approach to modernization and economic development and that of Gandhi is evident in his discussion of his personal philosophy and his attitude
toward industrialization.

THE DISCOVERY OF INDIA*

Philosophy of Life

Often, as I look at this world, I have a sense of mysteries, of unknown depths. The urge to understand it, insofar as I can, comes to me; to be in tune with it and to experience it in its fullness. But the way to that understanding seems to me essentially in the way of science, the way of objective approach, though I realize that there can be no such thing as true objectiveness. If the subjective element is unavoidable and inevitable, it should be conditioned as far as possible by the scientific method.

What the mysterious is I do not know. I do not call it God because God has come to mean much that I do not believe in. I find myself incapable of thinking of a deity or of any unknown supreme power in anthropomorphic terms, and the fact that many people think so is continually a source of surprise to me. Any idea of a personal god seems very odd to me. Intellectually, I can appreciate to some extent the conception of monism, and I have been attracted toward the Advaita (nondualist) philosophy of the Vedanta, though I do not presume to understand it in all its depth and intricacy, and I realize that merely an intellectual appreciation of such matters does not carry one far. At the same time, the Vedanta and other similar approaches rather frighten me with their vague formless incursions into infinity. The diversity and fullness of nature stir me and produce a harmony of the spirit, and I can imagine myself feeling at home in the old Indian or Greek pagan and pantheistic atmosphere, but minus the conception of god or gods that was attached to it.

Some kind of ethical approach to life has a strong appeal for me, though it would be difficult for me to justify it logically. I have been attracted by Gandhi's stress on right means, and I think one of his greatest contributions to our public life has been this emphasis. The idea is by no means new, but this application of an ethical doctrine to large-scale public activity was certainly novel.

* Excerpts from Jawaharlal Nehru, *The Discovery of India* (New York: The John Day Company, 1946); copyright 1946 by The John Day Company; reprinted by permission of The John Day Company, Inc., publisher.

It is full of difficulty, and perhaps ends and means are not really separable and form together one organic whole. In a world which thinks almost exclusively of ends and ignores means, this emphasis on means seems odd and remarkable. How far it has succeeded in India I cannot say. But there is no doubt that it has created a deep and abiding impression on the minds of large numbers of people.

A study of Marx and Lenin produced a powerful effect on my mind and helped me to see history and current affairs in a new light. The long chain of history and of social development appeared to have some meaning, some sequence, and the future lost some of its obscurity. The practical achievements of the Soviet Union were also tremendously impressive. Often, I disliked or did not understand some development there, and it seemed to me to be too closely concerned with the opportunism of the moment or the power politics of the day. But despite all these developments and possible distortions of the original passion for human betterment, I had no doubt that the Soviet Revolution had advanced human society by a great leap and had lit a bright flame which could not be smothered, and that it had laid the foundations for that "new civilization" toward which the world would advance. I am too much of an individualist and believer in personal freedom to like overmuch regimentation. Yet it seemed to me obvious that in a complex social structure individual freedom had to be limited, and perhaps the only way to real personal freedom was through some such limitation in the social sphere. The lesser liberties may often need limitation in the interest of the larger freedom.

Much in the Marxist philosophical outlook I could accept without difficulty: its monism and nonduality of mind and matter, the dynamics of matter, and the dialectic of continuous change by evolution as well as leap—through action and interaction, cause and effect, thesis, antithesis, and synthesis. It did not satisfy me completely, nor did it answer all the questions in my mind, and almost unawares a vague idealist approach would creep into my mind, something rather akin to the Vedanta approach. It was not a difference between mind and matter, but rather of something that lay beyond the mind. Also, there was the background of ethics. I realized that the moral approach is a changing one and depends upon the growing mind and an advancing civilization; it is conditioned by the mental climate of the age. Yet there was something more to it than that, certain basic urges which had greater permanence. I did not like the frequent divorce—in Communist, as in other, practice—between action and these basic urges or principles. So there was an odd mixture in my mind which I could not rationally explain or resolve. There was a general tendency not to think too much of those fundamental questions which appear to be beyond reach, and rather to concentrate on the problems of life—to understand, in the narrower and more immediate sense, what should be done and how. Whatever ultimate reality may be, and whether we can ever grasp it in whole or in part, there certainly appear to be vast possibilities of increasing human knowledge, even though this may be partly or largely subjective, and of applying this to the advancement and betterment of human life and social organization.

There has been in the past, and there is to a lesser extent even today among some people, an absorption in finding an answer to the riddle of the universe. This leads them away from the individual and social problems of the day, and when they are unable to solve that riddle, they despair and turn to inaction and triviality, or find comfort in some dogmatic creed. Social evils, most of which are certainly capable of removal, are attributed to original sin, to the unalterableness of "human nature," or the social structure, or (in India) to the inevitable legacy of previous births. Thus one drifts away from even the attempt to think rationally and scientifically, and takes refuge in irrationalism, superstition, and unreasonable and inequitable social prejudices and practices. It is true that even rational and scientific thought does not always take us as far as we would like to go. There is an infinite number of factors and relations which influence and determine events in varying degrees, and it is impossible to grasp all of them. Still, we can try to pick out the dominating forces at work and, by observing external material reality and by experiment and practice, trial and error, grope our way to ever-widening knowledge and truth.

For this purpose, and within these limitations, the general Marxist approach, fitting in as it more or less did with the present state of scientific knowledge, seemed to me to offer considerable help. But even accepting that approach, the consequences that flow from it and the interpretation of past and present happenings were by no means always clear. Marx's general analysis of social development seems to have been remarkably correct, and yet many

developments took place later which did not fit in with his outlook
for the immediate future. Lenin successfully adapted the Marxian
thesis to some of these subsequent developments, but again, since
then, further remarkable changes have taken place—the rise of
fascism and Nazism and all that lay behind them. The very
rapid growth of technology and the practical application of vast
developments in scientific knowledge are now changing the world
picture with an amazing rapidity, leading to new problems. . . .

Industrialization and the Machine

The Congress, under Gandhi's leadership, had long championed
the revival of village industries, especially hand spinning and hand
weaving. At no time, however, had the Congress been opposed to
the development of big industries, and whenever it had the chance
—in the legislatures or elsewhere—it had encouraged this development. Congress provincial governments were eager to do so. In the
twenties, when the Tata Steel and Iron Works were in difficulties,
it was largely due to the insistence of the Congress Party in the
central legislature that government aid was given to help to tide
over a critical period. The development of Indian shipbuilding
and shipping services had long been a sore point of conflict between nationalist opinion and the government. The Congress, as
all other sections of Indian opinion, was anxious that every assistance should be given to Indian shipping; the government was
equally anxious to protect the vested interests of powerful British
shipping companies. Indian shipping was thus prevented from
growing by official discrimination against it, although it had both
capital and technical and managerial ability at its disposal. This
kind of discrimination worked all along the line, whenever any
British industrial, commercial, or financial interests were concerned. . . .

The Congress Party has thus always been in favor of the industrialization of India, and at the same time has emphasized the
development of cottage industries and worked for this. Is there a
conflict between these two approaches? Possibly there is a difference in emphasis, a realization of certain human and economic
factors which were overlooked previously in India. Indian industrialists and the politicians who supported them thought too much
in terms of the nineteenth-century development of capitalist industry in Europe and ignored many of the evil consequences that

were obvious in the twentieth century. In India, because normal progress had been arrested for a hundred years, those consequences were likely to be more far-reaching. The kind of medium-scale industries that were being started in India under the prevailing economic system resulted not in absorbing labor, but in creating more unemployment. While capital accumulated at one end, poverty and unemployment increased at the other. Under a different system and with a stress on large-scale industries absorbing labor, and with planned development, this might well have been avoided.

This fact of increasing mass poverty influenced Gandhi powerfully. It is true, I think, that there is a fundamental difference between his outlook on life generally and what might be called the modern outlook. He is not enamored of ever-increasing standards of living and the growth of luxury at the cost of spiritual and moral values. He does not favor the soft life; for him, the straight way is the hard way, and the love of luxury leads to crookedness and loss of virtue. Above all, he is shocked at the vast gulf that stretches between the rich and the poor—in their ways of living and their opportunities of growth. For his own personal and psychological satisfaction, he crossed that gulf and went over to the side of the poor, adopting, with only such improvements as the poor themselves could afford, their ways of living, their dress or lack of dress. This vast difference between the few rich and the poverty-stricken masses seemed to him to be due to two principal causes: foreign rule and the exploitation that accompanied it, and the capitalist industrial civilization of the West, as embodied in the big machine. He reacted against both. He looked back with yearning to the days of the old autonomous and more or less self-contained village community where there had been an automatic balance between production, distribution, and consumption; where political or economic power was spread out and not concentrated as it is today; where a kind of simple democracy prevailed; where the gulf between the rich and the poor was not so marked; where the evils of great cities were absent, and people lived in contact with the life-giving soil and breathed the pure air of the open spaces.

There was all this basic difference in outlook as to the meaning of life itself between him and many others, and this difference colored his language as well as his activities. His language—vivid and powerful as it often was—drew its inspiration from the religious and moral teachings of the ages, principally of India, but also of other countries. Moral values must prevail; the ends can never justify unworthy means, or else the individual and the race perish.

And yet he was no dreamer living in some fantasy of his own creation, cut off from life and its problems. He came from Gujrat, the home of hardheaded businessmen, and he had an unrivaled knowledge of the Indian villages and the conditions of life that prevailed there. It was out of that personal experience that he evolved his program of the spinning wheel and village industry. If immediate relief was to be given to the vast numbers of the unemployed and partially employed; if the rot that was spreading throughout India and paralyzing the masses was to be stopped; if the villagers' standards were to be raised, however little, en masse; if they were to be taught self-reliance instead of waiting helplessly like derelicts for relief from others; if all this was to be done without much capital—then there seemed no other way. Apart from the evils inherent in foreign rule and exploitation, and the lack of freedom to initiate and carry through big schemes of reform, the problem of India was one of scarcity of capital and abundance of labor—how to utilize that wasted labor, that manpower that was producing nothing. Foolish comparisons are made between manpower and machine power; of course, a big machine can do the work of a thousand or ten thousand persons. But if those ten thousand sit idly by or starve, the introduction of that machine is not a social gain—except in long perspective which envisages a change in social conditions. When the big machine is not there at all, then no question of comparison arises; it is a net gain both from the individual and the national point of view to utilize manpower for production. There is no necessary conflict between this and the introduction of machinery on the largest scale, provided that machinery is used primarily for absorbing labor and not for creating fresh unemployment.

Gandhi's attitude to the use of machinery seemed to undergo a gradual change. "What I object to," he said, "is the craze for machinery, not machinery as such. . . . If we could have electricity in every village home, I should not mind villages plying their implements and tools with electricity." The big machine seemed to him to lead inevitably, at least in the circumstances of today, to the concentration of power and riches: "I consider it a sin and injustice to use machinery for the purpose of concentration of power and riches in the hands of the few. Today the machine is used in this way." He even came to accept the necessity of many kinds of heavy industries and large-scale key industries and public utilities, provided they were state-owned and did not interfere with some kinds of cottage industries which he considered essential. Referring to his own proposals, he said: "The whole of this program will be a structure on sand if it is not built on the solid foundation of economic equality."

Thus, even the enthusiastic advocates for cottage and small-scale industries recognize that large-scale industry is, to a certain extent, necessary and inevitable; only they would like to limit it as far as possible. Superficially, then, the question becomes one of emphasis and adjustment of the two forms of production and economy. It can hardly be challenged that, in the context of the modern world, no country can be politically and economically independent, even within the framework of international interdependence, unless it is highly industrialized and has developed its power resources to the utmost. Nor can it achieve or maintain high standards of living and liquidate poverty without the aid of modern technology in almost every sphere of life. An industrially backward country will continually upset the world equilibrium and encourage the aggressive tendencies of more developed countries. Even if it retains its political independence, this will be nominal only, and economic control will tend to pass to others. This control will inevitably upset its own small-scale economy which it has sought to preserve in pursuit of its own view of life. Thus an attempt to build up a country's economy largely on the basis of cottage and small-scale industries is doomed to failure. It will not solve the basic problems of the country or maintain freedom, nor will it fit in with the world framework, except as a colonial appendage.

Is it possible to have two entirely different kinds of economy in a country—one based on the big machine and industrialization, and the other mainly on cottage industries? This is hardly conceivable, for one must overcome the other, and there can be little doubt that the big machine will triumph unless it is forcibly prevented from doing so. Thus, it is not a mere question of adjustment of the two forms of production and economy. One must be dominating and paramount, with the other complementary to it, fitting in where it can. The economy based on the latest technical achievements of the day must necessarily be the dominating one.

If technology demands the big machine, as it does today in a large measure, then the big machine with all its implications and consequences must be accepted. Where it is possible in terms of that technology to decentralize production, this would be desirable. But in any event, the latest technique has to be followed. To adhere to outworn and out-of-date methods of production—except as a temporary and stopgap measure—is to arrest growth and development.

Any argument as to the relative merits of small-scale and large-scale industry seems strangely irrelevant today, when the world and the dominating facts of the situation that confront it have decided in favor of the latter. Even in India, that decision has been made by these facts themselves, and no one doubts that India will be rapidly industrialized in the near future. She has already gone a good way in that direction. The evils of unrestricted and unplanned industrialization are well recognized today. Whether these evils are necessary concomitants of big industry, or derive from the social and economic structure behind it, is another matter. If the economic structure is primarily responsible for them, then surely we should set about changing that structure, instead of blaming the inevitable and desirable developments in technique.

The real question is not one of quantitative adjustment and balancing of various incongruous elements and methods of production, but a qualitative changeover to something different and new, from which various social consequences flow. The economic and political aspects of this qualitative change are important, but equally important are the social and psychological aspects. In India especially, where we have been wedded far too long to past forms and modes of thought and action—new experiences, new processes, leading to new ideas and new horizons, are necessary. Thus, we will change the static character of our living and make it dynamic and vital, and our minds will become active and adventurous. New situations lead to new experiences, as the mind is compelled to deal with them and adapt itself to a changing environment.

It is well recognized now that a child's education should be intimately associated with some craft or manual activity. The mind is stimulated thereby, and there is a coordination between the activities of the mind and the hands. So also the mind of a growing boy or girl is stimulated by the machine. It grows under the machine's impact (under proper conditions, of course, and not as an exploited and unhappy worker in a factory) and opens out new horizons. Simple scientific experiments, peeps into the microscope, and an explanation of the ordinary phenomena of nature bring excitement in their train, an understanding of some of life's processes and a desire to experiment and find out instead of relying on set phrases and old formulas. Self-confidence and the co-operative spirit grow, and frustration—arising out of the miasma of the past—lessens. A civilization based on ever-changing and advancing mechanical techniques leads to this. Such a civilization is a marked change, a jump almost, from the older type, and is intimately connected with modern industrialization. Inevitably, it gives rise to new problems and difficulties, but it also shows the way to overcome them. . . .

India and the West

A nation, like an individual, has many personalities, many approaches to life. If there is a sufficiently strong organic bond between these different personalities, it is well; otherwise, those personalities split up and lead to disintegration and trouble. Normally, there is a continuous process of adjustment going on, and some kind of an equilibrium is established. If normal development is arrested, or sometimes if there is some rapid change which is not easily assimilated, then conflict arises between those different personalities. In the mind and spirit of India, below the surface of our superficial conflicts and divisions, there has been this fundamental conflict due to a long period of arrested growth. A society, if it is to be both stable and progressive, must have a certain more or less fixed foundation of principles, as well as a dynamic outlook. Both appear to be necessary. Without the dynamic outlook, there is a stagnation and decay; without some fixed basis of principle, there is likely to be disintegration and destruction.

In India, from the earliest days, there was a search for those basic principles—for the unchanging, the universal, the absolute. Yet the dynamic outlook was also present, and an appreciation of life and the changing world. On these two foundations, a stable and progressive society was built up, though the stress was always more on stability and security and the survival of the race. In later years, the dynamic aspect began to fade away, and in the name of eternal principles the social structure was made rigid and unchanging. It was, as a matter of fact, not wholly rigid, and it did change gradually and continuously. But the ideology behind it, and the general framework, continued unchanged. The group idea as represented by more or less autonomous castes, the joint family, and the communal self-governing life of the village were the main pillars of this system, and all these survived for so long because—in spite of their failings—they fulfilled some essential needs of human nature and society. They gave security and stability to each group, and a sense of group freedom. Caste survived because it continued to represent the general power relationships of society, and class privileges were maintained, not only because of the prevailing ideology, but also because they were supported by vigor, intelligence, and ability, as well as a capacity for self-sacrifice. That ideology was not based on a conflict of rights, but on the individual's obligations to others and a satisfactory performance of his duties, on cooperation within the group and between different groups, and essentially on the idea of promoting peace rather than war. While the social system was rigid, no limit was placed on the freedom of the mind.

Indian civilization achieved much that it was aiming at, but in that very achievement life began to fade away, for it is too dynamic to exist for long in a rigid, unchanging environment. Even those basic principles which are said to be unchanging lose their freshness and reality when they are taken for granted, and the search for them ceases. Ideas of truth, beauty, and freedom decay, and we become prisoners following a deadening routine.

The very thing India lacked, the modern West possessed—and possessed to excess. It had the dynamic outlook. It was engrossed in the changing world, caring little for ultimate principles, the unchanging, the universal. It paid little attention to duties and obligations, and emphasized rights. It was active, aggressive, acquisitive, seeking power and domination, living in the present and ignoring the future consequences of its actions. Because it was dynamic, it was progressive and full of life, but that life was a fevered one, and the temperature kept on rising progressively.

If Indian civilization went to seed because it became static, self-absorbed, and inclined to narcissism, the civilization of the modern West—with all its great and manifold achievements—does not appear to have been a conspicuous success or to have thus far solved the basic problems of life. Conflict is inherent in it, and periodically it indulges in self-destruction on a colossal scale. It seems to lack something to give it stability, some basic principles to give meaning to life, though what these are I cannot say. Yet, because it is dynamic and full of life and curiosity, there is hope for it.

India—as well as China—must learn from the West, for the modern West has much to teach, and the spirit of the ages is represented by the West. But the West is also obviously in need of learning much, and its advances in technology will bring it little comfort if it does not learn some of the deeper lessons of life which have absorbed the minds of thinkers in all ages and in all countries.

India had become static, and yet it would be utterly wrong to imagine that she was unchanging. No change at all means death. Her very survival as a highly evolved nation shows that there was some process of continuous adaptation going on. When the British came to India, though technologically somewhat backward, she was still among the advanced commercial nations of the world. Technical changes would undoubtedly have come and changed India as they had changed some Western countries. But her normal development was arrested by the British power. Industrial growth was checked, and, as a consequence, social growth was also arrested. The normal power relationships of society could not adjust themselves and find an equilibrium, as all power was concentrated in the alien authority, which based itself on force and encouraged groups and classes which had ceased to have any real significance. Indian life thus progressively became more artificial, for many of the individuals and groups who seemed to play an important role in it had no vital functions left and were there only because of the importance given to them by the alien power. They had long ago finished their role in history and would have been pushed aside by new forces if they had not been given foreign protection. They became straw-stuffed symbols or protégés of foreign authority, thereby cutting themselves further away from the living currents of the nation. Normally, they would have been weeded out or diverted to some more appropriate function by revolution or democratic process. But so long as foreign authoritarian rule continued, no such development could take place. And so India was cluttered up with these emblems of the past, and the real changes that were taking place were hidden behind an artificial façade. No true social balances or power relationships within society could develop or become evident, and unreal problems assumed an undue importance.

India must break with much of her past and not allow it to dominate the present. Our lives are encumbered with the dead-wood of this past; all that is dead and has served its purpose has to go. But that does not mean a break with or a forgetting of the vital and life-giving in that past. We can never forget the ideals that have moved our race: the dreams of the Indian people through the ages; the wisdom of the ancients; the buoyant energy and love of life and nature of our forefathers; their spirit of curiosity and mental adventure; the daring of their thought, their splendid achievements in literature, art, and culture; their love of truth, and beauty, and freedom; the basic values that they set up; their understanding of life's mysterious ways; their toleration of other ways than theirs; their capacity to absorb other peoples and their cultural accomplishments, synthesize them, and develop a varied and mixed culture. Nor can we forget the myriad experiences which have built up our ancient race and lie embedded in our subconscious minds. We will never forget them or cease to take pride in that noble heritage of ours. If India forgets them, she will no longer remain India, and much that has made her our joy and pride will cease to be.

It is not this that we have to break with, but all the dust and dirt of ages that have covered her up and hidden her inner beauty and significance, the excrescences and abortions that have twisted and petrified her spirit, set it in rigid frames, and stunted her growth. We have to cut away these excrescences, and remember afresh the core of that ancient wisdom, and adapt it to our present circumstances. We have to get out of traditional ways of thought and living which, for all the good they may have done in a past age—and there was much good in them—have ceased to have significance today. We have to make our own all the achievements of the human race and join up with others in the exciting adventure of man, more exciting today perhaps than in earlier ages—realizing that this has ceased to be governed by national boundaries of old divisions and is common to the race of man everywhere. We have to revive the passion for truth and beauty and freedom which gives meaning to life, and develop afresh that dynamic outlook and spirit of adventure which distinguished those of our race who, in ages past, built our house on these strong and enduring foundations. Old as we are, with memories stretching back to the early dawns of human history and endeavor, we have to grow young again, in tune with our present time, with the irrepressible spirit and joy of youth in the present and its faith in the future. . . .

The Caste System

Caste is the symbol and embodiment of exclusiveness among the Hindus. It is sometimes said that the basic idea of caste might remain, but its subsequent harmful development and ramifications should go; that it should not depend on birth but on merit. This approach is irrelevant and merely confuses the issue. In a historical context, a study of the growth of caste has some value, but obviously we cannot go back to the period when caste began; in the social organization of today, it has no place left. If merit is the only criterion and opportunity is thrown open to everybody, then caste loses all its present-day distinguishing features and, in fact, ends. Caste has in the past not only led to the suppression of certain groups but to a separation of theoretical and scholastic learning from craftsmanship and a divorce of philosophy from actual life and its problems. It was an aristocratic approach based on traditionalism. This outlook has to change completely, for it is wholly opposed to modern conditions and the democratic ideal. The functional organization of social groups in India may continue, but even that will undergo a vast change as the nature of modern industry creates new functions and puts an end to many old ones. The tendency today everywhere is toward a functional organization of society, and the concept of abstract rights is giving place to that of functions. This is in harmony with the old Indian ideal.

The spirit of the age is in favor of equality, though practice denies it almost everywhere. We have got rid of slavery in the narrow sense of the word—that a man can be the property of another. But a new slavery, in some ways worse than the old, has taken its place all over the world. In the name of individual freedom, political and economic systems exploit human beings and treat them as commodities. And again, though an individual cannot be the property of another, a country and a nation can still be the property of another nation, and thus group slavery is tolerated. Racialism also is a distinguishing feature of our times, and we have not only master nations but also master races.

Yet the spirit of the age will triumph. In India, at any rate, we must aim at equality. That does not and cannot mean that everybody is physically or intellectually or spiritually equal or can be

made so. But it does mean equal opportunities for all and no
political, economic, or social barrier in the way of any individual
or group. It means a faith in humanity and a belief that there is
no race or group that cannot advance and make good in its own
way, given the chance to do so. It means a realization of the fact
that the backwardness or degradation of any group is not due to inherent failings in it, but principally to lack of opportunities and
long suppression by other groups. It should mean an understanding
of the modern world, wherein real progress and advance, whether
national or international, have become very much a joint affair and
a backward group pulls back others. Therefore, not only must equal
opportunities be given to all, but special opportunities for educational, economic, and cultural growth must be given to backward
groups so as to enable them to catch up to those who are ahead of
them. Any such attempt to open the doors of opportunity to all in
India will release enormous energy and ability and transform the
country with amazing speed.

Democratic Collectivism

If the spirit of the age demands equality, it must necessarily also
demand an economic system which fits in with it and encourages
it. The present colonial system in India is the very antithesis of it.
Absolutism is not only based on inequality, but must perpetuate it
in every sphere of life. It suppresses the creative and regenerative
forces of a nation, bottles up talent and capacity, and discourages
the spirit of responsibility. Those who have to suffer under it lose
their sense of dignity and self-reliance. The problems of India,
complicated as they seem, are essentially due to an attempt to
advance while preserving the political and economic structure
more or less intact. Political advance is made subject to the preservation of this structure and existing vested interests. The two are
incompatible.

Political change there must be, but economic change is equally
necessary. That change will have to be in the direction of a democratically planned collectivism. "The choice," says R. H. Tawney,
"is not between competition and monopoly, but between monopoly which is irresponsible and private and a monopoly which is
responsible and public." Public monopolies are growing even in
capitalist states, and they will continue to grow. The conflict between the idea underlying them and private monopoly will con-

tinue till the latter is liquidated. A democratic collectivism need not mean an abolition of private property, but it will mean the public ownership of the basic and major industries. It will mean the cooperative or collective control of the land. In India especially, it will be necessary to have, in addition to the big industries, cooperatively controlled small and village industries. Such a system of democratic collectivism will need careful and continuous planning and adaptation to the changing needs of the people. The aim should be the expansion of the productive capacity of the nation in every possible way, at the same time absorbing all the labor power of the nation in some activity or other and preventing unemployment. As far as possible, there should be freedom to choose one's occupation. An equalization of income will not result from all this, but there will be far more equitable sharing, and a progressive tendency toward equalization. In any event, the vast differences that exist today will disappear completely, and class distinctions, which are essentially based on differences in income, will begin to fade out.

Such a change would mean an upsetting of the present-day acquisitive society, based primarily on the profit motive. The profit motive may still continue to some extent, but it will not be the dominating urge, nor will it have the same scope as it has today. It would be absurd to say that the profit motive does not appeal to the average Indian, but it is nevertheless true that there is no such admiration for it in India as there is in the West. The possessor of money may be envied, but he is not particularly respected or admired. Respect and admiration still go to the man or woman who is considered good and wise, and especially to those who sacrifice themselves or what they possess for the public good. The Indian outlook, even of the masses, has never approved of the spirit of acquisitiveness. . . .

Behind these problems in India, as in many other countries, lies the real issue—which is not merely the establishment of democracy of the nineteenth-century European type, but also far-reaching social revolution. Democracy has itself become involved in that seemingly inevitable change, and hence among those who disapprove of the latter, doubts and denials arise about the feasibility of democracy, and this leads to fascist tendencies and the continuation of an imperialist outlook. All our present-day problems in India—the communal or minority problem, the Indian princes, vested interest of religious groups and the big landowners, and the

entrenched interests of British authority and industry in India—
ultimately resolve themselves into opposition to social change. And
because any real democracy is likely to lead to such change, therefore democracy itself is objected to and considered unsuited to the
peculiar conditions of India. So the problems of India—for all
their seeming variety and difference from others—are of the same
essential nature as the problems of China, or Spain, or many other
countries of Europe and elsewhere. . . . Many of the resistance
movements of Europe reflect these conflicts. Everywhere the old
equilibrium of social forces has been upset, and till a new equilibrium is established, there will be tension, trouble, and conflict.
From these problems of the moment, we are led to one of the
central problems of our time: how to combine democracy with
socialism, how to maintain individual freedom and initiative and
yet have centralized social control and planning of the economic
life of the people, on the national as well as the international
plane. . . .

INDIAN SOCIALISM*

In a country like India—an underdeveloped country—socialism, a
real socialist basis of society, can only come gradually. There is no
help for it. Take the instance of China: They are very keen on
changing their economy, and there are no such difficulties as we
have—that is, parliamentary institutions and all kinds of "three
readings" and select committees, which take a long time. They can
pass a law overnight, if they want to. Even then, they go on saying that it will take them twenty years to lay the socialist basis of
their society—to have a socialist economy—in spite of all the
speed with which they may work. . . .

If by adopting some method which in theory appeals to us we
reduce our production, then we are in effect undermining the
growth toward socialism—although that particular step may be
called a socialist step. For instance, I am quite clear in my mind
that if we start nationalizing the existing institutions, industries,

* From a speech delivered by Nehru to the Congress Parliamentary Party
on December 22, 1954; excerpted from *Towards a Socialistic State* (New
Delhi: All-India Congress Committee, 1956).

etc., by giving compensation, we reduce our capacity to go ahead. Here you have to be clear about one thing in your minds. Are we going in for possible seizure, expropriation without compensation, or are we not? Generally speaking, if we go in for possible seizure, then we think out its consequences, the consequences of conflict, the consequences of suffering of large numbers. Now, so far as our Constitution is concerned, that is ruled out. Apart from the Constitution, our general policy has been opposed to it. . . .

People do not generally realize how many years it took the Soviet Union to get the machines running. We see Russia today, forty years after the Revolution. It took them years to get the machines moving. Take one simple instance. In their Constitution, they said, in a sense as we say, compulsory free primary education for everybody. As far as I remember, it took them fifteen years to do that, in spite of all the power of the state. These things do take time; you cannot help it, because it involves not only the money factor, but numerous other factors.

I think it is advantageous for the public sector to have a competitive private sector to keep it up to the mark. The public sector will grow. But I feel that, if the private sector is not there, if it is abolished completely, there is a risk of the public sector becoming slow, not having that urge and push behind it. It depends on men, of course. On the whole, it is a good thing to have a private sector, something where the surplus energies of people who are not employed in the public sector may have some play, provided, of course, we control that private sector in the interest of the National Plan. You can control it in a hundred ways. Control it by all means. But where you do not control, give them room to exercise initiative and bring results. That is only a sort of broad approach to this problem. I can understand that a government may gradually take steps which might be said to be in a wrong direction. It may strengthen the existing structure of society rather than weaken it. But in the final analysis, we want to break through the existing structure—the economic as well as the social—because it restricts progress. A country cannot grow if it allows rigid structures. . . . Similarly, we have to break through what might be called a capitalist structure and have something else. But breaking through it has to be in a way so as to replace it for all time, and to begin with—even while it exists—to control it.

PART II

THE ISLAMIC WORLD

The area of Islamic religion and culture extends from Morocco to Pakistan. There are also substantial Moslem elements in Malaya, Indonesia, and some African countries, but the common tie of the Arab language—which links areas as distant as Morocco and Iraq—is not present, and Islam does not have the political significance in these areas that it possesses in North Africa, the Middle East, and Pakistan.

In the Islamic world, as in Africa, nationalism has taken several forms. Where the nation-state was the product of artificial divisions imposed by the Europeans, loyalties have been directed to a Pan-Arab or even Pan-Islamic ideal as much as to the individual nation. In these areas, the binding force of culture, language, and religion gives a common universe of discourse to political leaders. These ties are the basis of efforts toward common consultation and action through such bodies as the Arab League or the projected Maghreb (North African) Federation. The appeal of the Pan-Arab ideal may also be used—as in the case of Nasser—to extend the influence of an individual national leader throughout the Middle East.

Yet divisions remain—whether caused by personal rivalries, permanent competition for influence (as between Iraq and Egypt), or different geographical situations and contacts with outside influences. North Africa, while maintaining links with the Middle East, seems destined to pursue a separate course, and Pakistan looks to Asia as much as to the Arab world.

All these areas are currently facing a common political problem (which Catholic Europe had to face earlier, in the nineteenth century): the adjustment of a traditional religion having a deep hold on the population to the needs of the modern world.* This, in turn, is part of the larger problem of how to combine traditional culture and the European influences, to which the area has been subjected intensively during the last fifty years. In most Islamic countries, democracy has not functioned effectively, and reformist military rule has been more successful. Moreover, as the history of the Middle East—particularly the success of Nasser's policy and the failure of the Baghdad Pact—has demonstrated in the last decade, the Islamic world prefers a neutral position in the East-West conflict. Even in Pakistan, long aligned with the West, there are substantial neutralist currents.

Nasser's recent action—nationalizing a substantial sector of the Egyptian economy—has set off new discussions concerning the relationship of his "Arab socialism" and Islam. Nasser himself defends socialization as being in accord with the principles of the Prophet. While he has been both defended and criticized by Islamic leaders, his action is in accord with the modernizing elite's desire to assert political control over the production and distribution of goods in the interest of economic development and social reform.

The Islamic world spans Africa, the Middle East, and parts of Asia, linking three of the four major areas of the underdeveloped world. Its contacts with Latin America have thus far been limited, though observers have commented on similarities in the political psychology and ideological assumptions of Latin America and the Middle East—in their hostility to foreign imperialism, in the intensity of their emotional involvement in politics, and in the importance of military men in national politics. Now that contacts are being developed between the governments of Cuba and the United Arab Republic, further efforts at rapprochement between the different sectors of the underdeveloped world can be anticipated.

* See Bourguiba's speech on Ramadan and Ayub Khan's speech on Islam in Pakistan.

7. Mohammed Ayub Khan

Mohammed Ayub Khan was born in 1908 in the northwest frontier province of British India. His father was a member of the British-trained Indian Army. He studied at the Moslem University of Aligarh and at Sandhurst (the equivalent of West Point in Britain). During World II, he commanded a battalion in Burma. Upon the partition of India in 1947, his regiment became part of the Pakistani Army. In 1951, Ayub became Commander-in-Chief of the Army, and in 1954–55, he served also as Minister of Defense. In 1958, Iskander Mirza, President of Pakistan, with Ayub Khan's support, abrogated the constitution and dissolved the political parties. A few months later, Mirza left the country and Ayub Kahn took over the presidency and proclaimed martial law.

Under his rule, land reform has been instituted, and a system of "basic democracy" introduced (described in his article "Pakistan Perspective"). Pakistan is an Islamic state, and Ayub Kahn is himself a devout Moslem. In his address to the assembly of Moslem legal and religious scholars (Ulema), Ayub Khan discusses the ways in which Islam can be modernized to meet the needs of a contemporary society.

ISLAM IN PAKISTAN*

. . . Islam came on earth by divine grace 1,400 years ago. It was not only a new religion but also a movement of great developing power that changed completely the conditions of human life and

* From a speech delivered by Ayub Khan to the Assembly of the Ulema on May 13, 1959; translated by the editor (by permission) from the French version in *Orient* (Paris), No. 12 (1959).

the realities of civilization. As long as that movement kept its fundamental vitality, Moslems demonstrated their greatness in the domains of theory, practice, and science. Gradually, however, the dynamic aspect of Islam was weakened, and its dogmatic aspect became stronger. The inevitable result of this was that life and religion became two absolutely separate worlds. This division extended to our entire existence. Islam, however, came to break down that difference.

If the link between life and religion weakens, life itself continues to pursue its course, one way or another, while religion becomes a silent and immobile idolatry, deprived of movement and flexibility, and imprisoned far from the world, in the mosques and monasteries. This, to some extent, is what has happened in Islam. Thanks to philosophy and science, the life of men today has progressed, while the progress of religion has been shackled for centuries. The miracle of Islam is that it ended idolatry, but Moslems have made an idol out of their religion.

One of the consequences of this situation is very dangerous for our community and civilization. Indeed, those Moslems who have accepted the new enlightenment and advanced with their times are called secular, and those who have remained in the shelter of traditional faith in the world of the past are called religious. To look to the future was soon considered an infraction of religion, and to look to the past a proof of love of religion. All new progress, new invention, and new education were suspect as contrary to Islam. This is why in past history most Moslem leaders who were too revolutionary were regarded as infidels.

Today I invite you to consider the content of the sermons read each Friday in all of the mosques in our country. In a good number of these sermons, exception is taken to the petty, inoffensive things of our day for the sole reason that these things are new. Thus Islam is considered as the enemy and rival of material progress, and to advance is the greatest crime that one can commit against Islam. Still worse, this crime falls on the young people who are Moslem and who want to remain Moslem in the modern world of today. To oblige twentieth-century man to go back some hundreds of years in the past in order to be Moslem is to perpetuate an injustice against the world and against the faith.

The question is to know now why and how this lack of progress has occurred in a religion as practical and dynamic as Islam. Is it because we have departed from our basic principles and have not been able to establish a social order and governmental regime that could survive in the midst of changing situations and values? Is it because, considering religion a collection of stories about spirits and angels, we have imprisoned it in all kinds of superstitions and, demanding a kind of servile imitation, have cut off the critical and creative faculties of human nature? Is it because of a type of mysticism that flees the world and tries to shut up life within the four walls of the monastery cell? Is it because of the erroneous belief that we can achieve salvation without taking action with our hands and feet? Have we forgotten that life in the other world is the fruit of this terrestrial life and that there we will receive our reward for our efforts and work accomplished on earth?

All these questions are basic. It is absolutely necessary to learn the reasons why the impatient soul of the youth of Islam has been forced into insensibility and lack of realism. In this search, many disagreeable and bitter things will become clear to us, but our moral duty is to overcome our bitterness and face this question honestly and courageously in order to find a proper solution.

One of the great reasons for confusion in the world of Islam is sectarianism. Whether it is right or wrong, it is a fact, and it is not wise to ignore it. Which sect is right? Which sect is wrong? Only evil can result from these differences. Instead of criticizing the beliefs of others, is it not preferable to declare that fundamentally we are all alike, since Allah is one, our Prophet is one, and our Holy Book is one? Development of this kind of correct sentiment is primarily in the hands of the doctors of Moslem law. You possess the treasure of wisdom. As to particular points of religion, your knowledge is very vast. But it is not right to limit this great knowledge to one single area. In this period of progress and evolution, it is indispensable that theologians also have some knowledge of philosophy, science, economics, history, and current events. It is likewise necessary that people have the benefit of modern education—so that they are not ignorant of the fundamental beliefs and principles of their religion. In your sermons, you should also insist that as far as possible, we should harmonize religious instruction and civic education. This point is still more important in this period. I have the firm hope that the Education Commission will give it particular attention. But even with the recommendations of the Education Commission, this matter will not be entirely resolved. The greatest responsibility to resolve it is on the shoulders of the religious and juridical leaders. And we will be thankful to you if in your perfect wisdom you present Islam in such language and in such a way that the scientists who carry out experiments in the laboratories, the professors who teach in the universities, the peasants who plow the fields, and the workers who work in the factories can understand Islam without difficulty and find their hearts revived and their souls lifted up in accordance with their capacities.

You know that the world today is divided into two hostile camps. This struggle is carried out not only on the material plane, but also on the ideological plane. The principal effort of Communism is to destroy all other ideologies and to impose itself on the whole world. Material values obviously have great importance for all, but not to such an extent that man must sacrifice himself for them. In these conditions, there is only one possible answer to Communism, and that answer is Islam. Between the ideology of Communism and the materialist conceptions of the West, Islam is the only point of view that can prevent the spirit of humanity from being destroyed. It is false to believe that Communism can be a danger only for Christian nations. The conditions of life that are developing in the Middle East show clearly that the Islamic world is in no way impervious to the attempts of Communism. To prevent that danger, it is necessary that Islam be taken out of the recesses of the past and presented to the world in a way and a language that are absolutely modern—not as an ideology, but as a true plan of political, civic, and spiritual action, because this is the fundamental meaning of Islam. For this effort, we also need the aid and the inspiration of religious and juridical leaders.

As to the affairs of Pakistan, there is no doubt that problems and difficulties—both internal and external—rise before us. By divine grace and mercy, many of these difficulties are being resolved. But the simplest method is still for you to have confidence in your own powers as spiritual guides both for yourselves and for others, and to carry out your different responsibilities with the greatest diligence. The law of nature decrees that man can work conscientiously only when a clear plan of action is presented before him.

We are not only Moslems; we are also Pakistanis. We are not only Pakistanis; among us there are Bengalis, Sinds, Punjabis, Baluchis, and Pathans. Our plan of action must be sufficiently broad to respond easily to all the local, national, and community aspects of the problems that we have to resolve. This can only be done if we carry on our lives according to the principles of fraternity, order, pity, nobility, courtesy, and honesty—that is, according to the principles in force in all countries and at all times. The most important thing is that these principles should also be those of Islam. If we conform to the principles of honesty and sincerity and if Allah wills it, Pakistan can become a model of peace and security, not only for ourselves, but also for the Islamic world and perhaps for the whole world. . . .

PAKISTAN PERSPECTIVE*

. . . It is a common fallacy to believe that the concept of Pakistan was formed in a poet's dream. The poet, Dr. Muhammad Iqbal, was no idle dreamer. Nor can countries like Pakistan (364,737 square miles; population 80 million) spring from the nebulous realm of poetry alone. Iqbal was in fact a philosopher of traditional as well as modern thought who had made a careful study of human affairs, both East and West, and focused the light of his inquiry on the causes of the economic and cultural subjugation to which the Moslems of India had been systematically subjected since their first abortive struggle for independence in 1857. It was in his presidential address to the annual session of the All-India Moslem League in 1930 that he spelled out the broad outlines of a plan under which the Moslems of India were led to aspire to an independent state in which they would be free to follow their own way of life.

The All-India Moslem League based its Charter on this idea and, under the leadership of Qaid-i-Azam Mohammed Ali Jinnah, launched a struggle which culminated in the establishment of Pakistan in August, 1947.

Iqbal's thesis—that in their free state the Moslems were to practice their own way of life—posed an ideological problem which was not easy to handle. On one hand, there were many outside Pakistan who charged us with planning to establish an obdurate theocracy in the medieval sense of the term. On the other,

* Reprinted, by special permission of the Council on Foreign Relations, from Mohammed Ayub Khan's article "Pakistan Perspective," in *Foreign Affairs*, XXXVIII, No. 4 (July, 1960), 547–56. Copyright by the Council on Foreign Relations, New York.

most of us within Pakistan itself were not quite clear how to go about welding our spiritual ideals into the business of statecraft. The result was a great deal of loose groping which infected our politics and our intellect alike.

Pakistan was thus involved in the paradox of almost losing its ideology in the very act of trying to fulfill it. This distraction was totally unwarranted, for Iqbal—one of the main creators of our ideology—had taken pains to define it in very clear terms: "In Islam, the spiritual and the temporal are not two distinct domains, and the nature of an act, however secular in its import, is determined by the attitude of mind with which the agent does it. It is the invisible mental background of the act which ultimately determines its character. An act is temporal or profane if it is done in a spirit of detachment from the infinite complexity of life behind it. It is spiritual if it is inspired by that complexity. In Islam, it is the same reality which appears as church looked at from one point of view and state from another."

According to this concept, the state owes a singular and specific duty to its people. "The essence of *Tauhid* [unity of God] as a working idea is equality, solidarity, and freedom," according to Iqbal. "The state, from the Islamic standpoint, is an endeavor to transform these ideals into space-time forces, an aspiration to realize them in a definite human organization."

It is this sort of human organization which Pakistan aspires to become, and one of my endeavors is to clear at least a part of the way by liberating the basic concept of our ideology from the dust of vagueness and ambiguities it has accumulated over the years. . . .

The British parliamentary system which we inherited and later adopted in the Constitution of 1956 is largely an unwritten law and takes for granted too many prerequisites which do not really exist in a country like Pakistan. Our rate of literacy is appallingly low. Our means of communication are poor—even primitive. The rural population, which constitutes over 80 per cent of the total, is hardly touched by the world outside the villages.

Just before independence, when Mr. Jinnah was anxious to put more and more of his party men in the Central and Provincial Assemblies of India to carry on the struggle for the idea of Pakistan, he issued an appeal: "Vote for a Moslem Leaguer even if it be a lamppost." People complied cheerfully—some even literally! When independence came, the gentlemen thus elected found themselves in a position of vantage to assume power in the new state of Pakistan, and the political system in their hands enabled them to keep delaying the making of a constitution for about eight years. The outgoing Parliament of Pakistan had eighty seats, with each member presuming to represent about a million of his countrymen for almost an indefinite period. Even under the Constitution of 1956, a member of the Provincial Assembly was required to be elected by more than 100,000 voters. Now this is the type of electoral college which just cannot work in Pakistan—or for that matter in any country where conditions like those of Pakistan obtain, as they do in many newly independent countries of Asia and Africa. An average villager with little or no education has no means of gaining any personal knowledge about a candidate who is mixed up in a population of 100,000 or more, spread over a large area without any advanced means of communication and contact. Votes cast under these circumstances cannot but be vague, wanton, and responsive to fear, coercion, temptation, and other modes of misguidance. This is exactly what had been happening in Pakistan. Whenever elections were held, they could be easily manipulated to return candidates with power to influence, money to bribe, and nuisance value to coerce. Conditions such as these reduce the practice of democracy to a farce.

But this does not dismay us. Nor should it be taken to imply that we can do—or wish to do—without democracy. The revolution of October 7, 1958, was not aimed against the institution of democracy as such. No, it was only against the manner in which its institutions were being worked. There are two main reasons why we in Pakistan cannot but adhere to a democratic pattern of life and government. In the first place, as Moslems, we are brought up on two basic ingredients of democracy—namely, equality and fraternity. Anything to the contrary would be the negation of our spiritual faith and practice. And secondly, we have to fight a long and arduous battle for progress and development in which every man, woman, and child of Pakistan must participate to the fullest possible extent. Democracy provides the only healthy and dignified way for arousing the willing cooperation of people and harnessing it to a sustained national endeavor.

We must, therefore, have democracy. The question then is: what type of democracy? The answer need not be sought in the theories and practices of other people alone. On the contrary, it must be found from within the book of Pakistan itself.

To my mind, there are four prerequisites for the success of any democratic system in a country like Pakistan:

1. It should be simple to understand, easy to work, and cheap to sustain.
2. It should put to the voter only such questions as he can answer in the light of his own personal knowledge and understanding without external prompting.
3. It should ensure the effective participation of all citizens in the affairs of the country up to the level of their mental horizon and intellectual caliber.
4. It should be able to produce reasonably strong and stable governments.

The scheme of "basic democracies" which has been launched in Pakistan is designed to meet most of these fundamental prerequisites. Under this scheme, the two wings of the country have each been divided into 40,000 constituencies with an average population of about 1,000. Every constituency elects one representative by universal franchise. In such a small and well-defined field of choice, voters of the meanest intelligence cannot go far wrong in putting their finger on the right type of candidate.

Ten such constituencies form a Union Council in the rural areas, and this elects its own chairman from among the elected members. Provision has also been made for nominated members to ensure, where necessary, the representation of special interests like women, minorities, etc. In towns and larger municipalities, organization follows a similar pattern.

The elected chairmen of Union Councils and Town Committees represent their areas on the next tier of administration, the *Thana* Council, which covers the entire area under the jurisdiction of a Police Station. From this stage, this system of associating the chosen representatives of the people with local administration travels upward, covering all intermediary tiers, like *tehsils*, districts, and divisions, up to the provincial level. This is designed to ensure a full sense of cooperation between the official and elected agencies at all stages of public administration.

The first elections to basic democracies were held last December, and I feel the results were quite heartening. The average percentage of votes cast was 67 per cent by men and 42 per cent by women. Those elected included 14 per cent university graduates,

78 per cent literate, and 8 per cent illiterate members. They came from the real hard core of the country, the majority of them being middle-class and lower middle-class agriculturists, lawyers, medical practitioners, businessmen, retired government servants, workers, and artisans.

One great lesson which these elections brought out was that, for the first time in Pakistan, it seemed possible for an average citizen to seek election purely on his or her personal merit, without the help of any financial, social, or political backing. Also for the first time, the elected candidate finds himself in a position to participate effectively and directly in the affairs of the country as they exist immediately around him.

The Union Councils and Town Committees have been given a wide charter of duties and responsibilities, ranging from local self-government to national reconstruction and development. Besides this, I am looking to this gigantic instrument of mass representation to achieve three other pressing objectives: First, to help create a fresh supply of local and national leaders. Second, to serve as a two-way traffic post between the government and the basic core of the people, and to bridge the gulf which under the best of systems is bound to exist between them in countries where education is limited, distances are large, and modern facilities for reaching the masses are not universal. And, third, I would personally like this body of 80,000 elected representatives to serve as the electoral college for the Parliament, and, possibly, for the President.* This is only my personal view, for I do not wish to prejudge the recommendations of the Constitution Commission, which is at the moment seized of this and other allied problems. . . .

An archaic type of feudalism which existed in Pakistan—particularly west Pakistan—had vested the entire political, economic, and social might of the country in a limited group of families. It was impossible to make any advance in any direction without first breaking this monopoly of power. Therefore, land reform was one of the first measures to be taken by the new regime. This was a major operation, but it was performed peacefully and scientifically, and was attended by no manner of tyranny or injustice. This is a

* The electors chosen in December, 1959, and January, 1960, elected Ayub Khan for a five-year term as President of Pakistan. In April, 1962 they chose representatives to the National Assembly.—ED.

far-reaching socio-economic change, and its full impact will be felt only with the passage of time.

Other fields in which reforms have been undertaken include education, public health, fiscal systems, law courts, civil administration, and the rehabilitation of refugees. The object is to get us to the starting point of development, whence we may be better able to grapple with some of the most pressing and immediate of our problems. These are: fighting the grave menace to the land of salinity and waterlogging; curbing the excessive rate of growth of population; and launching the next Five-Year Plan for national development—estimated to cost over 19 billion rupees (about $4 billion). According to experts, these figures are not astronomical, but only reasonable.

The next fifteen to twenty years are going to be most crucial for Pakistan. Either we "make the grade" in this period, or we do not. If we fail to make the grade, we are bound to be submerged under the tidal wave of Communism, which is constantly lashing its fury all around us. Since we do not seek this fate, we must move forward, and do so quickly. It is here that our eyes turn toward our friends and allies. They have already given us magnanimous aid, for which we are most grateful. But there are reasons of history which entitle us to claim still more. . . .

Moreover, in the context of present-day world politics, Pakistan has openly and unequivocally cast its lot with the West, and unlike several other countries around us, we have shut ourselves off almost completely from the possibility of any major assistance from the Communist bloc. We do not believe in hunting with the hound and running with the hare. We wish to follow, and are following, a clear and unambiguous path.

All these factors lead to one conclusion: that the English-speaking world ought to feel a special responsibility to assist Pakistan in attaining a reasonable posture of advancement. It is not just a claim. It is in fact the dictate of history. . . .

8. Abdul Karim Kassem

Abdul Karim Kassem was born in 1914, in Baghdad, and studied at the Iraqi Military College there. After participating in the Arab-Israeli war of 1948, he attended the Royal Military College at Sandhurst, England. On July 14, 1958, he headed a military revolution that overthrew the regime of King Faisal and Nuri-es Said, who, directly or indirectly, had ruled Iraq since the end of World War I. The revolutionary government denounced the Baghdad Pact as well as Iraq's military alliance with Great Britain.

Kassem has adopted a policy of economic and social reform, nationalism, and nonalignment and he has repressed political parties—including the Communists, after their unsuccessful rebellion in 1959. Despite the similarity of their programs and policies, Kassem is suspicious of Nasser's attempts to extend his influence over the Arab world. The following selections from his speeches explain his preference for rule by military reformers rather than by parliamentary means.

THE ARMY AND THE PARTIES*

The army and the people have merged into a single entity. They have become a source of strength which is worrying the foreigners. . . . Imperialism now tries to split up our ranks by calling for narrow parties and restricted groupings. The purpose of this is to play one against the other, while the foreigners and the imperialists will sit as spectators. But we shall thrust a stone in the mouth of imperialism. . . . The parochial groupings and party affiliation at this time are of no benefit to the country. They place the

* Excerpts from speeches delivered by Kassem on May 1 and June 16, 1959; reprinted from *Principles of 14th July Revolution* (Baghdad, 1959).

country in an embarrassing situation. As I have told you, the purpose of this is to create disunity and weaken our strength and play one against the other. We are in a period of transition. We have resolved to protect the gains of our revolution at any cost.

Some people have come to me and said: "O leader, we wish you would form a party, thus saving us from these parties and groupings." My answer was that we are in a period of transition and that my party is the entire people, and I belong to the party of the people. All of us are the party of Allah, the party of right and justice. We are the party of the struggle. We shall endeavor to achieve our freedom. We are marching on the road of freedom; we are heading toward healthy democratic rule. We cannot be disunited by anyone. The people as a whole, and I, being with the people, are making a tremendous revolution undermining imperialism and threatening its structure. We, the entire people, constitute a formidable revolution, shaking off imperialism from its foundations. We shall secure our full rights. We are heading toward a healthy democratic rule. Our meeting today is one of the examples of this healthy rule.

I warn you against the intrigues of mischief-makers. They are bent upon disuniting our ranks at a time when our republic is not yet one year old. We have scored many gains for our revolution. It is our duty to protect these gains. These gains can only be protected by unity, tolerance, and renouncement of the old enmities and splits. You must not become disunited into groups and factions.

We are the party of right and justice. You are the party of right and justice. You are the party of the revolution. You work in the way of Allah and the way of the people to secure the gains of the immortal Iraqi Revolution, which we are determined to preserve and to defend at any cost. . . .

The primary objectives of the army and of sincere people were to seize an opportunity someday with a view to delivering the people from the tyrants, saving the soil of the homeland, and obliterating imperialism and its stooges. The army had performed its duty in the July 14 Revolution and merged with the masses of the people in a spectacular patriotic movement that will be preserved in history. It was a move designed to achieve liberation and freedom and to crush the imperialists.

The army is the only force which can be relied upon at mo-

ments of emergency, and the entire people can depend upon it.
This force must necessarily be solid. We—the officers, other ranks,
NCO's, enlisted men, and workers with the army—are bound together with the fighting units by the ties of brotherhood and of
army discipline. We are bound together by the tie of the homeland. We always work with sincerity and straightforwardness, to
which corruption and twists are alien. The armed units are always
working in the way of Allah, for the sake of the people and the
public interests. They are completely alien to private interests.
They have devoted their lives and their efforts to the service of
the homeland.

The army had been humiliated and looked down upon with
contemptuousness for many years before the July 14 Revolution,
for the simple reason that the army was a patriotic force which
could be relied upon in moments of hardship. For that reason,
they sought to humiliate that force. But that force was attached to
the interest of the homeland by the bond of love of this soil and
devotion in defending it. Such a bond cannot be broken. We are
patriotic people, always working for the sake of the soil of the
homeland. It was because of this, brothers, that they were unable
to vanquish the army. Nor could they ever be able to dispel the
idea borne by the sincere people, secretly or openly, when they
rely upon the sincerity of other brothers.

I deliberately wanted to stress this point and emphasize this aspect. The army is the base on which the people depend. The
people always think of depending on the army. The army must
therefore remain a united force incapable of being disunited. It
must remain a united force, dealing blows to the foe, watching
readily the greedy people, and keeping an eye over those who seek
to split up the ranks as well as those who contemplate trespassing
on our frontiers. . . . I know full well the extent of the attachment,
brotherhood, and love which each of you harbors toward me in
particular. I am confident of this, and I am sure of it. This is so
because I have worked for you, for the army in particular, and for
the people even more, and for the homeland as well. . . .

We will proceed with the liberated world as friends. We will
know nothing other than that. A friend is different from the agent
and the stooge. We propose not to become a stooge of any power.
We do not wish to become subordinate to any power. We will be
friends with the powers of the world. We will be sincere friends

to the powers that are sincere in their intentions and their friendship to us. . . .

You must be sure that all powers, big and small, do respect friendly countries, but not agent countries. Small in size and in population, we have carried out a formidable accomplishment for the sake of the homeland, having acquired the respect of the friendly powers. Friendly powers no doubt respect us and wish to preserve this friendship. This, however, depends on what strength we maintain and on the unity of our ranks as well as on the extent of our sincerity to this people and to this homeland.

9. Gamal Abdel Nasser

Gamal Abdel Nasser was born in 1918, the son of a postal clerk in Alexandria. He went to secondary school in Cairo, studied law for a time, and then attended military school, receiving his commission in 1938. He served in the Sudan, and fought in the Israeli War. Nasser had been a nationalist since his secondary-school days, and the corruption and inefficiency of the Egyptian politicians at the time of the war against Israel led him to form a Free Officers' Committee, out of which grew the Council of Revolutionary Command, which seized power on July 23, 1952. General Naguib, the nominal head of the revolutionary junta, was removed in November, 1954, and since then, Nasser has ruled as Premier and Chairman of the Council of Revolutionary Command. He achieved fame as a neutralist leader by the nationalization of the Suez Canal in July, 1956, as a response to the American withdrawal of aid for his Aswan High Dam project.

After the seizure of power in 1952, Nasser wrote a series of articles for the Egyptian magazine Akhar Saa, later published as The Philosophy of the Revolution. *Nasser has outlawed all political parties except his Party of National Union, now reorganized as the Arab Socialist Union. In July, 1961, he nationalized most major business enterprises. His program of "Arab socialism," which he described in a speech on May 21, 1962, rejects the Marxist view of the inevitability of the class struggle and calls for a mixed economy and the establishment of elected councils in factories and in local and national government.*

THE PHILOSOPHY OF THE REVOLUTION*

The Two Revolutions

Every people on earth go through two revolutions: a political revolution that helps them recover their right to self-government from the hands of a despot who had imposed himself upon them, or free themselves from the domination of alien armed forces which had installed themselves in the land against their will; and a social revolution—a class conflict that ultimately ends in the realization of social justice for all the inhabitants of the country.

People who preceded us on the path of human progress have all passed through those two revolutions, but not simultaneously. In certain cases, centuries have separated the one from the other. In our case, we are passing through the grueling ordeal of experiencing the two revolutions together. This ordeal, this acid test lies in the fact that each of these two revolutions has peculiar circumstances which are strangely conflicting and highly contradictory.

Unity, solidarity, and cooperation of all elements of the nation and self-denial and self-sacrifice on the part of the individual to ensure the safety, prosperity, and integrity of the motherland are the fundamental factors for the success of a *political* revolution. The disintegration of values, disruption of principles, dissension and discord among both classes and individuals, and domination of corruption, suspicion, and perversion of egoism form the foundation of *social* upheaval. Between these two millstones we find ourselves today, destined to go through two revolutions—one calling for unity, solidarity, self-sacrifice, and devotion to sacred duty, while the other imposes upon us, against our will, disunity, dissension, and nothing else but envy, hatred, vindictiveness, and egoism.

Between these two millstones, to cite a case in point, the 1919

* Reprinted from *The Philosophy of the Revolution* (Cairo: Information Department, 1954).

Revolution failed to reach the results it ought to have realized. Hardly had the ranks designed to meet oppression been formed before they dispersed to engage in nothing else but strife. . . . Ignominious failure was the result; the oppressors tightened the screw, whether through the occupation forces or through their tools and instruments, who were then led by Sultan Fuad, and later by Farouk, his son. All that the people reaped was distrust, doubt, dissension, hatred, rancor, and strife among themselves—both classes and individuals. Thus faded the hope that was expected to be realized by the 1919 Revolution.

I said the hope faded. I did not say the hope disappeared, because the natural forces of resistance driven by the people's great hopes were still active and getting ready for yet another trial. Such was the situation that prevailed after 1919—a situation which made it imperative for the army to be the only force capable of any action.

In fact, the situation demanded a force concentrated within a framework that separates its members to a certain extent from the continual conflict between individuals and classes, a force drawn from the very heart of the people, whose members can trust one another and have full confidence in themselves—a force so equipped as to be capable of a swift and decisive action, and these conditions only prevailed in the army.

Thus it was not the army that determined the role it was to play in the course of events. The reverse was nearer to the truth. It was the events and their development that determined the army's part in the supreme struggle for the liberation of the homeland.

I realized from the outset that our success depended on our complete understanding of the nature of the circumstances in which we live in the present phase of our country's history. We could not with a mere stroke of the pen change these circumstances. We could not put back or forward the hands of the clock, and be masters of time. We also could not act the part of a traffic officer on the road of history, holding up the passage of one revolution to allow another revolution to pass through, and thus avert a collision. All that we could do was to act as best we could to escape being crushed between two millstones. There was no alternative to carrying out the two revolutions together.

In fact, the day we proceeded on the road to the political revolution and dethroned Farouk, we took a similar step on the road to the social revolution and limited the ownership of land. I still believe that the July 23 Revolution should continue to retain the initiative and its ability of rapid movement, so that it would be able to accomplish the miracle of carrying out the two revolutions simultaneously, no matter how contradictory our action may seem at times. . . .

Egypt at the Crossroads

Fate has decreed that we should stand at the world's crossroads. We have oftentimes been the invader's passageway and the adventurer's target. So numerous have been the circumstances through which we have lived that it would indeed be impossible to explain the factors latent in our people's souls unless these circumstances were taken into account.

In my opinion, Egypt's history under the Pharaohs cannot be overlooked. Then comes the interaction between the Greek culture and ours. The Roman invasion and the Islamic conquest, with the waves of Arab migration which followed, should also not be left out of the picture.

I am also of the opinion that we should dwell long on the circumstances through which we lived in the Middle Ages. It was those circumstances which brought about the situation in which we now are. If the Crusades marked the first dawnings of the Renaissance in Europe, they heralded the beginning of the ages of darkness in our country. Our people had borne alone almost the whole brunt of those battles, which left them completely impoverished and utterly helpless. And at the very time when they were shaking and tottering after the shattering blows of battle, it was their lot to suffer further humiliation and misery under the heels of Circassian tyrants and Mogul despots. . . .

My soul is torn with grief when I come to think, as I oftentimes do, of that period in our history in which a despotic feudalism was formed; a feudalism the sole object of which was to bleed the people white and deprive them of the last vestige of power and dignity. We shall indeed have to fight hard and long before we are able to rid ourselves completely of the deleterious effects of that system.

In fact, what still remains latent in our souls has on many an occasion provided me with an explanation of some of the aspects of our political life. It would seem to me sometimes, for instance, that many adopt toward the revolution the attitude of mere on-lookers who are interested in nothing else but the result of a fight between two sides with whom they are in no way connected. . . .

Then what happened to us after the Mamelukes? There came the French expedition, the iron curtain drawn around us was smashed, new ideas followed, and horizons as yet invisible to us opened. The Mohammed Ali Dynasty inherited all the evils of the Mameluke regime, although it attempted to garb them in nineteenth-century garments. Our contacts with Europe and the whole world began anew. So also began our modern awakening, but it began with a new crisis.

In my opinion, our case very much resembled that of a sick man who had spent a long time in a closed room. The heat in that closed room had become so intense that the man was in anguish. Suddenly a violent storm blew, smashing all windows and doors, and strong currents of cold air began to lash the body of the sick man, who was still perspiring. The sick man needed a breath of air. Instead, a raging hurricane assailed him, and fever began to devour his feeble body. This was exactly the case of our society. It was indeed a dangerous case.

Undoubtedly, this state of affairs is responsible for the non-existence of a strong united public opinion in our country. The difference between one individual and another is vast; that between one generation and another is greater still.

There was a time when I complained that the people did not know what they were about, that they never agreed to follow the same road. I later realized, however, that I was asking for the impossible, that I had not taken the society in which we live into account. Actually, we live in a society which has not yet crystallized. It is still in a state of ferment and agitation and has not yet stabilized to continue its gradual development, like the other peoples who have gone before on the same road. I believe, with no intention to flatter the people in expressing such a belief, that our people have wrought a veritable miracle. Any other society subjected to the same severe trials as ours might have succumbed. It would have been swept by the powerful currents that had overtaken us. We have, however, weathered the tempest. It is true we have almost lost our balance, but we have not fallen down.

I sometimes consider the state of an average Egyptian family—one of the thousands of families which live in the capital of the country. The father, for example, is a turbaned *fellah*—a thoroughbred country fellow. The mother is a lady of Turkish descent. The sons and daughters attend schools following, respectively, the English and French educational systems—all this in an atmosphere in which the thirteenth-century spirit and twentieth-century manifestations intermingle and interact.

I see all this and feel in my heart of hearts that I know the cause of this bewildering perplexity which is torturing our minds and this astounding confusion which is destroying our very existence. Then I say to myself, "Surely our society will crystallize; surely it will be solidified; surely it will be welded into a strong homogeneous whole. All that is required is to strain every nerve to hold our ground during this period of transition."

The Three Circles

When I come to analyze the elements of our strength, I cannot help being struck by three sources standing in bold relief, which should be taken into account before everything else.

The first of these sources lies in the fact that we are a group of neighboring nations welded into a homogeneous whole by every possible material and moral tie that would unite any such group of nations. Moreover, our peoples possess peculiarities, potentialities, and a civilization inspired by the spiritual principles of the three divine religions which can never be overlooked in any attempt to build a new stable and peaceful world.

The second source is our land itself and the position it occupies on the map of the world—that important strategic position which rightly makes of it the world's crossroads, the main route of its trade and the highway of its armies.

There remains the third source. This is oil—which is considered the backbone of material civilization, and without which all the world's largest factories, all means of land, sea, and air communication, all war weapons would become mere iron . . .

If I have succeeded in explaining the extent of the importance of this vital element of strength, as I sincerely hope I have, it would thus follow that we are strong—strong not through wailing, shouting, or appealing for help at the top of our voices, but strong through our composure or our correct estimation (supported by figures) of our capacity for work, and our true understanding of the strength of the ties that bind our peoples together, those ties which make of our homeland an integral and indivisible whole, which should be defended as such and not as an isolated unit. So much for the First Circle—the Arab Circle, within the framework of which we should endeavor to turn, move, and act with all our force.

As for the Second Circle—the African Continent Circle . . . we cannot, under any condition, even if we want to, stand aloof from the terrible and terrifying battle now raging in the heart of that continent between 5 million whites and 200 million Africans. We cannot stand aloof for one important and obvious reason—we ourselves are in Africa.

Surely the people of Africa will continue to look to us—we who are the guardians of the Continent's northern gate, we who constitute the connecting link between the Continent and the outer world. We certainly cannot, under any condition, relinquish our responsibility to help to our utmost in spreading the light of knowledge and civilization to the very depths of the virgin jungles of the continent.

There remains another equally important reason: The Nile, the life artery of our country, springs from the heart of the continent. And still one more reason: the beloved Sudan, whose boundaries extend to the heart of the continent and which is bound by neighborly relations with the sensitive spots in its center.

There is no denying the fact that Africa is now the scene of a strange and stirring commotion. The white man, who represents several European nations, is again trying to change the map of the continent. We surely cannot, under any condition, stand as mere onlookers, deluding ourselves into the belief that we are in no way concerned with these machinations.

Indeed, I shall continue to dream of the day on which I shall see in Cairo a great Africa institute, seeking to reveal to us the various aspects of the continent, to create in our minds an enlightened African consciousness, and to associate itself with all those working in all parts of the world for the progress, prosperity, and welfare of the peoples of Africa.

There remains the Third Circle—the circle encompassing continents and oceans—the Circle of our Brethren in Islam, who, wherever their place under the sun, turn with us toward the same *kiblah*,* their lips solemnly saying the same prayers.

* *Kiblah* is the direction of Mecca, which Moslems must face during prayer.—Ed.

My faith in the magnitude of the positive effectiveness that could result from strengthening the Islamic tie that binds all Moslems grew stronger when I accompanied the Egyptian mission to Saudi Arabia to offer condolences on the death of its great King. As I stood before the Kaaba,* with my thoughts wandering around every part of the world which Islam has reached, I fully realized the need for a radical change of our conception of the pilgrimage. I said to myself: The journey to the Kaaba should no longer be construed as an admission card to paradise or as a crude attempt to buy forgiveness of sins after leading a dissipated life.

The pilgrimage should have a potential political power. The world press should hasten to follow and feature its news not by drawing attractive pen pictures of its rites and rituals for the delectation of readers, but by its representation as a periodic political conference at which the heads of all the Islamic states—leaders of opinion, scientists, eminent industrialists, and prominent businessmen—assemble to draw up at this world Islamic parliament the broad lines of the policies to be adopted by their respective countries, and lay down the principles ensuring their close cooperation until they have again gathered together in the following session.

They assemble, devout, but mighty; unambitious of power, but active and full of energy; submissive to divine will, but immutable in difficulties and implacable with their enemies.

They assemble, confirmed believers in the life to come, but equally convinced that they have a place under the sun which they should occupy in this life. . . .

THE NATIONAL UNION PARTY†

Every healthy democracy should rest on the liberation of the individual. The individual should not be submitted to any sort of exploitation. I have responded to this requirement by establishing

* The Kaaba is the square structure in the center of the Great Mosque at Mecca which houses the sacred Black Stone.—Ed.

† Excerpts from a speech delivered by Nasser at the opening of the High Dam project on November 26, 1959. The English translation, taken from Nasser's *Speeches and Press Interviews, 1959* (Cairo: U.A.R. Information Department, 1960), has been revised by the editor.

the basis for a democratic, socialist, cooperative society, a society which is free of political, economic, and social exploitation. Having arrived at this stage, we must study by what means we can retain what we have acquired, and how it will be possible for us to remain united in order to oppose any attempt at domination—whether it comes from outside or within. . . .

Many political systems exist in the world. Some have a single party; others have many parties. The single-party organization does not respond to our hopes or our purposes. In the government by the single party, a small minority—5 or 10 per cent of the population—dominates political life, while the majority does not participate in it, but must submit to it nevertheless. As to the multiparty organization which we ourselves have experienced, it is evident that it serves the nations who want to keep us in their zones of influence. We know the typical example of Egypt after the revolution of 1919.

There was a nationalist revolution, and there were nationalist parties, but they became divided and multiplied. The unity of the people broke down. From that moment, the revolution of 1919 did not attain its ends. The English remained in our country until 1956, and the parties gave up the programs on the basis of which they had been established, in order to concern themselves only with their particular interests in their competition for power.

Of course, each of them proclaimed that the end justified the means of his coming to power (which he achieved thanks to British colonialism or to the Embassy of Great Britain or the Palace). In fact, each one thought only of benefiting his own particular cause.

It is clear that to have several parties at the present time would only result in favoring the penetration of foreign influence. Since the beginning of the Cold War, the reactionary parties have tried to rally to the cause of the West. They do not hesitate to go to the foreigner to increase the possibility of their accession to power, thinking that once victory is attained, they will keep their influence, and that collaboration can be established between the power of the external enemy and that of the internal exploiter. At the same time, the Communist parties opt for the East and try to arrive at power by all methods so as to establish instead the dictatorship of the proletariat and to cooperate with international Communism—naturally for the purpose of making us enter into a zone of influence.

It is obvious that at this moment of our history, at a time when we have great battles to carry out, the system of the single party—the expression of a desire for political monopoly—could not be suitable for us. At the same time, several parties which open the way to foreign infiltration could be no more suitable.

We therefore must attempt a new experiment which will guard us at the same time against the faults of the single party and against the inconveniences of a system of several parties—an experiment which answers the need for an organism with which all the children of the nation will be associated. It will protect us against foreign infiltration and preserve our unity, making it impossible for the foreigner to divide us and place us in a zone of influence. This experiment is the National Union.

The National Union is based on the liberation of the individual from economic, political, and social exploitation. It is a national and patriotic organization. All the children of the nation are associated there and elect their representatives. The entire people are the guardian of its unity, which they should protect against all foreign intervention. The whole people protect the rights which they have acquired. Together, they protect themselves against feudalism, against economic takeover, and against political monopoly. When a single party, or certain categories of the population, take over all political activity, that is political monopoly.

I have said that the liberation of the individual is accomplished when feudalism has been annihilated, when monopolies have been broken, when capitalism can no longer find ways to exercise its influence and in that way impose its domination—when, finally, social and economic exploitation is destroyed. All this has meant the establishment of the basis for a democratic party life, and in that way the elimination of political exploitation.

Today, seven years after the revolution, we see the characteristics of the new society to which we have aspired and at which in the past we had given up hope of arriving. It is a new socialist, democratic, and cooperative society, freed of all political, social, and economic exploitation. . . .

ARAB SOCIALISM*

Political democracy cannot be separated from social democracy. No citizen can be regarded as free to vote unless he is given the following three guarantees:

1. He should be free from exploitation in all its forms.
2. He should enjoy an equal opportunity to have a fair share of the national wealth.
3. His mind should be free from all anxiety likely to undermine the security of his life in the future.

Only when a citizen possesses these three guarantees can he be said to have political freedom and can he take part, by means of his vote, in shaping the authority of the state he aspires to have.

Political democracy cannot exist under the domination of any one class. Democracy means, literally, the domination and sovereignty of the people—the entire people. The experiment started with the beginning of the organized revolutionary action has proved that it is indispensable that the revolution undertake to liquidate the force of reaction, deprive it of all its weapons, and prevent it from making any attempt to come back to power and subject the state machinery to the service of its own interests.

The bitterness and sanguinary nature of class strife, as well as the grave dangers likely to ensue, are in fact the creation of the force of reaction, which does not wish to give up the monopolies or privileged positions from which it continues to exploit the people. The force of reaction possesses the means of resistance; it possesses the power of the state, and if this is taken away from it, it turns to the power of capital. If, however, this is taken away from it, then it turns to its natural ally, imperialism.

Because of their monopoly of wealth, reactionary interests are bound to clash with the interest of the whole people. Consequently, the peaceful resolution of class struggle cannot be

* Excerpts from Nasser's speech on the draft charter, delivered on May 21, 1962; English translation published by the U.A.R. Information Department, Cairo.

achieved unless the power of reaction is first and foremost deprived of all its weapons.

The removal of such clashes will pave the way to peaceful solutions to class struggles. It does not remove the contradictions in the rest of the social classes, but it creates a chance for the possibility of resolving them peacefully—namely, by means of democratic action. If, on the other hand, this clash of interests is allowed to remain, then it will not be resolved except by a civil war that will cause great damage to the country at a time of great international conflict and bitter Cold War.

The collaboration between the force of reaction and exploiting capital must, therefore, collapse. The road must then be paved for democratic interaction among the various powers of the working people—namely, the farmers, workers, soldiers, intellectuals, and national capital.

Cooperation among the powers representing the working people is the legitimate substitute for the collaboration between feudalism and exploiting capital. It alone is capable of replacing reactionary democracy by true democracy.

The national unity created by the cooperation between those representative powers of the people will be able to set up the Arab Socialist Union. This union will constitute the authority representing the people and the driving force behind the possibilities of the revolution and the guardian of the values of true democracy.

These enormous popular powers—forming the Arab Socialist Union, and responsible for the unleashing of its energy and effectiveness—make it necessary that, when dealing with the form of the political organization of the state, the new constitution of the United Arab Republic must refer to a set of necessary guarantees:

1. The popular and political organizations based on free and direct election must truly and fairly represent the powers forming the majority of the population—the powers that have for long been exploited and have a deep interest in the Revolution, through their experience of deprivation. These powers are also naturally the storehouse of revolutionary energy, which is both dynamic and forceful.

This is only just and fair, since it means that the majority will be represented. It also provides a sure guarantee of the strength of the revolutionary impetus because it will then be springing from its genuine and natural sources.

It follows, then, that the new constitution must ensure that farmers and workers will get half the seats in political and popular organizations at all levels—including the house of representatives—since they form the majority of the people. Moreover, they are the majority who have been longest deprived of their inalienable right to shape and direct their future.

2. The authority of the elected popular councils must be consolidated and raised above the authority of the executive machinery of the state, for that is the natural order regulating the sovereignty of the people, and ensures that the people will always lead national action. . . . Local government should gradually but resolutely transfer the authority of the state to the people, for they are in a better position to feel their own problems and find the proper solutions.

3. There is a dire need to create a new political organization within the framework of the Arab Socialist Union—recruiting the elements fit for leadership, organizing their efforts, clarifying the revolutionary motives of the masses, sounding their needs, and endeavoring to satisfy them.

4. Collective leadership is imperative in the period of the revolutionary drive. Collective leadership not only guards against the individual running loose, but also confirms and ensures the reign of democracy in its most sublime form.

Popular organizations, especially cooperatives and trade unions, can play an effective and influential role in promoting sound democracy. These organizations should form a vanguard force in the various fields of national democratic action. The development of the cooperative and trade-union movements provides an endless source to the conscious leadership that directly feels the reactions and responses of the masses. The pressure that stifled these organizations and paralyzed their movements has vanished.

Besides their productive role, the farmers' cooperatives are democratic organizations, capable of spotting and solving the problems of the farmers. So it is high time for agricultural labor unions to be established.

Industrial, commercial, and service trade unions were able, thanks to the July laws, to reach a position of leadership in the national struggle. The workers are no longer commodities in production processes. The forces of labor have become masters of the production process. They also share in its administration and profits, under the best terms of wages and working hours.

Criticism and self-criticism are among the most important guarantees to freedom. The greatest danger in the way of free criticism and self-criticism in political organizations is the infiltration of reactionary elements.

As a result of their control of economic interests, the reactionary forces controlled the press. Freedom of opinion was thus deprived of its most valuable instrument. The elimination of reaction puts an end to the dictatorship of one class and paves the way for the democracy of all the national powers of the people. It provides the surest guarantees for the freedom of assembly and freedom of discussion. . . .

Nationalization and Private Ownership

It is of prime importance that our outlook toward nationalization should be freed from the stigmas that private interests have tried to attach to it. Nationalization is but the transfer of the means of production from the sphere of private ownership to that of public ownership.

This is not a blow to individual initiative, as alleged by the enemies of socialism, but a guarantee to and an expansion of the range of general interest in cases affected by the socialist change, carried out for the benefit of the people.

Nationalization does not lead to a decrease in production. Experience has proved the ability of the public sector to shoulder the greatest responsibilities with maximum efficiency, whether in the achievement of the production targets or in the raising of the standard of its quality. Although some mistakes may occur during this great evolution, we must recall the new hands that have assumed the responsibility. At any rate it was inevitable that the major national interests should be handed over to the people even at the cost of facing temporary difficulties.

The great importance attached to the role of the public sector, however, cannot do away with the existence of the private sector. The private sector has its effective role in the development plan. It must be protected to fulfill that part. The private sector is now required to renovate itself and strike a new path of creative effort not dependent, as in the past, on parasitic exploitation.

The crisis which befell private capital before the Revolution actually stemmed from the fact that it had inherited the era of the foreign adventurers, who, in the nineteenth century, helped transfer abroad the wealth of Egypt. Private capital was accustomed to live under a protective trade policy that gave it benefits at the expense of the people. It was also accustomed to dominate the government with the aim of pursuing a policy of exploitation. ... The people could not forever remain indifferent to maneuvers to direct the government to favor the minority controlling wealth, and to guarantee the maintenance of their privileged position at the expense of the people's interests.

Progress through socialism is a consolidation of the bases of sound democracy, the democracy of all the people. . . .

Moreover, the maintenance of the role of the private sector beside that of the public sector renders control over public ownership more effective. By encouraging free competition within the framework of the general economic planning, the private sector is also an invigorating element to the public sector. The July, 1961, revolutionary laws did not aim at destroying the private sector, but had two basic aims: The creation of some form of economic equality among citizens that ensures legitimate rights and removes the effects of a minority's monopolizing all opportunities at the expense of the majority contributes to the dissolution of class distinctions in a way that enhances the possibilities of a peaceful struggle between them, and paves the way for democratic solutions to the major problems confronting the process of development. The second objective is to step up the efficiency of the public sector, owned by the people, to consolidate its capacity to shoulder the responsibility of planning, and to enable it to play its leading role in industrial development on a socialist basis. These two objectives have been crowned with sweeping success, confirming the power of the revolutionary drive and the depth of national unity.

The realization of these two objectives wipes out the residue of the complexes (created by exploitation) that cast a shadow of doubt on the role of the private sector. Consequently, the path open to this sector today, to promote the process of development, is only restricted by the socialist laws now in force or by the steps deemed necessary by the popular authorities elected in future. . . .

Foreign Capital

Foreign capital is regarded with dark doubts in underdeveloped countries—particularly those which were colonized. The sovereignty of the people over their land and their restoration to the helm allow them to set the conditions under which foreign capital may be invested in the country.

The matter calls for the setting up of a system of priority, drawn from the essence of the national experience. It also takes into account the nature of world capital—always striving after unexploited raw materials in areas not yet ready for any economic or social revival, where it can obtain the highest share of profit.

In the first place, in the process of national evolution, all foreign aid with no strings attached is accepted to help attain the national objectives. The aid is accepted with sincere gratitude for those who offer it regardless of the colors of their flags.

In the second place, all unconditional loans are accepted, provided they can be refunded without difficulty or strain. Experience shows that loans are a clear operation; their problem ends with their amortization and the reimbursement of their interest.

In the third place, the participation of foreign capital as investment is accepted in indispensable operations, especially those requiring experience difficult to find in the national domain. Acceptance of foreign investment implies that a foreigner would participate in the administration. It also implies that a share of the annual profits would be transferred to the investors indefinitely. This matter should not be left without limitation.

First priority goes to unconditional aid. The second place is reserved to unconditional loans. Then follows the acceptance of foreign investment (in unavoidable circumstances) in aspects of modern evolution requiring international experience.

In their conscious revolutionary outlook, our people consider it the duty of the advanced states to offer aid to those still struggling for development. In their conception of history, our people believe the states with a colonialist past are, more than others, compelled to offer to the nations aspiring to development part of the national wealth they sapped when that wealth was a booty for all looters. . . .

The Class Struggle

We must clearly realize that no individual can be free unless he is first liberated from the shackles of exploitation. It is this fact that makes social freedom a way—in fact, the only way—to achieve political freedom.

Our immediate aim is to do away with exploitation and to make

possible the exercise of the natural right of equal opportunity; to
dissolve class distinctions and to end the domination of one class,
and hence remove the struggle between classes, which constitutes
a threat to the freedom of the individual citizen and even to freedom of the whole of the country by violating the rights of the
people, and which creates the chance of exposing the country to
the lurking dangers of foreign forces, vigilantly on the lookout to
drag it to the arena of the Cold War and make of it its battlefield
and of its people fodder for their guns. The removal of the struggle between classes which arises out of interests that can never be
reconciled, between those who exercise exploitation and those
crushed by exploitation in the past society, cannot overnight lead
to the dissolution of all class distinctions, or lead to social freedom and true democracy.

Yet, the removal of the struggle between classes makes it possible—by eliminating the exploiting class—to dissolve class distinctions peacefully and to open the gates for democratic exchange,
which brings the whole society nearer the age of true freedom.
That was one of the great social objectives of the July laws, which
directed a deadly blow at the centers of exploitation and monopolies. That great revolutionary action made it possible to have
democracy for the first time in Egypt.

10. Habib Bourguiba

Habib Bourguiba was born in 1903, in a small fishing village in
Tunisia. His father had been an officer in the army of the Bey of
Tunis, but had resigned in protest against the establishment of the
French protectorate. Bourguiba was educated at French schools
in Tunis and at the Faculty of Law in Paris. On his return to
Tunis, in 1928, he became active in the nationalist movement. In
1934, Bourguiba organized the Neo-Destour Party, which stood for
complete independence of Tunisia. From 1934 until 1952, he was
repeatedly imprisoned by the French for nationalist activities, but
when Tunisia received internal autonomy in 1956, he became

Prime Minister. When full independence was accorded a year later, he became President.

A modernizing Moslem, Bourguiba has campaigned—with only limited success—to persuade the Tunisians to abandon the traditional fast of Ramadan as not suited to a country trying to develop as rapidly as possible. Sometimes regarded as pro-Western, Bourguiba describes his policy as one of nonalignment and gradualism (Bourguibism). These policies are defended in the following selections from his speeches.

THE FAST OF RAMADAN*

...The cause of these obstacles to our progress and of the paralysis of our minds is not the Moslem religion. As I know it, as I have studied it and learned it—as it was lived and practiced by the earliest members and by the Prophet himself, his companions, contemporaries, and successors—the Moslem religion is not a doctrine of intellectual asphyxia.

The first leaders of Islam were infinitely bolder and infinitely freer in the application of the principles of their religion, in their creativeness and adaptation to circumstances than our Ulema of the period of decadence. The Prophet's life and history are witness of this. They did not hesitate to suspend the effects of a Koranic edict. The caliph Omar suspended the application of certain penalties because of special circumstances. The Prophet himself had done likewise before him.

Why should such boldness be forbidden today? Why should we always be bound by what so and so said or someone else forbade?

I do not want you to agree with me blindly. I shall be satisfied if the question is studied, thought about, and freely discussed. What surprises and pains me at the same time is to hear that problems of this sort are outside the field of reason. Here we see the poverty of the chained mind. "How can we discuss this problem, since it has never been discussed before?" This is the supreme argument. I cannot accept it. We must discuss it, with complete freedom. Allah has given us brains. Let us use them to discuss and

* From a speech delivered by Bourguiba on February 6, 1961; translated and published by the Tunisian Secretariat of State for Information.

understand his commands. After all, we allow ourselves to discuss his existence.

Let us see what all the talk is about. It is said that I want to abolish Ramadan and want to force civil servants, among others, not to fast. There has never been any question of this. Need I say that the Ramadan fast is perfectly valid. The institution of fasting is to be found in other religions. Its beneficial effects are well known: self-mastery, improvement perhaps of physical condition, treatment of certain illness. All this is reasonable, and we subscribe to it.

But, as we said, we are living today in special circumstances. Neither the Prophet nor the first Moslems would ever have imagined that this nation, which Allah said was the best ever to have existed among men, should be far behind the other nations and reduced to its present fate. You need only look around you. . . .

Thus, as soon as we took power, we considered it of the utmost importance to set resolutely to work. Work and still more work: productive, rational, and methodically organized work, undertaken to create new wealth and cause an upheaval comparable to what the Arabs achieved in passing from the pre-Islamic to the Islamic era.

I am convinced that the greatest contribution made by Islam is in the liberation of the human mind. The first Moslem Arabs owe their extraordinary advance to this liberation. In reading the *Koran* and the *Life of the Prophet,* we are struck by the boldness and the exceptional power of the thought expressed.

It is only natural that, in talking to the mass of believers, Islam should have made attractive promises and terrible threats. Paradise and hell were both described in minute detail. Of course, for the Arabs of that time, paradise represented every imaginable form of beauty: gently murmuring springs, trees, and gardens watered by rivers. The inhabitants of a harsh, bare country could imagine no greater delight than water and a green landscape. To this picture, a few houris were added, as well as rivers flowing with honey and melted butter—in fact, all that was needed for perfect happiness.

On the other side, however, there were the flames and burning coals of hell. One might imagine that, once the sinner was burned to ashes, his tortures would be ended. Far from it! His flesh would be reconstituted and his sufferings start all over again an infinite number of times.

In this way, primitive people were induced to behave well, so as to avoid hell and make themselves worthy of paradise.

However, when a higher outlook came into being—as during the golden age of Moslem civilization—the great doctrinal masters, such as Ghazali and others, taught that this belief is at a lower level than that of the faith which expects neither heavenly nor earthly reward for good works, but seeks only peace of conscience. The accomplishment of duty, the practice of charity, the forgiveness of injuries, all these Moslem virtues are gifts of self designed to bring the believer close to Allah.

At the same time, we should note that by working solely to deserve paradise and avoid hell, scrupulously carrying out divine teachings, man works for his happiness here on earth. This is of the utmost importance. After all, religion is made for men and to keep man from being a "wolf to man." There was no state organization at that time, but religion held out the prospect of reward or punishment so that men would do good and refrain from evil. By observing the commandments, abstaining from theft, drink, etc., by practicing charity and doing good around them, men were contributing to social harmony. When the Last Judgment sounded, they would have won happiness in heaven as well as here on earth. As for those who are skeptical about the afterlife, they would have accomplished their duty; they would have produced and triumphed; their consciences would be at peace.

Then, spiritual decay set in. There was a tendency to disregard essential truths and abandon the substance while clinging to the form. And the Moslem world entered on a period of decadence.

As head of the state, responsible for the progress of the nation in the world, in the same way the Prophet was responsible for the Moslems of his day, I must think of every possible way of strengthening and building up the nation, making it creative and energetic. I must impress on you the need for a new approach to the problem of achieving national renewal. The means we use must be treated as sacred and as categorical obligations, like religious commands. Thus, work and behavior will no longer be dictated by the fear of the police or of the law, but will be ordered with the conviction that they come under the authority of religion, society, and individual conscience. Any disharmony between conscience, reason, and religious teaching would lead to complete disorganization.

I have developed these ideas as an introduction to the remarks I want to make today about Ramadan. This question has led to heated discussion and is being exploited in bad faith by a certain group. The seeds of doubt and hesitation are being sown in the minds of the unlearned, so that they will become agents of destruction and civil war.

Today, I shall repeat what I have already said about the fast of Ramadan. This practice was imposed by Islam. It is still so imposed today, as it will be till the end of time. However, Allah has allowed certain dispensations, which are laid down in the *Koran*. In certain circumstances, a man is not obliged to observe the fast. These dispensations are well known and have been thoroughly studied. In the Tunisian schools, they are not mentioned in certain teachings, but they are nonetheless authentic and valid. Originally, dispensations were only allowed in cases of sickness or when traveling. Then the Jihad (or holy war) was included. Later on, with the agreement of the Ulema, the risk of illness was added, by extension of principle.

If we study the question thoroughly and analyze the reasons given for the dispensations, we see that they have a common purpose—that of relieving Moslems of the obligation to fast if the effort involved is excessively arduous. For example, traveling was included in the dispensations because it was originally very tiring.

Under these circumstances, a traveler was not bound to observe the fast. He was excused because Allah did not want him to suffer excessively. If there were no dispensation, there would be a serious risk that Moslems would abstain from traveling during the month of Ramadan. This would reduce their means, and force idleness and unemployment upon them. But, far from encouraging laziness, religion gives dispensation from fasting in cases where it would stand in the way of traveling, that is to say, of work and effort.

Another case for dispensation is sickness. Why? Because fasting is likely to aggravate an illness, since the physical condition of a sick person is such that it is dangerous to deprive him of food. In fact, instead of fasting, he needs to eat properly.

If we meditate over these Koranic provisions and examine them closely, we realize how much trouble Islam has taken to spare men unnecessary causes of fatigue and impediments to their activity. You all know the origin of the dispensation allowed for the Jihad. The day before the capture of Mecca, Mohammed ordered the faithful to break their fast, so that they would be in the best physical condition to meet the enemy.

From a careful study of the purposes of the fast, the circumstances which surround this practice, the dispensations allowed, and the reasons for them, we find there is no room for hesitation. There are good grounds today for not observing the fast of Ramadan.

The *Koran* prescribes fasting, so as to accustom men to controlling their senses and appetites. But if fasting involves a risk, is harmful or impairs a man's physical condition, health, or working capacity, or lowers his potentialities or those of the Moslem community, he is dispensed from fasting.

We must keep a sense of proportion. Thus, traveling is one of the reasons for dispensation. But traveling is no longer as tiring today as it used to be. Today, we travel by air, ensconced in a comfortable seat. Modern travel bears no comparison with journeys across the desert by camel. All the same, some people argue that the dispensation allowed to travelers still holds good. Personally, I think that traveling today no longer gives dispensation from fasting. These same people maintain that no dispensation can be allowed to workers even when they toil to the point of fainting. Why should an allowance be made for a traveler surrounded by the most up-to-date comfort, and refused to an underfed worker with a weak constitution? The latter, it is argued, may only break his fast after fainting for the second time. Is this logical?

I invite the Tunisian people, its Ulema, and sheiks to study the whole problem from the point of view of the purpose of the fast and the reasons for dispensation. Everyone must acquaint himself with the problem of how to interpret divine law properly. Allah gave man his reasoning faculty so that he would be able to distinguish good from evil.

At a time when we are fighting against poverty and drawing up programs and plans to remedy our underdevelopment, when we contemplate calling to account those who do not produce enough, and restricting individual freedom, when the recovery of the Moslem nation depends on strenuous work—I urge you to make use of a dispensation which is based on a sound conception of religious law.

BOURGUIBISM*

The policy which has been described as Bourguibism is not a matter of accepting charity from the colonizing country and then
begging for more. It is more like a war for positions, which consists
of directing the weight of the attack against strategic points. This
is the meaning of our policy of stages, each of which should facilitate accession to the next, until we achieve our final goal of independence, without which there can be no dignity.

This has been our concern from the very beginning. Since 1930,
I have accepted many things: cosovereignty; participation in a
ministry—most of whose members were tools of the colonialists—
which we eventually left in order to take up armed resistance; internal autonomy, from which we achieved incomplete independence, which, in turn, enabled us to obtain partial evacuation. We
have achieved all this after only seven years, starting with a regime
of direct French administration, the like of which neither Syria,
Lebanon, nor any other Middle East country has known. For
although these countries have experienced French colonization, it
had nothing in common with the regime installed in Tunisia. The
form they knew did indeed make use of ruse, perfidy, and division
in order to maintain its position, but the regime knew it was provisional because it was authorized by mandate. Here things were
quite different. We experienced colonization by settlement. This
came to an end barely seven years ago. All of you here and most of
those listening to me remember this period. The protectorate which
Tunisia underwent was harsher than was imposed on any other
Arab country. In Egypt, for instance, the English protectorate
came to an end in 1922, yet total evacuation was not obtained
until 1957—over thirty years, in stages. Our stages barely lasted
seven years, while our situation was much worse to start with.

We do not say this in order to boast of our successes, but only
to give a comparable example, illustrating Bourguibism—which
has sometimes been badly understood, to the extent of likening
it to a policy of collusion or complicity with colonialism. It is
nevertheless the policy of our means, the one which follows from

* From a speech delivered by Bourguiba on October 12, 1961; translated
and published by the Tunisian Secretariat of State for Information.

our geographical position, our history, and the form of colonization imposed on us. . . .

My method is to advance by steps, thinking out every step as I go. Speed does not mean hasty, unthought-out actions. In the past, when I was a school child and had quarrels with my schoolfellows, I did not rush to fight the enemy, but on the contrary I needed a certain amount of time to ponder and watch the situation evolve. It is too serious a matter for me to allow myself to throw the whole nation in with one bloc or another, with the excuse of French aggression.* In spite of the aggression we have suffered, we must not brutally change our policies. Naturally we must foresee matters, temper our policies, and allow them to evolve according to both circumstances and the means at our disposal.

We ourselves were fed on and formed by French culture. Through it, we found the principles of humanity, liberty, and dignity. We have always harbored feelings of affection for French culture and the French people and nation. We were even searching for explanations for the French attitude by saying that it is not possible for the French people to commit acts of aggression such as this. We distinguished between the French people and the supporters of colonialism. In spite of all this, the French used cultural relations as an object for low bargaining. We must refuse all bargaining. This refusal could lead to the reshaping of our programs. We may even have to envisage the use of a language other than French, and thus look toward other civilizations, countries, and friends. The problem is still of great importance and must be seriously examined and thought out.

Our decisions will be taken calmly by stages, in the light of our interests and the interests of the Tunisian state, and according to what suits our best interests. . . .

THE AGRICULTURAL ASPECT OF THE ECONOMIC BATTLE†

We are not inspired by any considerations of demagogy in the field of agrarian reform, a tempting formula covering a very simple

* Bourguiba is referring here to the Bizerte crisis.—ED.
† From a speech delivered by Bourguiba on October 27, 1961; translated and published by the Tunisian Secretariat of State for Information.

operation: parceling out lands and distributing them. A regime which carries out such measures aims at gaining the support of the masses by satisfying those who are worst off. It is not greatly concerned with the effect of the reform on the curve of production. In fact, no thought is given to this. Agrarian reforms of this sort are generally accompanied by a vast propaganda campaign in which there is talk of social justice, of poor people to whom rights are restored, and of rich men despoiled—to the delirious applause of the populace.

What is important to me is the level of production. Admittedly, in some special cases, individual estates may be as much as 15,000 to 25,000 acres—which one man cannot farm properly. The state may intervene to help him and improve working conditions. If it decides to confiscate part of the estate, this is not done out of a desire for revenge. To create a hate psychosis like this would be contrary to the general interest. Poor and rich, we are one family. The state's role is to maintain the nation's unity. However, when a landowner has an agricultural estate which is too large for him to manage properly—or in conditions corresponding to the community's interest—it is the state's duty to dispossess him in whole or in part. The state performs its duty in the interest of all, whether poor or rich. It is concerned solely with the community's interest. An owner who has part of his lands confiscated must not feel he is being despoiled. In any case, the increase in production which would result from confiscation would help to raise the general level of the community. As a member of this community, a dispossessed owner will have his share of the general income. The sense of fraternity and association uniting the nation will be strengthened thereby. Sacrifices are accepted all the more readily if they are seen to be in the general interest. We do nothing with the intention of restricting the freedom of individuals. We do not apply any pressure. We do not impair individual freedom or the right of ownership, except in the general interest.

This is the path we have chosen in order to achieve socialism. Our method is based on respect for the individual, not on class hatred or the dictatorship of the poor over the rich. Our sole guide is the interest of the country, in which we are united for better or worse.

How can we compare the sacrifice of a few interests, a few minor rights, a few relatively unimportant freedoms, to the deportation, imprisonment, and death to which Tunisians were exposed in the past, and to which they are still prepared to expose themselves anew should the country be threatened once again?

If the state, which is in a position to weigh the situation, decides on measures implying a restriction of a given freedom, the reconversion of a given crop, the redivision of certain agricultural lands, it is because it has been led to do so for imperative reasons of general interest.

In carrying out this gigantic task, using the method of Neo-Destourian socialism, we are at the same time respecting the dignity of the individual. The latter must be convinced that the sacrifice he accepts, by agreeing to the restriction of some of his freedoms, is in his country's interest. He is not so different from a conscript who relinquishes his individual freedom when he is called up. He makes this sacrifice willingly.

Freely accepted discipline is the motive power of progress. We must realize this and fully familiarize ourselves with the idea that the individual's interest lies in the progress and well-being of the community.

11. Ahmed Ben Bella

Ahmed Ben Bella, Premier of the Republic of Algeria, was born in 1919 at Marnia, near the Moroccan border of Algeria. During World War II, he served with distinction in the French Army, receiving four citations for valor. After the war, he was active in Algerian political groups, and was one of the organizers of the Special Organization, an underground military group that was preparing the Algerian rebellion. In 1949, he took part in a daring holdup of a post office in Oran, carried out to secure funds for the Algerian cause. Captured by the French and sentenced to life imprisonment, he escaped and rejoined the underground. Ben Bella was one of the nine members of the Revolutionary Committee that launched the Algerian Revolution in 1954. In 1956, he became one of the most celebrated leaders of the Algerian cause when the French captured a plane on which he and his companions were flying from Morocco to Tunisia. Imprisoned near Paris, he became a symbol of the nationalist movement, and he maintained contacts with the other Algerian leaders until his release in 1962.

In the following interview, which was given to a correspondent of an Italian Communist newspaper, it should be noted that Ben Bella's discussion of the revolutionary role of the peasantry departs from the canons of orthodox Marxism, and his favorable comments on "the socialist camp" do not imply any wish to compromise the Algerian neutralism, which he emphasizes earlier. His proposal for an immediate redistribution of land and his intense opposition to "neocolonialism" ally him with the radical wing of nationalist thinking. Other Algerian leaders have expressed some reservations about Ben Bella's statement, but it is an important summary of the political ideas of the best known leader of the Algerian revolt.

THE FUTURE OF ALGERIA*

What political form is Algeria likely to adopt?
Socialism. But analogies in this area are nearly always likely to be superficial and erroneous. We want an Algerian socialism which is based on our own experience and, at the same time, also draws on that of the socialist countries. . . .

It is essential that a program of agrarian reform be carried out immediately. We are taking over a country that has a basically peasant economy. Seven million peasants, one million peasant families—they constitute the foundation of the country. The peasant population is the decisive force supporting us. It made up the core of the Liberation Army in each region, in each village, in the country, and in the *bled*. . . .

We favor a system of agrarian reform under which the land will be collectivized and granted to agricultural cooperatives which will be responsible for its management and exploitation. . . . This should be carried out through assemblies and peasant meetings. We wish to promote agricultural reform from below so that the peasant masses may be involved and participate directly in its

* Excerpts from an interview of Ben Bella with Maria Macciochi, correspondent of *L'Unita* (daily newspaper of the Communist Party of Italy) August 13, 1962; translated by the editor.

application through large-scale movements in the countryside. The impoverished peasantry is the basic element for the revolutionary transformation of society. . . . The revolutionary masses are fundamentally composed of peasants. The Cuban revolution arose from this kind of base—peasant masses in arms for independence and agricultural reform. Czarist Russia was also an agricultural country. . . .*

Is not the vanguard of the revolution made up of workers?

True, but it is not a question of the vanguard but of the entire force. Thus, in the highly industrialized countries of Europe, the powerful worker masses could not bring about a revolutionary transformation. Today, the restraint of the Social Democratic parties, the formation of a worker aristocracy, worker participation in the different benefits which capitalism allows, and a paternalistic social policy have tended to turn the working class in Europe away from its revolutionary objectives. . . .

What do you mean by the Arab element in the Algerian revolt?

When I say that we are Arabs, I do not, even remotely, want to make any allusion to questions of race, blood, or color of skin. I do not know how much Arab or Roman blood is in my veins; this does not interest me. But it happens that I have a way of acting and thinking in life, a certain ethic, a definite heritage of culture and civilization, a specific type of humanism and certain special moral values. Thus, Arabism for me is, first of all, a way to emphasize our neutralism with regard to foreign policy. Arabism is an active and dynamic neutralism which can act to enforce peace but which should not be confused with the neutralism of those who remain apart from the problems of our day. . . .

Does Arabism oppose all compromise with the forces of neocolonialism?

That is the great question—neocolonialism. I think that the basic disagreement among us [Algerians] is on this question: What attitude should we adopt with regard to neocolonialism? That is, what ideological content should be given to the Algerian revolution? I have declared that neocolonialism is our great scourge. In

* Details on the Algerian proposals for agrarian reform are contained in the program of the National Council of the Algerian Republic, adopted in Tripoli in June, 1962. See *Le Monde*, September 5, 1962, for text.—ED.

discussions, I have always maintained that it represents a method of perpetuating old privileges in new forms. Colonialism has been modernized. It has become more progressive, less crude. It understands that people can no longer be dominated by force, by machine guns, and by bloody repression. It seeks new ways of domination—an enlightened colonialism, so to speak—although based on a fictitious equality, a new form of slavery controlling the key positions in our society. Either there is a revolution under way in the country and we will be able to pursue this course under our own power, or else Algeria will become a revised and improved version of the other African governments which have accepted neocolonialism.

What will be Algeria's relations with the U.S.S.R. and the socialist countries?

The Algerian leaders have the same attitude toward the socialist camp as those of other underdeveloped countries which have received support and economic cooperation from it. They favor coexistence and neutralism, but they recognize that they have received the aid of the ideology of the socialist camp and have been guided by its past experience, which means that the Algerian revolution has a definitely socialist orientation.*

What will be the role of the Algerian Army of National Liberation?

The Army of National Liberation must be demobilized. Not because it constitutes the basis of a military dictatorship, but because without the support of that mass of men, we cannot build the new Algeria. We have magnificent politically trained officers of all ranks. The best among them should take their place in the party. We need a new army of pioneers to create the infrastructure of the country, to build the roads, the houses, and the schools, as well as to defend our frontiers. . . .

* This answer, paraphrased rather than quoted in the original interview, should be compared with the following passages in the Tripoli program of the National Council of the Algerian Republic: "The support of the socialist countries, which have come to our assistance in various ways during the war and with which we should reinforce existing links, creates real possibilities of release from imperialist control. . . . The increasing strength of the current of neutralism in which we are participating reflects the dynamism of the nations struggling to consolidate their independence. . . . The foreign policy of Algeria should be oriented in a neutralist direction toward alliance with the countries which have succeeded in consolidating their independence, and have freed themselves from the hold of imperialism."—Ed.

Will Algeria have a single party?

Undoubtedly—and that single party is the National Liberation Front. . . . All those who wish to work for the building of Algeria should join and work within it. . . . The members of the Algerian Communist Party are invited to join the Front, and aid us in the Front to consolidate our links with the masses. Its trained members can be the trained members of the Front, the leaders of the Front, according to their merit and effort.

What is your opinion of President Nasser?

Unlike others, Nasser has succeeded in eliminating the colonialists from his country. As to his internal regime, I will not make a judgment on it. In any case, it is a kind of special experiment. This experiment is completely different from concrete reality in a country such as ours, which has fought for seven years and whose people are impelling us toward a socialist future.

PART III

AFRICA

African political and social thought, like African nationalism, has developed only in recent years. Yet, it has already made some important contributions to the common ideological stock of modernizing nationalism. In London and in Paris and in the African capitals, African students, intellectuals, and political leaders have drawn on Western democratic thought, on Marxism, on Gandhiism, and (in the case of those studying in America) on Black Nationalism and combined them with a romanticized version of the African cultural heritage and history to produce a common Pan-African ideology shared by most African nationalist leaders—however much they may differ on its practical implementation.

The African nationalists face many of the same problems of underdevelopment as their counterparts in the Middle East, Asia, and Latin America, but there are also important differences. Since much of Africa has only recently achieved independence, no entrenched military class or feudal oligarchy impedes national development. In some areas, tribalism has broken down, either because cooperation with the colonizing power has discredited the traditional tribal leadership or because urbanization has loosened traditional loyalties. The nationalist leaders have thus been presented with a ready-made following, responsive to nationalistic and anticolonial appeals.

Yet, the vast majority of Africans remain enmeshed in tribal and traditional structures of authority. The modernizing elite finds itself caught between the goals of democracy and development. The objective of modernization is by no means certain to win a majority.

The theory of the democratic single party—perhaps the distinctive African contribution to the ideology of modernizing national-

*ism—offers a way out of this dilemma. Utilizing the slogans of
development and national unity, the party educates a largely
illiterate population to desire the goals that the modernizing elite
considers desirable, at the same time making it possible for at least
minimal controls to be exercised over the leadership by party members. Although it has not been universally accepted by African
leaders,* the theory of the single party has received its best formulation in the writings and speeches of African nationalists such as
Sékou Touré, Julius Nyerere, and Madeira Keita, and its influence
is wide.*

*In economic thought, the attempt to find a middle way between
the individualism of the West and the collectivism of the Soviet
bloc has received eloquent expression in Senghor's "African Socialism." A similar conception also underlies Julius Nyerere's emphasis on the harmony of the individual and the group in African
social life.*

*The revival of African culture under the labels of Negritude and
"the African personality"† has a political as well as a cultural
significance in the support it gives to the ideal of African unity.
Already, however, there is among the Pan-Africanists a division,
derived partly from varying conceptions of the method to reach
African unity, partly from differing views regarding internal development and external ties, and partly from power rivalries.‡*

*There is no disagreement on the desirability of national inde-
pendence, of the liberation of the remaining colonial territories,
or of a nonaligned position in international relations. Above all,
modernization and development are the objectives agreed upon by
all educated Africans as the goals of African national and regional
policy. This process has been termed "Westernization," but African leaders specifically reject some aspects of Western life—for
example, its racialism, its individualism, and, in many instances,
its political forms. Yet, the categories of their thought—the nation,
the party, and the concept of modernization itself—are derived
from Western sources and modified to fit African political and
social realities.*

*The relations of Africa with the other developing areas are espe-
cially important in the United Nations. Voting records indicate
that there is no clearly defined Afro-Asian bloc, but consultation*

---

*See selections by Nnamdi Azikiwe and Chief Awolowo.
† See selection by Senghor.
‡ See Dr. Azikiwe's speech to the Lagos Conference.

does go on among Africans, Asians, and Middle Easterners. At the Bandung Conference of 1955, which was the first attempt to bring together the leaders of African and Asian governments, Ghana and Liberia were the only African nations represented. Many more—though by no means all—African nations attended the Belgrade Conference of Unaligned Nations in September, 1961. There is also a bridge to the Islamic world, through the North African countries and the United Arab Republic. The Algerians cultivated African support throughout the lengthy history of their revolt, and Nasser has harbored anticolonial African leaders in Cairo for many years. Gandhi's system of thought has exercised influence upon a number of African leaders, but Indian-African relations may be strained in the future by the position of the Indian traders in East Africa.

The rise of Africa to self-assertion and independence has brought with it new contributions to the political theory of modernizing nationalism. It is still too early to judge whether the post-independence period will bring a further development of ideology—as a spur to the national development effort or as a justification of the ambitions of one nation or group of nations—or whether, on the other hand, independence will be followed by a political demobilization of the masses and a consequent decline in the importance of ideological appeals.

12. Sékou Touré

Sékou Touré was born in 1922 in Kan-Kan, Guinea, of peasant
parents. He received a primary education, but was expelled from
a trade school for leading a food strike at the age of fifteen. He
then secured a civil-service job and became active in Guinean trade
unionism, becoming leader of the Guinean branch of the Confédér-
ation Générale du Travail (CGT), the Communist-influenced
French trade-union federation. Touré organized the Parti Démocratique de Guinée (PDG), as the Guinean branch of the Rassemblement Démocratique Africain; his party lost the apparently
rigged elections of 1954, but won complete control of the Guinea
Assembly in 1957. He then broke ties with the CGT and formed
an African trade-union federation. Using the French grant of internal autonomy to consolidate his political control and break the
power of tribal chieftains, he was able to secure a 95 per cent endorsement of his position for immediate independence in the referendum of September, 1958—at a time when all other French-speaking African territories were voting by equally lopsided margins for
continued association with France. Since 1958, Sékou Touré has
pursued a policy that is regarded as the furthest left of any of the
African states, in both internal and international politics. Those
who had considered Guinea a member of the Soviet bloc were
surprised, however, when Touré expelled the Soviet Ambassador
in December, 1961.

The selection below is taken from his speech to the congress of
the Parti Démocratique de Guinée, delivered on September 14,
1959, a year after independence. It explains how the PDG operates
as the single party in Guinea, and defends Touré's version of
"democratic centralism."

pol. party—something like vangd. of the prolet.

AFRICAN EMANCIPATION*

The Contradictions of Colonialism

If the problem of the individual is a central concern in other continents—in countries that are free and independent—the first and the only true problem for the colonial peoples is that of the attainment of independence. It is consequently a collective problem, a political reality engendered by nationalist sentiments.

But if our party has been more successful than the other fraternal parties of Senegal, of the (French) Sudan, of Niger, etc., in guiding our country to its independence, it is because it has found itself in favorable objective conditions. Political struggle involves laws, power relationships, a given level of maturity, problems of unity, etc.—a number of objective conditions which, combined, produce the rise of the dependent countries and govern the rhythm of their political development.

The expansion of our political movement was achieved because of the many contradictions between the interests of the people and the interests of the colonial regime. The principal contradiction was between the African interest and the interests of French imperialism, which had repercussions in all areas of social life. In addition to the moral domain (that of the dignity of our people) and the juridical domain, by which the illegitimate occupation of our country established by the colonial power was firmly entrenched, there were practices on the economic level and on the level of public activity, on the military level, and on the social level which constantly revealed these conflicts of interest. It was on the basis of these oppositions and in terms of these dichotomies that the struggle was organized and conducted, against both the colonial regime and those who by their actions, consciously or unconsciously, favored the programs of that regime.

Internal contradictions also existed. In the first place, the peasants—who constitute 80 per cent of the population of Guinea —turned against feudalism, which, perverted by the colonial

*Excerpts from *La Lutte du Parti Démocratique de Guinée pour l'Emancipation Africaine* (Conakry: Imprimerie Nationale, 1959); translated by the editor.

regime, had ceased to be the true expression of the thought of our national social units. Created, supported, and used by the colonial regime, this feudalism, in opposition to the interests of the people, was better known under the name of "cantonal chiefdom." The chiefs lived on the exploitation of the peasant masses, and they justified the colonialist practices with which their own interests were intimately linked. There were still other internal contradictions, which were less apparent, but which had to be eliminated rapidly in order to reinforce the unity of the people. There was, notably, the nascent opposition between what we can call the intellectual elite on the one side and the peasant masses on the other. The education that was given to us was designed to assimilate us, to depersonalize us, to Westernize us—to present our civilization, our culture, our own sociological and philosophical conceptions, even our humanism as the expression of a savage and almost unconscious primitivism—in order to create a number of complexes in us which would drive us to become more French than the French themselves. In addition to this, there were the advantages and security of the material surroundings of the intellectual elite, which were absolutely foreign to the life of the immense majority of the people and constituted a privileged situation in comparison with general conditions. The satisfaction of the requirements of one group appeared immediately as a new obligation, a new burden on the others, who constituted not only the majority of the population, but also the most disinherited strata.

Contradictions existed in the economic domain, as they exist elsewhere in all colonial and imperialist regimes. Appropriate structures were used to facilitate the exploitation by the colonialists of the two aspects of the market: import and export. The shameful system of trading functioned through practices that none could deny because they were too simple and too apparent. There was speculation, with produce handled at three stages: purchase, storage, and resale to the producer in time of need. The difference between the cost of imported merchandise and the price to the consumer was exorbitant.

The feudal regime (despite the fact that the land is the first and natural property of the people) annexed the land and, under the name "national property," made it the property of the French state. The military regime contained the same contradictions because the African soldier had neither the material nor the moral advantages of his French colleague—just as the African veteran was treated in an inferior fashion in relation to his French counterpart. Finally, the administrative structure could be summed up by this simple formula: The French administration, the sole origin of all decisions involving the destiny of the country, was in fact the guarantor and manager of the interests of the colonialists. . . .

In its military organization, as in its administrative, economic, and political structure, assimilationist colonialism decreed laws that were to be applied unilaterally throughout the whole empire, without taking account of the particular characteristics of each part, or of its economic and social conditions or political evolution. This unification policy, the corollary of the aim of assimilation, created a feeling of equality in misery, and was bound to result in the emergence of an identity of interests of all those under colonial rule—whether in the north, south, or west of Africa. Thus the military and administrative organizations, with their broader and more general structures involving the whole of the former French empire, created new institutions favoring the unity of action of those under colonial rule against a common oppressor. . . .

Our party is a committed party which does not look for the golden mean between truth and falsehood. It is aware of the backwardness of the African peoples and does not want to lose time in useless evasions. From the moment that it has decided on a goal, it wants to attain that goal with the support and action of the people. Hence the anticolonial struggle did not end on the 28th of September;* it has only started again with more power as a double struggle against the consequences of the colonial regime (by the adaptation of methods, structures, spirit and population to the new requirements of a free national life) and against the colonial domination that still weighs upon a good part of Africa.

We are aware that as long as all Africa is not free, Guinea will feel threatened. Consider the man who has injured a finger. The finger alone does not feel pain; if there is pain, it is the whole body of the man that feels it. Guinea feels the pain of the colonized people of Africa. In order to attempt to eliminate the pain of soul and body of the inhabitants of Africa, whose welfare constitutes the object and the reason for our combat, we must first examine the state of the instruments—the Democratic Party of

---

* September 28, 1958 was the date of the referendum on the Constitution of the Fifth Republic of France. By voting "no" on the constitution and thus refusing to join the new French Community, Guinea became the first of the French colonies in sub-Sahara Africa to achieve independence.—ED.

Guinea, and its institutions, the people and their political, social, economic, and cultural practices—that serve to lead us to victory in the combat.

Principles of the PDG and Their Application

Conc. of party

The Democratic Party of Guinea is a national movement grouping together (without distinction of race or sex) all those of good will who are determined to work against colonialism and for the building up of a solid democratic state in Guinea. There should be no astonishment that in Guinea there is only one single national party, the PDG. I want to emphasize that political unity is not an end. It is only a means to develop a progressive movement that serves the general interest. This unity can be maintained and developed to serve the national interest only if it involves unity of action on the part of the whole population, mobilized for positive ends and constantly confirming the democratic character of the development of our country. We can also say that the life of a society, of a social unit, or of a nation is not essentially governed by laws, decrees, or regulations. The life of a society is governed by habits, customs, historic traditions, and the necessity for its maintenance and development. Thus, the value of a government is determined by the balanced development it assures on the national level. The various changes in living conditions that result from our progress clash with the conservative forces of the present and the reactionary forces of the past, the former representing vested interests and privileges and the latter the interests and privileges that have been lost. These forces are not working for the general interest because their demands only involve particular and special cases which are, by their nature, opposed to social justice and the national interest.

The most progressive and revolutionary law will remain without application if it is not understood by the people and if the attitudes and habits of the people are contrary to that law. Similarly, if the principles of the party are not well understood by the party membership, and especially by all the leaders, the party will only list its principles at its congresses without ever translating them into reality in the living conditions of the nation. We must constantly recall that the Democratic Party of Guinea is a popular movement, uniting the entire mass of the population who wish to work together for the realization of its program in the general interest.

The party should not change its political line if this line remains in conformity with the national interest. The essential principle that we should never forget is that the Democratic Party of Guinea is different from the ethnic movements we formerly knew in Guinea. Our party operates scientifically—by analyzing concrete situations to determine the objectives and forms of its action.

We constantly reiterate that the PDG is a party of men who place their intelligence at the service of the masses. When we say they are "intellectuals," it is in the true sense of the word. It is not a question of those who know how to read and write, but of those who determine their action on the basis of reason, starting out with concrete study; of those who, guided by intelligence, can know at any moment what has already been accomplished and what has not yet been carried out; of those who can appreciate the real value of the action of our party, so as to make it more efficient; in short, of those men and women who look for the truth—starting out with historic and present facts, determining their action by the objectives that have been assigned to them. This intelligence is found among peasants, workers, civil servants, laborers, women, and children.

In the world today, there are three types of organizations and movements. There is the party that speaks of the past and lives on the basis of the past. The members of this party continually say, "We have done such and such a thing in 1900, we have done such and such in 1910"; they are not capable of saying, "This is what we have done today, and this is what we should do tomorrow." The second category lives only in the present, and its workers are concerned exclusively with day-to-day problems and make no effort to analyze these problems or carry out the changes that would resolve them in the future. The Democratic Party of Guinea belongs neither to the first nor to the second category. Not forgetting what has taken place in the past, and keeping in mind what is taking place today, it is also concerned with what should take place tomorrow. Indeed, it is insofar as one is concerned with what will take place tomorrow that one can take the appropriate measures to make the future of the country more happy and prosperous. Party workers who only think of what is taking place today are those who are often surprised, have no general view, and are very quickly discouraged, for, at the least unhappy and unexpected event, they are disoriented and suffer panic, thus distorting the real significance of the party. When something happens that they cannot work out, they are immediately discouraged and lose all desire to continue their activity. It is the opposite with the worker who thinks of the program of the future while keeping in mind the present. Mistakes—far from discouraging him or limiting his action—are sources of profit, because once he has discovered them, thanks to criticism and self-criticism, he can henceforth avoid them in carrying out his future actions.

Indeed, it is when we discover a mistake committed by the whole party or by a worker or leader, that we seek to know its nature, its causes, and its consequences. There is no action without mistakes. Only a party that carries on no activity can avoid mistakes. Just as one cannot develop knowledge without study and apprenticeship, one cannot learn anything without the possibility of mistakes. That is why the party should stimulate action every day on the part of its workers. The officeholders and party workers ought to know that action feeds the intelligence and gives practical effect to the thinking of the party. We have often said that practice is superior to thought and theory. Suppose that the members of the party establish a program which everyone approves. Even when there is agreement on the program, it is action that will determine what part of the program is possible for the country and in the interest of the party, and what should be corrected, modified, or abandoned. The superiority of practice over theory is attainable only in action and results. Hence, the party should be organized at all levels—in the local districts, in the villages, in the administrative divisions, and at a national level—a perfect organization of militant activity, so that each one can contribute effectively to the realization of the party program.

When we say that the party works for democracy and the unity of the country, and against colonialism, this is only the general framework and spirit in which all daily actions should be taken, and a statement of future activities. On the level of local and village committees, as well as those of the sections and districts, there should be general assemblies and conferences to study and establish a concrete program, to work for the permanent mobilization of the energies of the PDG. Without a concrete and definite program according to the respective possibilities of the different branches of the party, action can be carried out in the abstract and come to an end before any positive result is attained. . . .

The workers ought to give an account of what they have done and an evaluation of the progress that has been realized every day.

Action is necessary, but it is only possible within the framework of a program, and how is this program established? It is not the Political Bureau that establishes it. The Political Bureau only prepares a project, and the General Assembly discusses and determines it. Thus each one can understand its value and its implications.

It is necessary also to popularize the program among the masses, but it is not just a question of discussion of the program or of adopting it and understanding it. It is also a matter of distributing assignments; and the party must exercise some check over the carrying out of the tasks undertaken by each one.

For example, a delegation of the Political Bureau recently went into the regions of the interior. Its accounting, observation, and notes were discussed, after which a statement was made and circulars were sent out to the various sections, which drew lessons from this visit and determined new directives for action. The party should let no phenomenon or action take place without an appropriate analysis for the purpose of drawing from it a positive conclusion and determining the political line of its further activities. One can say that confidence does not exclude the review of action. When you benefit from the unlimited confidence of the masses, you have to act in such a way that the masses are aware that they have made a good decision, that they were not mistaken in granting you their confidence. . . .

In following the principles of the party, the officers of a local committee ought to have a meeting every evening and bring together all their information, review the execution of assignments, establish a program, distribute new assignments to be fulfilled, and, finally, organize a general assembly. At the assembly, everyone who is absent should be noted. If review is made in a rigorous manner, methodically and democratically, only real workers will continue in the party, for the bad elements will be eliminated of themselves.

When you cease to have criticism and self-criticism in the party, the party will die little by little. Everyone, as a matter of principle, must serve the party, and no one must serve himself. If there is no criticism and self-criticism, one cannot determine what is good and what is evil; one cannot locate mistakes that have been committed or evaluate the consequences; one cannot act against the enemies of the party, who are making use of it to operate against its objectives. . . .

Political Supremacy and Democratic Dictatorship

For the argument from force which the old colonialist state used, our new democratic state intends to substitute another basis of authority and draw its strength from arguments and from its guiding principles. Thus, the supremacy of political action is the consequence, the reality, of the political democracy that we have chosen for ourselves and have wished to be as real as possible and as vivid as the popular desire for a general revival in our country.

Democracy has different natures indeed and is interpreted in different ways, according to whether it is inspired by one or another form of thought, objective, or social force. We do not have to carry our analysis very far to become aware of the different social conceptions that utilize the name "democracy." Christianity acts politically under the name "Christian democracy," the bourgeoisie operate under the name "bourgeois democracy," and some social sectors talk about a "social democracy." Thus, if democracy represents a conception of the organization of society and peoples, its real content can be perverted or interpreted in different fashions.

As for ourselves, we are in favor of a democracy as real and as complete as possible and based solely on the interests of the people. This is the only form of democracy we recognize, the only interpretation we give to the word "democracy." . . .

Whether we are concerned with the democratic or nondemocratic state, both are governed by a man or a group of men who exercise power over the whole population. Both are dictatorships. Dictatorship is the concentration of powers exercised by a man or group of men over the whole. We can say, following that definition, that the driver of a vehicle imposes a dictatorship on the passengers of the vehicle. In a trade union, in a youth organization, in a women's organization, in an athletic team, there is this type of dictatorship. We can say, therefore, that states are democratic or nondemocratic—but whatever their nature, their direction toward specific objectives set out in advance necessarily implies a dictatorship.

To define the nature of this dictatorship, which is exercised differently in democratic states and nondemocratic states, we must consider the objective conditions surrounding the exercise of dictatorship to determine whether a state is democratic. . . . If the dictatorship exercised by the governmental apparatus emanates directly from the whole of the people, this dictatorship is popular

in nature and the state is a democratic state—democracy being
the exercise of national sovereignty by the people. It is power
exercised of the people, by the people, and for the people.

A democratic state comes from the will of the people. Its program is therefore necessarily in conformance with the interests of
the people. Likewise, its force, its authority, the powers it exercises, the discipline it imposes—in short, the dictatorship it exercises—arise exclusively from the interests, the requirements, and
the principles of popular sovereignty. For every human society,
democracy always corresponds in its form to given conditions and
requirements, which are the result of the economic and social
level at which the society has arrived. Hence, democracy can be
more or less developed, more or less advanced. Democratic dictatorship—that is, the concentration of powers of the sovereignty
of the people at the level of the people—can be more or less great
and more or less developed. Thus, a state whose program of work
and whose political power are determined, not in the interests of
one level or part of the population, but exclusively in the interests
of the whole people is a democratic state.

This means that on the level of the governing apparatus, there
is an obligation to assure direct and free representation of the
whole population, without discrimination of any sort. In a democratic state, the sovereign power is exercised directly by representatives whom the people have chosen freely.

But if the dictatorship is exercised by a king, a part of the population, a coalition of interests, or a feudal economic power, and
if there is an interest other than the general interest operating
in the exercise of the sovereignty, the dictatorship ceases to be
exercised in the interests of the people. Economic dictatorship,
financial dictatorship, personal dictatorship, military dictatorship
are nothing else than the exercise of national sovereignty for the
economic, financial, and personal benefit of one caste or social
class. The state ceases to be democratic when the dictatorship it
exercises arises solely out of the interests of the king, a social class,
or any other group that does not represent the whole population. . . .

In a democratic state, sovereignty is the property of the nation
as a whole. The responsibilities involved in running the state are,
by the nature of its structure, shared collectively. Thus, all intelligence, all values, and all energies are mobilized for the benefit of
the whole, so as to assure the best possible ways of achieving

progress, creating the best conditions for the development of the country, and bringing about the maximum guarantee of the expansion of the society and the security of each of its members. . . .

On the other hand, there are states that are democratic in form, ruled by ministers, parliamentarians, and responsible people in power, elected according to sometimes quite complicated procedures; but the dictatorship practiced by these states is not democratic in fact, since it is exercised by one feudal group or coalition of private interests, or even by a clan or social caste. This is a dictatorship one can call ethnic or factional.

A first requirement for democracy is liberty. If men are to be considered as equals and are to participate with equal concern and involvement in the life of the nation, they must first be free. Without effective liberty, there is no possibility for men or societies to determine themselves freely. . . .

The Exercise of Democracy

We can say that our state is democratic, unitary, and progressive. We want Guinea to be a viable national entity. In three or four years, no one will think any longer of the tribal, ethnic, and religious rivalries that have in the past caused so much evil for our country and population. A considerable decentralization of administration and policy has been permitted on the level of electoral districts, and the district council has all authority to decide what needs to be done. But there is also a perfect concentration of powers in the national institutions: the assembly and the government. Our constitution has authorized this concentration of powers by stipulating that the chief of the state is also the chief of the army—as he is the one who names the ministers and can at any point remove them. Obviously, if we did not understand that behind the state there is a higher entity, the party, we could not comprehend the political value of the provisions of the Guinean constitution. That is why the party assumes a directing role in the life of the nation and exercises all the powers of the nation. Political, judiciary, administrative, economic, and technical powers are in the hands of the Democratic Party of Guinea. It is the party that designates the chief of state, by direct universal suffrage. The deputies to the National Assembly are elected for five years, directly by the population, under the same conditions as the chief of the state. Every seven years . . . popular elections take place for the selection of the President of the republic. . . .

There are contradictions in all societies. We refuse to regard them passively, for we want to direct our evolution in a harmonious and just fashion. But to govern is to choose, and to choose is to use authority for the realization of previously determined objectives. To govern is to apply a dictatorship. When an aroused people has chosen its future, it must follow the line that leads it efficiently and rapidly to that future. But to impose a discipline in the framework of principles set up in advance is to agree to subordinate oneself to the authority of principles and to accept the dictatorship that flows from them. Our fundamental principles are simple. We recognize as valuable only what serves the cause of the people and develops the history of the nation. This is the discipline to which we submit ourselves freely, and this orientation constitutes the principal task of a forward-looking party and a democratic state. This is the nature of the dictatorship. It can have a different content if it is applied by one man who considers himself superior to all others, or if it is the people themselves who have conceived its program of development and chosen the methods by which it will accomplish its daily tasks. Depending on how it is applied, dictatorship can be antidemocratic or democratic. As for ourselves, we say that in giving supremacy to the people and making them participate directly in all important decisions involving the nation, we want a popular democratic dictatorship.

For our decision to be more than a theoretical one—for it to be applied in every aspect of the life of every citizen and every branch of the state—we must immediately struggle against ourselves, against whatever in us is in contradiction to the decision we have taken. Thus, more than ever, there is a task of education on all levels and stages of thought, conception, and action. That is why, in the political field, the party has decided that our state, as a democratic state, will be at the same time a unitary and communitarian state.

Many nations in the world have 100–200 million inhabitants and are centuries ahead of us, disposing of enormous riches, which we do not have, and utilizing modern methods, which we lack today. We are just beginning, and our first chance to raise ourselves to the level of modern states in the world consists in our unity. Our desire for progress will be fruitless if individual wills are not identical and do not aim at attaining the same objectives, for internal contradiction will become more and more violent and hold us back, endangering our very independence. That is why we have said that at all levels the party must be extremely vigilant, intransigent, and severe, in order to force the unitary and dynamic character of its policy into the awareness and action of every citizen. . . .

The Unification of the Youth of Guinea

The constant concern of the Democratic Party of Guinea has been to . . . place all the institutions of the country at the service of the population. Thanks to its integral and solid structure, it has brought all organizations under its control. . . . It was the only party to choose independence in the name of the people of Guinea and of all of colonial Africa, by rejecting the French Community in a massive and historic vote.

Youth will play a primary role in the immense task of construction that we have begun since our accession to full sovereignty. It is important for each worker of the party, and particularly for the youth, that the specific problems of young people be approached with a clear conception of the general objectives of the nation. More than ever, the actions of young people must necessarily reflect the essential concerns of the country. We are guided by the central principle that the party has always considered of great importance—the absolute necessity of carrying out the program of youth on a national level, in the framework of the general program of the party. Youth ought to have an active part in the nation, be aware of its responsibilities, and be ready to play the dynamic role we assign to it.

The unification of youth movements was a response to the necessity of putting an end to the dispersion of energies that paralyzed the youth and prevented it from playing a worthy role as a front-ranking part of the Guinean people in the struggle for the emancipation of Africa. When the officers of the PDG, at the Congress of the JRDA* in March, 1959, emphasized the weakness of youth organizations in the fields of sport and art, they were right in thinking that it was urgent to abolish the individualism and mediocrity inherited from the colonial system and to place sport and art on the level of the most noble institutions of our nation. Henceforth, the spirit of competition should be developed among young people on the basis of an aroused sentiment of na-

* Jeunesse du Rassemblement Démocratique Africain, the youth section of the PDG.—Ed.

tional pride. The PDG has therefore acted perfectly well in unifying the youth movements and in concretely realizing, within the
JRDA, the unity of action of all the young people of the country. . . .

The Principles of Democratic Centralism

Democratic centralism consists of the following principles:

1. All the leaders of the party are directly elected, democratically, by the party workers, who have complete freedom of conscience and expression within the party.
2. The concerns of the state of Guinea are the concerns of all
the citizens of Guinea. The program of the party is discussed
democratically. As long as a decision has not been taken, each one
is free to say what he thinks or wishes. But when—after a long
discussion in the Congress or Assembly—the decisions have been
taken by a unanimous vote or by a majority, the workers and the
leaders are required to apply them faithfully.
3. There is no sharing of the responsibility of the leaders—
only of the responsibility for a decision. Thus, discipline will not
be undermined.

Democracy and the freedom of all party workers are expressed
in the framing of problems, in their discussion, and in the choice
of solutions for them. On the other hand, the leadership of the
party has complete liberty in the execution of assigned responsibilities and in the evaluation of the forms of action appropriate for
the objective conditions of their execution. Thus, at certain points,
the leadership of the PDG has said to the masses: "Do not create
any incidents. Even in the case of flagrant provocation, do not
respond." Then, at other moments, when the power relationships
and the development of the struggle required a strong attitude,
the same leaders invited the militant masses to respond with force
to the blows of the adversaries. Each movement of retreat or
offense was linked to the political context of the moment. In
other words, once the decisions had been democratically arrived
at, it was up to the leadership to study the situation, the conditions, and the means, and to adopt the tactic to be employed to
carry out effectively and efficiently the tasks assigned to the party.
The choice of tactics to be employed was up to the leadership

of the party. This required that the authority of the leadership be complete. If the leaders of the party abdicated their authority, if they were neither heard nor respected, what would the authority of the party be? If the party were without authority, what would be the character of the authority of the government or of the state of Guinea? Without the authority of the party, where would the government derive its own authority? The country would soon fall into disorder and anarchy, and rapidly lose its independence. As far as authority is concerned, there is no isolated problem. Everything holds together and makes one body. In the subdivisions of the party, if the leaders are without authority, there is no reason to be surprised if inefficient and mediocre administration results. There is no reason to be surprised if taxes are collected with difficulty, if human investment* is not fully carried out, and if discord arises. All that is normal. When supremacy is given to the party, nothing can go well in the places where the party is insufficient or lacks authority. The party ought to be continually mobilized if it wants the country to develop rapidly at an extraordinary rate of social, economic, and cultural progress.

In order to maintain this indispensable supremacy of the party, we have decided that the general secretaries of the local committees of Conakry are henceforth the official representatives of the mayor. No public act can take place in the future without the authorization of the party. In the local subdivisions (*quartiers*), the general secretary is the representative of the mayor. He represents him at the administrative and political level, at the level of authority and of public order. . . .

Conclusion

The foreign policy of our state is based on positive neutralism with regard to the antagonistic blocs that at present dominate the world with their influence. This is in order to safeguard the chance of the Republic of Guinea to lead the struggle for African independence to success. Indeed, Africa cannot accept the organic extension of any political or ideological system that does not respect its personality, its civilization, and its proper structure.

* *Investissement Humain* is the title of the program organized by the PDG in Guinea in which the inhabitants of villages, towns, and other social units donate their free time to collective-work projects organized by the party.—Ed.

And, as we have said recently at the Indian Congress of Transvaal, "Africa, land of the oppressed, cannot become, against its ardent will for liberation, a place for oppression." In its struggle for reconquest, there is no demand other than that its people have the right to life and to possession of their land, their sun, their sky, and to free utilization and free disposal of their goods. If Africa is a place of asylum for all those who have a sacred respect for man and wish to develop human society, it cannot allow brute force, exaction, and discrimination to be the laws governing the relations of men, people, and races. Against the old divisive practices utilized by the colonial dominators, against the continual diversionary maneuvers that attempt to reduce all coordinated action by arousing internal oppositions among the exploited and oppressed masses, we will respond with firmer cohesion and a renewed determination to assure the triumph of justice, dignity, and liberty.

13. Madeira Keita

Madeira Keita was born in 1917. Although a native of Mali (formerly the French Sudan), he was active in the politics of Guinea before it acquired independence in 1958. A founder of the Democratic Party of Guinea, he collaborated closely with Sékou Touré. More recently, he has been engaged in the building up of the local organizations of the Union Soudanaise, the governing party in Mali. In April, 1959, he became Interior Minister of Mali, and in August, 1960, he gained also the post of Minister of National Defense. In Mali politics, he is considered somewhat to the left of President Modibo Keita in political orientation. The selection below, from a speech Madeira Keita gave in Paris at a meeting organized by the journal Présence Africaine *in early 1960, is the classic defense of the single party. (It concludes with brief comments by others present at the meeting.)*

THE SINGLE PARTY IN AFRICA*

Before 1945, there was a colonial regime with government by decree, the regime of the *indigénat*. The *indigénat* form of government permitted the colonial administration to put Africans in prison without any trial. Sometimes you were put in prison for two weeks because you did not greet the administrator or the commander. You were happy enough if they did not throw stones at you or send you to a work camp, because there was also forced labor at that time. In 1947, I met French journalists who were very surprised to learn that forced labor was nonvoluntary and not paid for. Transportation was not even covered; nor were food and lodging. The only thing that was covered was work.

Then Africa began political life. When I say Africa, I mean Negro Africa, West Africa, French-speaking Africa. In 1945, we were asked to participate in political life. Naturally, Senegal was an exception. We should not lose sight of the fact that in Senegal, Africans have been rather directly involved in the public life of France since the French Revolution. . . . They were French citizens, and could elect a municipal council and send one representative to the French National Assembly. But the others, the great mass of Senegalese (since the electors constituted a minority), began political life with the elections in 1945. And this was going to create difficulties which African political leaders and political parties would have to take time to remove, because we began political life with elections and we did not have much experience in the first elections of September, 1945. In the second elections, in November, 1945, we were not aware for the most part of the intervention of the administrative apparatus of France, which gave administrative support to its candidates.

Little by little, with increasing awareness, we saw more clearly what the situation was, and we perceived the contradictions between the declarations on the subject of liberty and democracy and the reality. . . .

* Excerpts from Madeira Keita, "Le Parti Unique en Afrique," *Présence Africaine*, No. 30 (February–March, 1960); translated by the editor, by permission.

I saw French colonialists (to the extent that colonialism can be honest) who were revolted by the elections, which they said were a caricature of democracy. Honesty and electoral freedom were not respected; methods that degraded the parliamentary regime and would hurt Africa were used. I do not think it necessary to speak longer on what has been called *élections à l'Algérienne*.

If I speak on this subject, it is in order to underline the fact that, from the beginning, Africans were rather disturbed to perceive the contradictions that existed between theoretical definitions and realities in Africa. Now we have progressed rather far. England, in the meantime, has granted independence in a peaceful way. The Gold Coast has taken the glorious name of the old empire of Ghana. Tunisia and Morocco have acquired their independence. All of this has stimulated the desire of the African peoples under colonial rule to achieve full sovereignty.

Thus, in 1956—because the English were planning to grant independence to Nigeria (after having done so in Ghana), and because the Soviet Union, with its political and social regime, had become a factor in the political consciousness of peoples who aspired to liberty and wanted to free themselves from the bonds of slavery—France, some of whose political leaders had accused England and the Soviet Union of sabotaging the French empire and wishing to liquidate it, created the *loi-cadre*.* Many of our African comrades and militants thought that it was an error to accept the *loi-cadre*. . . . Personally, I think that although it included erroneous conceptions—especially as far as the "Balkanization" and division of French West Africa were concerned—the *loi-cadre* also had positive aspects.

The most stable governments (and I am not now talking about the most efficient governments) were those constituted by a single party that had a very large majority. This was the situation in the Ivory Coast, in Senegal, and in the Sudan.† (I am mentioning these particular territories because they stand for different political doctrines.) The governments created under the *loi-cadre* had very little in the way of disturbances or crises. However, in countries such as Upper Volta, which had the good fortune to have a remarkable man at its head—the late President Ouezzin Coulibaly—the government underwent an extremely long and difficult min-

* The *loi-cadre* was a French law permitting considerable internal autonomy to African territorial governments.—ED.
† Now the Republic of Mali.—ED.

isterial crisis, and only three parties made up a coalition government. In Dahomey, likewise, we had a coalition government. In Chad, as well as in Ubangui-Chari,* with the late President Boganda, there was government by a single party, the government of the MSA (*Mouvement Socialiste Africain*). These governments under the *loi-cadre* were a valuable education for Africans. We became aware that in the present historical conditions of Africa, it was not impossible, but extremely difficult, to take over successfully the responsibility of carrying on public affairs under coalition governments. We left the colonial system and took a part of our affairs into our own hands, and we likewise left what one might call the evil period of electoralism.

I want to emphasize that the elections had the effect of dividing Africans and of weakening the consciousness of the masses, since, in the absence of organized parties, the leaders—who wanted votes and wished to sit in councils and territorial assemblies and in the French Parliament—were obliged to play on regionalism and on what we have called internal racism. It was useful to set regions and ethnic groups in opposition to each other in the same electoral areas, and for a time we were obliged to act this way.

In the beginning, the French administration supported a certain number of politicians, who did not, however, always follow the directions given by that administration or by the interest groups which the French administration was trying to defend. These politicians were sometimes confused and tried more and more to involve Africa in purely electoral stands that were caricatures of democracy, for what was important for them was to have a majority for their party and to get positions they considered honorific or lucrative. Thus I must say that we had very great difficulties to surmount, both within and among the parties.

Now all African countries have finally taken the road toward independence. This situation creates a certain number of problems to be resolved by African political leaders. We are the so-called underdeveloped countries. We are aware of our economic backwardness. We are aware of our cultural backwardness. Nevertheless, we want to move very quickly. In general, our European friends and our French friends do not always understand the African position. Perhaps this is because they do not know Africa well. This may be the situation because the French, proud of

---

* Now the Central African Republic.—ED.

their own country and their own culture, want to suggest their own institutions as a model. Thus, when we speak of democracy and liberty, I have the impression, sometimes, that we are not in complete agreement with our friends the French. For us, the essential thing is to mobilize all the forces of the country to advance, and we do not think that liberty is threatened in Africa. We think that we are acting with complete respect for democratic rules.

Does democracy necessarily imply several parties? We say no. We think that there are democratic forms without political parties. We think also that if a political party is the political expression of a class, the class itself representing economic interests, that, though we cannot assert that the society of Negro Africa is a classless society, we can say that the differentiation of classes in Africa does not arise from a diversification of [economic] interests and especially not from an opposition of interests.

In 1946, the dominant and most relevant concern was the union of all social levels against colonialism and for an increase in liberty, without religious or social distinction. With a few exceptions, the African leaders—if one classified them by the criteria of the French—would have been in the category of the petty bourgeoisie. And it is very interesting to note that these leaders are neither bankers nor industrialists—that M. Senghor, M. Modibo Keita, and M. Sékou Touré, if they have bank accounts, have them only for their salaries, that very few have shares in corporations, and that if they do, it is merely a reflection of their [governmental] responsibilities, a device to create confidence in one corporation or another. Such shares represent insurance for these corporations. The rare cases that I know involve the mixed companies, those established by private capital and the public authority. There is a very definite tendency on the part of large companies—a little frightened by the rapid evolution of the countries of Africa and wishing to invest—to prefer the mixed form, since the government and the nationals of the country can take out shares, and this, they think, constitutes a solid guarantee and an assured climate.

As to the religious problem, this does not constitute a major reason for division among Africans. In particular, the Africans are avoiding the involvement of religion in politics. On this subject, we should be very clear since, in general, when we take positions that are considered advanced, people speak of Communism. These last weeks, we have seen a great prelate of the

Roman Catholic Church coldly compare Islam and Communism. On the level of African politics, no religious problems exist. Moslems in Mali, some 70 per cent of the population, live in peace, and the other Africans are very tolerant. A hundred years ago, of course, Islam could be used as a pretext by some conquerors in Nigeria—or even in Western Sudan, Senegal, or Guinea—to carve out empires. But today, all religions are in competition in Negro Africa, and we are very concerned about this. We refuse to allow religious rivalries to become operative on the political level.

Nevertheless, I am a bit disturbed because I have just read an article in *Temoignage Chrétien* that perhaps does not sound the alarm but is still rather dangerous. That article points out to Christians their responsibilities by saying to them, "You Christians represent 10 per cent of the population. You face a population that is 70 per cent Moslem. You have a role to play in independence. You ought especially not to forget that you are Christians." This type of article is dangerous, for it tends to create problems where they do not exist.

The Africans tolerate their neighbors, and in our political parties up to the present time no Catholic or animist has ever been ostracized because of his religious convictions. Naturally, the Moslems are in a majority in the country, but our leadership is chosen purely according to democratic criteria—that is, on the basis of capacity, merit, and devotion within the party.

Therefore, we do not have the same reasons as France, Italy, and Belgium for having several parties, and for experiencing the luxury of a ministerial crisis every six months. Our position is completely different. It is true that we must have more experience in order to analyze African problems. We are no longer like the countries of the Middle East or Latin America who, even at a time when the number of parties was limited, had many revolutions and government turnovers. We think that these revolutions, these uprisings, these *coups d'état* do not correspond to our needs.

There is still the question of the organization of democracy in the action of the party. And since we have no reason to increase the number of parties, since the differentiation of interests is not very great, the most important problem for the countries of Africa arises from aspirations for unity—both for the countries that have been deprived of freedom and for those countries that only experienced freedom of association fifteen years ago. The most important problem is that of international independence and sovereignty. We have very clear objectives for the most part, although the awareness of some people is confused, but we all agree that Africa will only have the possibility of developing rapidly in very large groupings. Philosophical, religious, and ideological problems do not divide us. The only objective that animates us is that of finding the way to put the apparatus of the state in the service of economic, cultural, and social development. We are looking for the methods that will permit us to carry out this development as rapidly as possible.

If we analyze the situation carefully, even keeping in mind that the electoral system of colonialism divided Africans by its fraud and deceit, we can note that there is no fundamental opposition among us. Certainly, we played the game for a long time. But when one considers the programs and resolutions of the party congresses, one can see our agreement on all points. Nevertheless, we carried our battle to the death, passionately, furiously—and the word "passion" expresses for Africans, for men of the land of the sun, all the violence of our struggles and oppositions.

Since we agreed on the essentials and pursued the same objectives, was there any reason to remain divided and split into parties that fought one another? It was by reason of this thinking that the countries began to move progressively toward the formula of the unified party. I started out by talking about the *single* party, but I have ended by using President Senghor's expression "unified." Language contains many nuances; the word "unified" has been adopted because it allows for the juridical possibility of the formation of other parties. We say "unified" because other parties and other political groups have voluntarily sacrificed themselves for the sake of unity.

And that is why in Sudan, as in Guinea, there is only one party. I should note that in both Guinea and Sudan this took place by free choice, without violence. On March 31, 1959, the Executive Committee of the Sudan section of the Parti du Regroupement Africain, the former socialist section of Filydabo Sissoko, decided after three days of uninterrupted meetings to dissolve and become integrated in the Union Soudanaise, the majority party. This fusion ran into difficulties at the top, but in the country itself, the population was happy to find unity once again, and the people gave the impression of having had a great burden removed, since the populace had become passionately involved and passion brought with it violence, separation, loss, attack on property, and murder. But the people no longer understood why they were so opposed to one another, and in the course of our campaign tours they asked us why we had waited so long to establish unity.

I am not going to outline the reasons why there were difficulties at the top. There was passion. Some of our comrades were aware of the necessity of unity, but made the development toward unity difficult on practical matters. There were questions of opportunism, difficult problems regarding appointment to the executive, especially at the moment when the party could distribute many positions of responsibility.

Now, since our objectives are common ones and we are in agreement on methods, we must create a single party. It is necessary to create a single party to be efficient, to remedy the situation, and not to give aid to the anonymous adversary, colonialism, which up to the present has been instrumental in the division of our country. We must have the unified party in order to limit the possibilities of corruption and to attempt to destroy opportunism, for these constitute dangers that threaten the African parties and the action of the governments and parliaments.

But how to safeguard the ideals of liberty and democracy in the single party? As to the meaning of democracy, I have already said that we understood it in its naïvely original sense. Democracy is the exercise of public authority in conformance with the will of the masses. But if we want to remedy the situation and deprive the colonialists and adversaries of the weapon of division, if we want to prevent corruption and give more assurance to the leadership, we must recognize that the system of the single party is not without dangers.

There is one aspect of the problem of African life that I want to emphasize—our sincerity with ourselves. If there is one party, it is necessary, first of all, that it be the true expression of the aspirations of the people. It is not sufficient that it be the expression of true aspirations for one moment; it must continue to be so. This is only possible to the degree that the party is solidly organized and there is a real discipline within the party, so that decisions are taken only after lengthy debate and free discussion. I would add that the system of the unified party demands more honesty, more disinterest, and more devotion from the leadership.

In addition, one can remain a leader in Africa for a long time only if one is really acting effectively.

I want to give some examples of internal democracy in our parties. The press has emphasized the freedom of speech, which the eminent leaders of French politics noted in September, 1957, at the third interterritorial congress of the RDA* at Bamako. I saw our friends, the students, denounce us violently at that time because we accepted the *loi-cadre*. I saw them very much impressed by the discussions of the Fifth Congress of the Union Soudanaise in August, 1958, because the discussions were absolutely free. There are other examples at the present time. When Modibo Keita makes a decision, it is generally thought that it is immediately accepted by the Union Soudanaise or, when it is a matter of the opinion of Senghor, by the Parti Fédéraliste Africain (PFA). Those who think that one can do what one wishes in the PFA, or in Mali, are sadly mistaken. As for those two men, I can assert that they are very disciplined party militants. Moreover, the highest body in the Union Soudanaise is the Political Bureau. In the PFA, it is the Executive Bureau and the Directing Committee. And without giving away any secrets, I can tell you that the leaders are obliged to follow the advice of the majority. They are obliged to execute the decisions taken by the majority.

In the case of the unified party, I believe that the leaders not only ought to be capable, but also ought to encourage discussions and give examples of party discipline. The party ought to be very well organized, since—if universal suffrage is a criterion of democracy—we have to change the parliaments continuously through elections.

Nevertheless, our democracy does not end there. First of all, it was necessary in Guinea and Sudan, when the political development and the development of awareness allowed, to replace a part of the leadership set up by the colonial regime and to modify the basic structure of the administration profoundly by suppressing the chiefdom, the chiefs of the local districts in Guinea and Sudan, and by changing the chiefs, as has just been done in Senegal. This latter change was carried out by giving them the full status of civil servants and establishing them in administrative posts, henceforth to be called *arrondissements*, and also by changing the electoral districts.

* Rassemblement Démocratique Africain, a political party organized in many French African territories before independence.—Ed.

Structural reform is very important. In Sudan, we established an elective council in the villages. Naturally, we have enumerated the functions of the chief—whom the government has the power to name, on the advice of the elective council—and we have also enumerated the functions of the elective council, so that the chief cannot do anything without consulting it. In other words, the chief and the elective council must make decisions in common. Soon we expect to establish by universal suffrage provincial elective councils, which will be responsible for local interests.

The organizer of all this is the party. For not only the Congress but the Political Bureau can add a certain number of leaders to establish the Directing Committee and make not a national conference (since Sudan is a territory, a province of Mali) but a territorial conference.* In each electoral district, we have a political bureau on the model of the central Political Bureau, and in each village we have a political committee. And so that the political committee and the elective council of the village will not enter into conflicts of influence, rivalry, and personal opposition, the most outstanding and competent party leaders are elected to the village council to act as liaison, to coordinate and harmonize, with the party always remaining the organizer.

In a recent resolution (adopted during our last conference), we asserted the superiority of the political apparatus to the administrative one. Also, we placed clerks at the head of each electoral district—African administrative officials who had already given proof of their administrative efficiency when they headed political sections or trade unions.

Thus, from the point of view of internal democracy with freedom of discussion, party discipline, democratic election of not only the top organs of the party but also the legislative and representative organs such as the provincial assemblies and the village councils, we think that the criteria of democracy are respected.

In the present historical situation in Africa, there is no need to multiply parties. There is no need to indulge in the luxury of a sterile and fratricidal opposition. There is no need to have a ministerial crisis every three months if we have decided to move to independence and to consolidate the independence of the African states, and if we wish to realize African unity and raise

* This speech was given before the union of Sudan and Senegal in the Mali Federation broke up and Sudan became the Republic of Mali.—ED.

Africa economically and culturally to the level of other countries and peoples.

Evidently, the unified party has effects on other democratic organizations. But if the party is the expression of the true aspirations of the people, if it is the spokesman and instrument for the realization of the state, there is no reason why trade-union organizations, whose program constitutes part of the program of the political party, should not find themselves in harmony with the political organization. For the same reasons, it is not impossible that youth organizations, women's organizations, and democratic movements such as the Peace Movement should not find a way to collaborate with the leading force in the country, the unified political party. And this is much easier for the African countries since the dominant ideas and aspirations today are independence, unity, and rapid realization of economic and social progress.

You must travel in the country and participate in the meetings of the village committees and the political bureaus and the subdivisions, in the discussion groups, in the meetings of the central Political Bureau to understand that the system of a unified party such as exists today in Guinea and in Sudan, is a really democratic system. I am not going to spend time on the reasons for the effectiveness of the unified party. We refuse to fight on the ideological territory of the West. Journalists, businessmen, French intellectuals—in Paris or traveling in our countries—have expressed their fears to us. "Be careful," they tell us. "Do not follow the example of Guinea, which has relations with the countries of the East. Be careful. Do not leave the West. You are going to be independent, and you will have to choose your way. We believe that it is in your interest to locate yourself in the camp of the West." My personal opinion is that it is not desirable for us to establish ourselves in this position. When we see France, England, and the United States exchanging numerous tourists and missions with the Soviet Union, and we see the Soviet Union and other countries of the East planning commercial agreements with all countries of the West, we wonder why they fear our having contacts with these countries. We are aware that it is because of a lack of confidence. They tell us that they are very clever—as if France could without difficulty have contacts with Poland and Yugoslavia while there would be a mortal danger for Guinea or Mali tomorrow to establish the same contacts with the same countries. When one asks these people if they think that we are not sufficiently mature to defend our interests ourselves, they protest, "That isn't what we meant to say!"

I say that Africa should not fight on the ideological battleground of the West because we do not have religious and philosophical problems that divide us in the administration of civic life. . . . As for economic and cultural development, even right-wing economists now admit that the underdeveloped countries can only advance rapidly and develop themselves sufficiently through planning. Even the old industrialized countries now think that they will overcome their backwardness by planning. When a man like Nehru, who seems to me like a good British bourgeois from the City,* asserts that the underdeveloped countries, which have recently achieved independence after a long period of colonial regime, cannot develop without the methods of socialist planning, I believe that this is a very important indication. From the point of view of development, it is the countries in which a single party is in power that make the most evident progress. On the other hand, countries in which the new leaders are content to replace the colonial regime without changing the structure in any way or reforming it, without bringing new methods or giving a new conception and orientation to the economy and to the program of education, without adapting the new needs to the real situation of the country, and without adapting the actions of the government and parliament to the true aspiration of the masses—these countries, in spite of every kind of aid that can be given to them, will be marking time so long as they have not adopted new, revolutionary methods.

We have been much criticized since 1946, but all this propaganda has remained without effect and has not prevented us from advancing. The important thing for us is to know what we want and to decide how we shall reach our objective. The important thing for us is to find our inspiration in all experience—in the success of industrial civilization in the United States and France; but one cannot prevent us, and we will not allow ourselves to be prevented, from studying the Chinese experience and the Soviet experience, or the experience of Israel, and taking everything that is adaptable to the conditions of our country, and using all these experiences to try to work effectively for the benefit of our country. . . .

* The financial district of London.—Ed.

Cheikh Anta Diop: You have spoken of the single party. As others have already underlined, when this is the incarnation of national goals, it is a very good idea. But when it dominates the entire political life of the nation, all the national life, and orients it to its own pleasure without taking into account the aspirations of the people, the single party can have very serious consequences. On this point, my opinion is the following: The single parties we are going to create may be parties of the Latin American type —that is, there is danger that we will create petty, ephemeral dictatorships that will be dominated by foreign capital in a very insidious fashion. Then Africa will live in a state of division and permanent weakness exactly as Latin America does. The single party is a very good formula for the purpose of dominating a little territory and safeguarding personal interests by making them, for all practical purposes, permanent. Or, on the other hand, we can orient Africa toward federation. In this case, another political form and another political conception are relevant. First of all, we must indicate our intentions very clearly now, without waiting for political frontiers to be established—for it will be more difficult afterward, perhaps too late, to federate the African continent.

Madeira Keita: The political unification of the African continent poses the problem of membership in the Community or membership in the Commonwealth, and likewise the problem of time. That is why I insist on this question. When we federate from the Sahara to the Cape, from the Atlantic Ocean to the Indian Ocean, to become a great power which, from the point of view of potential economic power, will be as strong as the Soviet Union or America, we must show the former mother countries that we are not ignoring them. Their interests will continue to be safeguarded, but not in the way they hoped for. . . .

M. Ben Barka: If you will allow, I would like to add the following observations. The first concerns the worry that certain of those present have expressed that there may be a bundle of contradictions in these unified parties which will render the parties absolutely ineffective. We think that the social classes that are trying to reconstitute feudal domination or are open to foreign domination do not necessarily belong in these organizations and ought not to be considered as an integral part of this organizing force in the people working toward its unification. Therefore, there should be more concern for unanimity in the establishment of this organizing party necessary for all development.

A second observation relates to the attitude of the unified party with regard to other syndical organizations of youth and other groups. In my opinion, the unified party would be wrong to attribute to itself a monopoly of political conceptions and political activity. Certainly, since it includes the members of these organizations, it is their political expression. But it ought to allow youth organizations, women's organizations, and trade unions to play their political roles as well, in order to realize the democratic synthesis sought in the conception of the unified political party.

Finally, the religious problem raised by certain of those here is not a problem, as you said, for Africans. It is created from outside, by those who want to make use of it as a means of penetration. We need not congratulate ourselves on the allegiance of religious leaders who, seeing which way the wind was blowing, now appeal to the new leaders. If they rally to us, so much the better. But we should not consider their allegiance as a positive factor for the future of our countries. We do not have to approve that religious phenomenon by giving a preponderant place to religious leaders who have been discredited during the colonial period. We want to arouse and form our youth without destroying the religious foundation of each community, and to give it a common revolutionary education which ought to be the ferment of the union of all of Africa.

14. Kwame Nkrumah

Kwame Nkrumah was born in the Gold Coast, near the Ivory Coast border, in 1909. He was baptized a Catholic and attended mission schools for eight years. A German priest sent him to Achimota College—a secondary school near Accra—where he first acquired nationalist sentiments. After several years of teaching in the Gold Coast, he borrowed enough money to get to the

United States where, in 1935, he received a scholarship from Lincoln University in Pennsylvania. After graduation, he taught political science at Lincoln University, and at the same time did graduate work toward advanced degrees at the University of Pennsylvania. In 1945, he went to England, where he became active in the nationalist movement. Two years later, he returned to the Gold Coast as organizing secretary of the United Gold Coast Convention, under J. B. Danquah. In 1949, he organized his own party, the Convention People's Party, which won all subsequent elections (including one in which Nkrumah campaigned while in prison, in 1951). On March 6, 1957, the Gold Coast was granted independence under the name of Ghana, and Nkrumah became its Prime Minister. In 1960, Ghana became a republic, and Nkrumah was elected President. A new constitution gives him virtual dictatorial powers—and these are reinforced by the fact that most of the leaders of the opposition United Party have been imprisoned under the Preventive Detention Act. The selection below, from Nkrumah's autobiography, describes the principal influences on his political outlook, and the methods that led to the independence of Ghana.

BACKGROUND TO INDEPENDENCE*

Independence for the Gold Coast was my aim. It was a colony, and I have always regarded colonialism as the policy by which a foreign power binds territories to herself by political ties, with the primary object of promoting her own economic advantage. No one need be surprised if this system has led to disturbances and political tension in many territories. There are few people who would not rid themselves of such domination if they could.

At this time, I devoted much energy to the study of revolutionaries and their methods. Those who interested me most were Hannibal, Cromwell, Napoleon, Lenin, Mazzini, Gandhi, Mussolini, and Hitler. I found much of value to be gleaned and many

---

* Excerpts from *Ghana: The Autobiography of Kwame Nkrumah* (New York: Thomas Nelson and Sons, 1957; copyright by Thomas Nelson and Sons, 1957); reprinted by permission.

ideas that were useful to me later in my own campaign against imperialism.

At first I could not understand how Gandhi's philosophy of nonviolence could possibly be effective. It seemed to me to be utterly feeble and without hope of success. The solution of the colonial problem, as I saw it at that time, lay in armed rebellion. How is it possible, I asked myself, for a revolution to succeed without arms and ammunition? After months of studying Gandhi's policy and watching the effect it had, I began to see that, when backed by a strong political organization, it could be the solution to the colonial problem. In Jawaharlal Nehru's rise to power I recognized the success of one who, pledged to socialism, was able to interpret Gandhi's philosophy in practical terms.

The Gold Coast revolt against colonialism is not a new thing. Its roots are deep. There was the Confederation of 1868, when certain chiefs came together to defend themselves not only against their tribal kin, the Ashantis, but also against political encroachments from abroad. After the bond of 1844, which gave Britain trading rights, the Gold Coast had come increasingly under her control.

The next great move of political cohesion and conscience was the formation of the Aborigines Rights Protection Society by chiefs and literate Africans with the object of defending Gold Coast land. When this collapsed—because of an ever-widening rift between the chiefs and the educated people—the latter, binding themselves together and supported by their educated brothers in other West African territories, established the National Congress of British West Africa. This was the first indication of West African nationalism. However, because it lacked the support of the masses, it disintegrated in 1930.

The vacuum that this left in Gold Coast politics was eventually filled by the formation of the United Gold Coast Convention by the merchant and lawyer class of the country. It was when I realized that this movement was doomed to failure because it ignored the interests of the masses that I broke away, in 1949, and formed the Convention People's Party.

I saw that the whole solution to this problem lay in political freedom for our people; for it is only when a people are politically free that other races can give them the respect that is due them. It is impossible to talk of equality of races in any other terms. No people without a government of their own can expect to be treated on the same level as peoples of independent sovereign states. It is far better to be free to govern or misgovern yourself than to be governed by anybody else.

The formation of the CPP coincided with a political reawakening among the workers and young people of the country. Ex-servicemen who had taken part in World War II returned to the Gold Coast dissatisfied with their position after having been given the chance of comparing their lot with that of other peoples, and they were prepared to take up any line which would better their conditions. There was a general dissatisfaction with the British colonial policy that had been adopted until that time, especially the policy of indirect rule which so encouraged tribal feudalism. Again, the Russian Revolution and its aftermath had left its mark by spreading ideas of workers' solidarity, trade-union movements, freedom and independence. Events in Asia also added a glow to the political awakening.

The CPP was not merely a mass movement. Mass movements are well and good, but they cannot act with purpose unless they are led and guided by a vanguard political party. And when the time comes for a ruling power to accord self-government, it will do so more willingly if it can hand over to a properly constituted political party with a majority backing, rather than to a revolutionary nationalist movement. Rallying around me all those who genuinely wished for progress, I resisted both the opportunist element and the reactionary forces, and sought to establish the CPP as the democratic instrument of the people's will and aspirations. We were freely elected to power in 1951. Three years later, and again in 1956, the same confidence was shown by the country.

The first objective then is political independence, for which I believe the organization itself must take two forms. First there is the period of "positive action"—a combination of nonviolent methods with effective and disciplined political action. At this stage, open conflict with the existing colonial regime is inevitable, and this is a test of strength for the organization. Since it is marked by nonviolence, and since the forces of might are on the side of the colonial power, there is little chance of complete success in this period.

The second stage is one of "tactical action"—a sort of contest of wits. From now on, the movement must make its ideology clear and convincing. The ideology of my party may be formulated as follows: No race, no people, no nation can exist freely and be respected at home and abroad without political freedom.

Once this freedom is gained, a greater task comes into view. All dependent territories are backward in education, in science, in agriculture, and in industry. The economic independence that should follow and maintain political independence demands every effort from the people, a total mobilization of brain and manpower resources. What other countries have taken three hundred years to achieve, a once dependent territory must try to accomplish in a generation if it is to survive. Unless it is, as it were, "jet-propelled," it will lag behind and thus risk everything for which it has fought.

Capitalism is too complicated a system for a newly independent nation. Hence the need for a socialistic society. But even a system based on social justice and a democratic constitution may need backing up, during the period following independence, by emergency measures of a totalitarian kind. Without discipline, true freedom cannot survive. In any event, the basis must be a loyal, honest, hard-working, and responsible civil service on which the party in power can rely. Armed forces must also be consolidated for defense. . . .

I concentrated on finding a formula by which the whole colonial question and the problem of imperialism could be solved. I read Hegel, Marx, Engels, Lenin, and Mazzini. The writings of these men did much to influence me in my revolutionary ideas and activities, and Marx and Lenin particularly impressed me as I felt sure that their philosophy was capable of solving these problems. But I think that of all the literature that I studied, the book that did more than any other to fire my enthusiasm was *The Philosophy and Opinions of Marcus Garvey* . . . with his philosophy of "Africa for the Africans" and his "Back to Africa" movement.

15. Kofi Baako

Kofi Baako is Leader of the House and Minister of State for Parliamentary Affairs of Ghana. He was born at Saltpond, in what was then the Gold Coast, in 1926. When Kwame Nkrumah returned to the Gold Coast in 1947 to act as organizer for the United Gold Coast Convention, Baako worked closely with him as editor of the Cape Coast Daily Mail. Baako then also organized a youth group, which provided the nucleus of the Convention People's Party when it was organized by Nkrumah in 1949. Baako was imprisoned for his political activities in 1950. After his release, he became General Secretary of the CPP, and, in 1954, a member of Parliament for Saltpond. Following independence, in 1957, he became Minister of Information and Chief Whip in Parliament. In 1961, he was appointed to his present positions.

The following selection is taken from the monthly publication of the CPP. It explains Nkrumah's philosophy of government, as seen by one of his most trusted lieutenants. Baako's support of socialism, combined with his recognition of a role for private investment, is characteristic of the attitude toward economic development of many African, Asian, and Latin American leaders. His endorsement of a complete political union of all the states of Africa contrasts with the gradualism of the approach to African unity outlined in Nnamdi Azikiwe's speech to the Lagos Conference of the Monrovia powers. Baako's discussion of the single party should also be compared to the criticisms of one-party government by Nnamdi Azikiwe and Obafemi Awolowo of Nigeria (reprinted below).

NKRUMAISM—ITS THEORY
AND PRACTICE*

I would define Nkrumaism as a nonatheistic socialist philosophy which seeks to apply the current socialist ideas to the solution of our problems—be they domestic or international—by adapting these ideas to the realities of our everyday life. It is basically socialism adapted to suit the conditions and circumstances of Africa.

Anticolonialism

As a philosophy, it has no boundaries and allows flexibility of application anywhere in the world where similar conditions exist. I refer to conditions such as long domination by colonial powers, exploitation of the natural resources by foreigners against the will of the people, discrimination of any kind, artificial boundaries drawn by foreigners, tribalism, feudalism, and similar evils that have the effect of reducing a land of natural riches into a land of artificial poverty and its people into slaves and chattel. As a socialist philosophy, it seeks to adapt socialist ideas to the evolution of an African society that has emerged from colonialist domination, and to realize its socialist aims amid the legacies of colonialism, yet, in the process, never sacrificing its African character and heritage. Nkrumaism is not a religion and has not come to replace any religion, but it preaches and seeks to implement all that true religion teaches. I can therefore safely describe Nkrumaism as applied religion, and it is a way of life which must be lived.

Nkrumaism aims at fighting to eradicate the evils of colonialism, tribalism, Balkanization, etc., and to replace them with freedom, unity, dignity, social justice, and higher living standards. And for the sake of freedom, justice, and world peace, Nkrumaism supports the right of self-determination of all peoples, rejects imperialist domination everywhere, and, in the present power-bloc rivalry, emphasizes positive neutralism and supports the forces of peace in the world.

* Reprinted from *The Party* (CPP Journal, Accra), Nos. 4–7 (April, May, June, and July, 1961).

African Socialism

In order to distinguish it from socialism practiced in other places, which in its entirety may not be suitable or applicable to the conditions and circumstances of Africa, it has been described as "African socialism." This should not be interpreted to mean a restriction of its application only to Africa; it only means that as a socialist nondoctrinaire philosophy, it is primarily designed to solve the peculiar social, economic, and political problems imposed by imperialism and colonialism on our continent. We must not take Nkrumaism as an abstract philosophical concept. It has a definite content and objective—namely, a social reform aimed at the abolition of the social power wielded by private capital property and replacing it with the social power held by the people through the state. It aims at stopping man's inhumanity to man, exploitation of man by man, and at evolving a society in which all the material and spiritual values created are social property and the people who create them dispose of themselves at their own discretion and enjoy all the fruits of their labor—working according to their abilities and receiving according to their needs. This presupposes the establishment of a socioeconomic structure that ensures not a mere redistribution of property, but a just distribution of income out of the yield of the socioeconomic process, with the aim of a proportionate distribution of property.

To achieve the lofty objective of Nkrumaism, the main means of production and distribution must be owned and controlled by the state. Nkrumaism believes that the public ownership of the main means of production and distribution places social power in the hands of the people through the state, thus enabling coordinated organization and planning of the economy, and an orderly and effective execution of the national programs.

Capitalism places social power in the hands of individuals by the ownership and control of the means of production and distribution. Thus, even though the state (i.e., the people) may hold the political power, the absence of social power makes the creation of a welfare state very difficult—even almost impossible. To the Nkrumaist, the possession of political power must go together with the possession of social power to ensure the speedy and orderly creation of a socialist state. The African traditional social system is basically communalistic—i.e., socialistic—"a society in which all live with all, and all for all," a society in which the welfare of the individual is bound up with the welfare of all the people in the community.

Nkrumaism and Religion

Nkrumaism as a philosophy recognizes "that among the natural rights of man, rooted in his existential ends and to be respected and guaranteed by the state, are those in the religious sphere." Nkrumaism guarantees the right of worship in the sense that all citizens should enjoy the same right, protected by the state, to practice their religion in private and public without suffering any disadvantage in their civil life; the right of parents in the religious education of their children; the right to association on the ground of common religious duties and interests; the right to champion the convictions of one's religious community in accordance with the right of expression and information maintained by modern free society. In fact, there is nothing I find in Nkrumaism which is incompatible with religion—be it Christianity, Islam, or Buddhism.

In the interest of religion, and in order to avoid dragging religion into disrepute, Nkrumaism is opposed to the practice—so common in many European countries—of forming political parties or political associations based on religion.

I know that in certain circles there have been some misgivings about the meaning and content of Nkrumaism, due mainly to the vicious meanings and interpretations some foreign newspapers gave to it and also due to some irresponsible talk within our own country. The foreign anti-African press, knowing the inherent religious qualities of the African, tried to play on the keyboard of the religious emotions of our people by presenting Nkrumaism as being antireligious—and yet none of these people can claim to be more religious and God-fearing than Kwame Nkrumah, whose ideas and teachings constitute Nkrumaism. In fact, atheism is foreign to Africa, and religion is the basis of all our culture. . . .

Nkrumaism and International Relations

The Nkrumaist philosophy teaches that all those who live by their work want and need peace to enjoy the fruits of their labor. Peace and Nkrumaism are therefore inseparable—for we need peace and not war to advance our economy and to raise the standard of living of our people. Indeed, it is no exaggeration to say that if the whole world were socialist, war would be a thing of the past, for imperialism and its twin sister, capitalism, are by their very nature and content the main causes of wars, and indeed thrive only on wars and misunderstandings. Unfortunately, one wonders whether the world—including the capitalist countries and socialist countries—will survive a third world war.

It is for this reason that Nkrumaism calls for the creation of a third world force, a nonnuclear force, comprising mainly the African and Asian states and the uncommitted countries of the world, which will work faithfully for disarmament and peace in the world.

Nkrumaism puts forward the view that imperialism and peace are poor bedfellows. For imperialism cannot exist—and therefore cannot thrive—in a world of peace. That is why, even though it has been chased away from Ghana and from other places in Africa through the forces of African anti-imperialist nationalism, it is doing everything possible to replant itself by such devilish techniques as instigation of quarrels and wars among small nations, by the signing of military pacts with independent African states, by the fanning of tribalism, by economic penetration, cultural assimilation, ideological domination, and subversive activities even to the point of promoting assassination and civil strife, such as we are witnessing in the Congo and Algeria. Without such intrigues and planned and subtle invasion of the colonies, imperialism cannot thrive. Imperialism and Nkrumaism are incompatible, for the socialist principles that underlie and underline Nkrumaism cannot tolerate a society dominated by a foreign power against the will of the people. Nkrumaism is vehemently opposed to the evils of discrimination and apartheid, which are born of imperialism and colonialism. Nkrumaism cannot contain tribalism and Balkanization because they favor the growth and expansion of imperialism and exploitation, which are the main causes of all wars and misunderstandings.

Nkrumaism believes that the surest way to achieve peace and understanding in the world is the achievement of the total liberation of Africa and the establishment of a continental federal government in a complete political union of Africa. This will enable the continent to pool its resources—material and human—for the common good of its people and for the general good of mankind. It will also help Africa to exert its influence on the international scene by consolidating its foreign policy and by coordinating its defenses and by presenting a solid economic and social front. . . .

Nkrumaism and the People

Nkrumaism teaches that the powers of all government spring or must spring from the people and should be exercised therewith. In almost every speech Dr. Nkrumah has made since he arrived in this country to become our undisputed leader, he has always stressed the importance of the ordinary people. Nkrumaism does not represent the special interest of individual groups. It is the movement of the people, and its goal is the reconstruction of society in the spirit of socialism. Nkrumaism therefore strives for the equality of men and for spiritual, political, and economic freedom, which could not be realized under imperialist domination.

All social institutions and systems tend to become self-centered and bureaucratic. Nkrumaism teaches us to recognize these dangers and to fight them. Let me repeat, Nkrumaism stands for social justice, political and economic democracy, spiritual freedom and tolerance, national unity and international cooperation undeterred by any narrow-minded concern for vested interests. . . .

Nkrumaism and Private Investment

In most cases, a large proportion of the turnover of an industrial company remains in Ghana in the form of wages and salaries to employees. These wages and salaries in turn attract taxation and also purchasing power, which encourage further enterprises. In good companies, of which there are many, a share of the profits is plowed back into the company for development of its enterprises. This is, in fact, further investment. If there are fears of permanent foreign domination in the commercial and industrial field of our economy, these fears should be immediately and permanently abandoned. The government has already taken adequate measures by limiting the tenure of leases and concessions and by clearing foreign elements from the ownership of land. It must be borne in mind, however, that the duration of leases and concessions must be balanced against the encouragement of overseas capital in such a way as to guarantee a reasonable return for the investment.

In spite of this, however, we are called upon by the same Nkrumaist philosophy to be watchful and vigilant so that private

investors who primarily think of their profits may not adopt subtle
tricks to further their capitalist aims of exploitation.

Indeed, it must be stated that the Nkrumaist prefers loan
capital to investment capital. The difference . . . is clear. Loan
capital allows the receiver of the loan—say, the government—to
use its loan to set up any state enterprises within the framework
of its socioeconomic plan. In the case of investment capital, the
investor sets up his business in the country and tries, by any means
that may suit his profit-making mission, to achieve his aims. For
instance, in the absence of effective import-control and price-
control systems, the private investor may be able to further his
capitalist aims by fixing prices of commodities far above the
average means of the consumer.

This state of affairs may lead to wage and salary increases that
may affect, in the long run, the smooth implementation of the
over-all development plan of the country. In the view of the
Nkrumaist, therefore, some effective measures are necessary to
arrest any tendency toward exploitation and inflationary consequences, and all the while the ideal of total ownership of the
means of production and distribution should be pursued by continually and energetically strengthening the public sector of the
economy. Also we must continue to encourage responsible cooperatives in the country.

One-Party System

I do not agree with those political theoreticians and theoretical
politicians who would want us to believe that it is wrong for all
the country to belong to one party, and that an opposition is
necessary in a democracy. I beg to differ. What is necessary for
democracy is not an organized opposition, which, in order to
offer itself as an alternative government, adopts every obstructive
and even at times destructive measure and maneuver to overthrow
a government that for the sake of the people and the good name
of the state is unprepared to make mistakes to encourage the
growth of a strong opposition. What is necessary for democracy
to be maintained is the opportunity to criticize or speak one's mind
without fear or favor, the opportunity to share in the government
by exercise of your franchise without fear or favor, the opportunity to change those who govern by the use of your votes. I
assure you and all that the CPP has plenty of room for construc-

tive criticisms and the free expression of opinions for the building up of our great party for the service and independence of our people and Africa. Human dignity, freedom, justice, and tolerance, as well as individual responsibility toward the state, are cherished principles of Nkrumaism. The Convention People's Party, whose platform is Nkrumaist socialism, will ensure (as does our constitution) freedom of opinion, freedom of speech, and freedom of individual activity in public life. But it will not allow freedom to destroy freedom. It will not allow freedom to retard the growth of freedom. It will take such measures as are morally and politically appropriate to ensure national security, under which alone individual freedom is possible. We must, as citizens and Nkrumaists, remember that true individual freedom lies in the recognition of one's own limitation within the framework of the security of the state. It follows, therefore, that any tendency toward bureaucracy, feudalism, oligarchy, or capitalism, leading to limitations on the rights of the masses, is incompatible with Nkrumaism.

As Nkrumaists, we believe that a monolithic party is necessary in an ex-colonial state which is inevitably faced with the task of correcting past maladjustment, years of neglect and of colonial mental conditioning, and of building a new, really independent, happy, and proud state. Such a young state cannot afford to dissipate its national efforts through the senseless wranglings and obstructive and destructive tactics that organized political opposition encourages. Besides, it is through such opposition parties that colonialism and imperialism seek to perpetuate their hold on the country. What is wrong with a newly independent state, united under one leader in one dynamic party utilizing the efforts of all, channeling the energies of each toward the great goals of social and economic reconstruction—a happy, dignified, and respectable life for all?

Nkrumaist Economic Policy

On this question of the socialist pattern of society, let me quote the *Osagyefo** himself:

I have stated on many occasions that the government's policy is aimed at evolving a socialist pattern of society. No secret has been

* A courtesy title for Nkrumah, meaning "Victorious Leader."

made of this fact. I have also stated that there are different paths to socialism, that each country must find its own way, and that socialism could differ in form from one country to another. Ghana intends to evolve its own socialist pattern of society adapted to its own particular needs. . . .

The economic structure is divided into four different sectors: (1) the state-owned sector; (2) the joint state–private-enterprise sector; (3) the cooperative sector; and (4) the purely private sector. . . .

First, the state-owned sector: In previous statements, I have defined this sector as embracing specific industries reserved to the state. Such industries include the manufacture of arms and ammunitions, alcoholic beverages, and the operation of facilities such as electricity, water supplies, hydroelectric projects, etc. It also includes industries of a pioneering nature which private enterprise is unwilling or unable to undertake.

The second sector, joint state–private enterprise, is intended to include those industries which by their nature make it essential for the state to hold a substantial interest in them—because they either confer monopoly rights on their owners or demand substantial protective tariffs. This sector will also include those industries which the private-enterprise partners are unwilling or unable to undertake without government participation.

The third, or cooperative, sector is intended to build up Ghanaian enterprise in all fields. In the past, the government has given considerable assistance to Ghanaian private enterprise, but the result has been negligible and disappointing—so disappointing, in fact, that the government feels that its assistance must be channeled in a more productive manner. My statement . . . does not mean that Ghanaian private enterprise is to be nationalized, but it must now stand on its own feet and not rely on the government for its development. With regard to the distributive retail trades, the government intends to foster cooperatives to enter this field, both wholesale and retail. . . . The cooperatives must develop side by side with private enterprise, either overseas- or Ghanaian-owned, in a freely competitive manner. I am quite satisfied that the large overseas firms are genuinely encouraging the growth of Ghanaian retail trade and that they will continue to do so.

Lastly, the purely private-enterprise sector: For the reasons I have mentioned in relation to the cooperative sector, this purely private-enterprise sector mainly concerns investment from abroad. So that there may be no exploitation whatsoever in the private sector of our economy, the government has taken such steps as are appropriate to ensure that the state derives adequate and reasonable benefits from private enterprises.

Those of us who profess to believe in Nkrumaism must show by both our words and actions—indeed, by the way we live generally—that we are true followers of this great citizen of Africa, who has made Africa's cause his cause and international peace his aim. We should continue to learn from him. We should not, in our determination (even anxiety) to achieve socialism for our country and for Africa, make the unhappy mistake of thinking that we are better socialists, or understand socialism better, or know how to achieve socialism better than the leader himself. In whatever we do, we must be guided by the policy statements of our great leader, whose ideas and ideals constitute Nkrumaism. We must not attempt, either by words or deeds, to frighten people away from socialism. We must give the correct interpretations and explanations of the Nkrumaist ideals and objectives, and ensure, through consistent and patient education, that this great African socialist philosophy is accepted by the masses of Ghana and of Africa. For, as Karl Marx said, "Theory becomes a material force as soon as it has gripped the masses." As true Nkrumaists, we always let objectivity and comradeship permeate our discussions, and truth, honesty, and modesty guide us on the road to Nkrumaist socialism.

16. Julius Nyerere

Julius Nyerere was born in 1922, the son of a Tanganyikan tribal chief. He was educated in Catholic schools, received his B.A. from Makerere College in Uganda, and his M.A. from the University of Edinburgh. After his return to Tanganyika, he became President of the Tanganyika African Association, which he transformed in 1954 into the Tanganyika African National Union (TANU). Since that time, TANU has had a virtual political monopoly among African organizations in Tanganyika. Nyerere has stood for multiracialism and moderation in his approach to self-government for Tanganyika, but his ideas on Pan-Africanism, the single party, and the relation of the trade unions to the political organi-

zation resemble those of the more radical wing of the African na-
tionalists. Tanganyika became independent in October, 1961. In
January, 1962, Nyerere resigned from his post as Prime Minister to
devote himself to full-time party work. In November, 1962, he was
elected President of the Tanganyika Republic.

ONE-PARTY RULE*

The African concept of democracy is similar to that of the ancient
Greeks, from whose language the word "democracy" originated.
To the Greeks, democracy meant simply "government by discussion among equals." The people discussed, and when they reached
agreement, the result was a "people's decision."

Mr. Guy Clutton-Brock, writing about Nyasaland, describes
traditional African democracy as follows: "The elders sit under
the big tree and talk until they agree." This "talking until you
agree" is the essential of the traditional African concept of democracy.

To minds molded by Western parliamentary tradition and
Western concepts of democratic institutions, the idea of an organized opposition group has become so familiar that its absence
immediately raises the cry of "dictatorship." It is no good telling
them that when a group of 100 equals have sat and talked together until they have agreed where to dig a well (and "until they
have agreed" implies that they have produced many conflicting
arguments before eventually agreeing), they have practiced democracy. Proponents of Western parliamentary traditions will
consider whether the opposition was organized and therefore automatic, or whether it was spontaneous and therefore free. Only if it
was automatic will they concede that here was democracy!

Basically, democracy is government by discussion as opposed to
government by force, and by discussion between the people or
their chosen representatives, as opposed to a hereditary clique.
Under the tribal system, whether there was a chief or not, African
society was a society of equals, and it conducted its business by
discussion.

It is true that this "pure" democracy—the totally unorganized
"talking until you agree"—can no longer be adequate; it is too

* Reprinted from *Spearhead* (Dar-es-Salaam), November, 1961.

clumsy a way of conducting the affairs of a large modern state. But the need to organize the "government by discussion" does not necessarily imply the need to organize an opposition group as part of the system.

I am not arguing that the two-party system is not democratic; I am only saying that it is simply one form which democracy happens to have taken in certain countries, and that it is by no means essential. I am sure that even my friends in the Labour Party or in the Conservative Party in Britain would admit that if their party could succeed in winning all the seats, they would be perfectly happy to form a one-party government. They—the winning party, that is—would not be likely to suspect themselves of having suddenly turned Britain into a dictatorship!

Some of us have been overready to swallow unquestioningly the proposition that you cannot have democracy unless you have a second party to oppose the party in power. But, however difficult our friends in Britain and America may find it to accept what to them is a new idea—that democracy can exist where there is no formal opposition—I think we in Africa should think very carefully before we abandon our traditional attitude.

It is often overlooked that the Anglo-Saxon tradition of a two-party system is a reflection of the society in which it evolved. Within that society, there was a struggle between the "haves" and the "have-nots," each of whom organized themselves into political parties—one party associated with wealth and the *status quo*, and the other with the masses of the people and change. Thus, the existence of distinct classes in a society, and the struggle between them, resulted in the growth of the two-party system. But need this be accepted as the essential and only pattern of democracy?

With rare exceptions, the idea of class is something entirely foreign to Africa. Here, in this continent, the nationalist movements are fighting a battle for freedom from *foreign* domination, not from domination by any ruling class of our own. To us, "the other party" is the colonial power. In many parts of Africa, this struggle has been won; in others, it is still going on. But everywhere the people who fight the battle are not former overlords wanting to re-establish a lost authority; they are not a rich mercantile class whose freedom to exploit the masses is limited by the colonial powers; they are the common people of Africa.

Thus, once the foreign power—"the other party"—has been expelled, it is by no means certain that democracy will adopt the same machinery and symbols as the Anglo-Saxon. Nor, indeed, is it necessarily desirable that it should.

New nations like Tanganyika are emerging into independence as a result of a struggle for freedom from colonialism. It is a patriotic struggle that leaves no room for differences and unites all elements in the country; and the nationalist movements, having united the people and led them to freedom, must inevitably form the first governments of the new states. Once the first free government is formed, its supreme task lies ahead—the building up of the country's economy, so as to raise the living standards of the people, to eradicate disease, to banish ignorance and superstition. This, no less than the struggle against colonialism, calls for the maximum united effort by the whole country if it is to succeed. *There can be no room for difference or division.*

In Western democracies, it is an accepted practice in times of emergency for opposition parties to sink their differences and join together in forming a national government. *This is our time of emergency,* and until our war against poverty, ignorance, and disease has been won, we should not let our unity be destroyed by a desire to follow somebody else's "book of rules."

If these, then, are the forms of democracy, what are its essentials? First, the freedom and the well-being of the individual. Freedom alone is not enough; there can be a freedom which is merely the freedom to starve. True freedom must be freedom not only from bondage, from discrimination, and from indignity, but also from all those things that hamper a people's progress. It is the responsibility of the government in a democratic country to lead the fight against all these enemies of freedom. To do this, the government, once freely elected, must also be free to govern in the best interests of the people, and without fear of sabotage. It is therefore also the duty of the government to safeguard the unity of the country from irresponsible or vicious attempts to divide and weaken it—for without unity, the fight against the enemies of freedom cannot be won. . . .

True democracy depends far more on the attitude of mind that respects and defends the individual than on the forms it takes. The form is useless without the attitude of mind of which the form is an external expression. As with individuals, so with organized groups, this question of attitude is all-important. It is not enough to ask what attitude an African government will adopt toward an opposition without also asking what attitude an opposition will adopt toward a popularly elected government.

In the past, all that was required of government was merely to maintain law and order within the country and to protect it from external aggression. Today, the responsibilities of governments, whether "Communist" or "free," are infinitely wide. However nearly its requirements of money and men may be met, no government today finds it easy to fulfill all its responsibilities to the people.

These common problems of a modern state are no less formidable in young and underdeveloped countries. The very success of the nationalist movements in raising the expectations of the people, the modern means of communications which put the American and the British worker in almost daily contact with the African worker, the twentieth-century upsurge of the ordinary man and woman—all these deprive the new African governments of those advantages of time and ignorance which alleviated the growing pains of modern society for the governments of older countries.

To the demands of the common man in Africa, intensified as they are by the vivid contrast between his own lot and that of others in more developed countries, add the lack of means at the disposal of the African governments to meet these demands: the lack of men, the lack of money, and, above all, the lack of time. To all this, add the very nature of the new countries themselves. They are usually countries without natural unity. Their "boundaries" enclose those artificial units carved out of Africa by the grasping colonial powers, without any consideration for ethnic groups or geographical realities, so that these countries now include within their borders tribal groups that, until the coming of the European powers, had never been under one government. To these, in the case of East and Central Africa, you must add the new tribes from Asia, the Middle East, and Europe. Here are divisions enough to pose a truly formidable task in nation-building.

As if the natural challenge were not enough, with the raising of each new flag come the intrigues of the international diplomacy of rivalry and all that goes with it—the cynical and the criminal attempts by powerful foreign governments to weaken the unity of any country whose government pursues policies they do not like. Who does not know that foreign nations have again and again poured in money to back up any stooge who will dance to their political tune? As their sole purpose is to confuse the people and weaken the legal government for their own ends, they are quite indifferent to the fact that their chosen puppets have no following at all in the country itself.

It should be obvious, then, why the governments of these new countries must treat the situation as one of national emergency, comparable almost to that of a country at war. In the early days of nation-building, as in time of war, the opposition, if any, must act even more responsibly than an opposition in a more developed and more stable, a more unified and better-equipped country in time of peace. Given such a responsible opposition, I would be the first person to defend its rights. But where is it? Too often, the only voices to be heard in "opposition" are those of a few irresponsible individuals who exploit the very privileges of democracy—freedom of the press, freedom of association, freedom to criticize—in order to deflect the government from its responsibilities to the people by creating problems of law and order.

The admitted function of any political opposition is to try and persuade the electorate to reject the existing government at the next election. This is reasonable in the case of a responsible opposition with a definite alternative policy in which its members sincerely believe; but that sort of mature opposition is rare indeed in a newly independent state. Usually, the irresponsible individuals I have mentioned have neither sincerity, conviction, nor any policy at all save that of self-aggrandizement. They merely employ the catch phrases copied from the political language of older, stable countries in order to engage the sympathy of the unthinking for their destructive tactics. Nor are the tactics they use those of a responsible democratic opposition. In such circumstances, the government must deal firmly and promptly with the troublemakers. The country cannot afford, during these vital early years of its life, to treat such people with the same degree of tolerance that may be safely allowed in a long-established democracy.

This does not mean, however, that a genuine and responsible opposition cannot arise in time, or that such an opposition would be less welcome in Africa than it is in Europe or America. For myself, as I have said, I would be the first to defend its rights. But whether it does or does not arise depends entirely on the will of the people themselves, and makes no difference at all to the freedom of discussion and the equality in freedom which, together, make democracy.

To those who wonder if democracy can survive in Africa, my

own answer, then, would be that, far from its being an alien idea, democracy has long been familiar to the African. There is nothing in our traditional attitude toward discussion and our current dedication to human rights to justify the claim that democracy is in danger in Africa. I see exactly the opposite: The principles of our nationalist struggles for human dignity, augmented by our traditional attitude toward discussion, should augur well for democracy in Africa.

THE ROLE OF AFRICAN
TRADE UNIONS*

I think the time has come to re-examine our ideas about the trade-union movement in Africa and its relationship with the nationalist movements. Here again, we are in danger of accepting, without thought, the Western pattern, regardless of the fact that it makes little or no sense in Africa.

In Great Britain and in America, the trade unionists have come to believe that the trade-union movement must be "independent of any political party." Superficially, this sounds attractive; any slogan that can bring in the word "independence" always does sound attractive, so that its very appeal to the emotions automatically tends to stifle further thought about what it means. Let us try to find out how this idea of independence from the political parties grew, and what it does mean.

A great deal of the confused thinking on the part of those who pontificate about African trade unions stems from their having forgotten a very important fact—that the trade unions and the labor, or socialist, parties of Europe are two wings of the same labor movement. Trade unionism first came into being as a result of the industrial revolution and the division of the Western countries between "labor" and "capital."

At first, unorganized labor was completely at the mercy of the employers, by whom it was exploited in more than one sense of the word. The workers then decided that they must organize themselves for the purpose of collective bargaining with the employers;

* Reprinted from *Labour* (Accra), June, 1961.

to put it bluntly, they realized that they must fight for their rights against their exploiters, and that to do so they must organize.

It was not long before the workers found that their trade unions alone were not enough. In industry, the unions could bargain with the employers; but the employers still had the last word, for they were also the rulers of the country.

If the new labor movement was to have any influence over the laws affecting industrial conditions, it must have a voice in parliament. The workers must organize themselves into political parties as well as into trade unions; when the political prong had been added to the industrial one, the labor movement was complete.

In those early days there was no confusion of thought. The Labour Party in England, for instance, was quite clearly part of the same movement as the trade unions, and if anybody then had talked of the need for trade unions to be "independent of any political party," he would have been told he was talking nonsense.

If, on the other hand, he had said the trade-union movement must be independent of the government, he would merely have been stating the obvious; because at that time the "government" was the same thing as the industrialists—the exploiters—against whom the whole movement had been organized. The need for the labor movement to be free from any control by the capitalists is not a doctrine; it is a self-evident definition.

This fact, however, has gradually been forgotten, and forgetting it has led to some ridiculous results. In Britain, for instance, one would have expected that when once the labor movement succeeded in forming a government of its own, the whole movement would rejoice. But no! When this did eventually happen, only one prong of the labor movement rejoiced—the political prong. The other, the industrial prong, from long force of habit remained sulky and suspicious! . . .

Habit, no less than emotion, has an unhappy tendency to stop people from thinking. The rule that you must not allow yourself to be controlled by the enemy springs from the very definition of "enemy." The labor movement applied this rule correctly in the days when Britain was controlled by the capitalists. But then, somehow, the rule slipped imperceptibly into some general doctrine of the independence of trade unions from *any* political control.

As a result, when the labor movement won its resounding victory after the end of World War II, the victory, instead of being seen in its true light as a victory of the whole movement, was looked at as only a Labour Party victory. . . . They [the unions] had for so long accepted the doctrine that trade unions must be independent and suspicious of the government that they had come to believe this meant *any* government—including, I suppose, a government 100 per cent trade unionist.

A socialist government either is socialist or it is not. A trade-union movement either is socialist or it is not. If a government *is* a socialist government, representing the working peoples of the country, then it must be acknowledged and treated as such, not only by the capitalists, but by the workers themselves. The workers can no more be independent of it than it can be independent of the workers.

Of course, if the particular individuals who happen at any given time to form the government do not carry out the policies for which the labor movement as a whole stands, they can be replaced, in the normal democratic way, by the labor movement itself. But there can be no logic in any *part* of the labor movement trying to have it both ways. . . .

I said the time had come to re-examine our ideas about the trade-union movement in Africa. So far, I have been dealing with European, and particularly British, trade unions. I have done this deliberately, in order to bring out one thing: that particular patterns or traditions grow up in different countries because of the historical circumstances peculiar to those countries during the period of growth, and that these habits of thought tend to become accepted as essential to trade unionism when, in fact, they are not.

I have tried to indicate why, in the case of Great Britain especially, the doctrine or habit of trade unions being independent of political control is the result of the original necessity for their independence from what was then a capitalist government, and how this habit of thought has slipped into a meaningless formula of independence from political control generally.

In Britain, the fact that the formula is meaningless saves it from doing much harm, for the British are accustomed to taking their political slogans with a pinch of salt, with a ruling class of industrialists or employers associated with political power, against whom it has been necessary for the workers to organize first an industrial and then a political movement. Our development has been the other way around. When, six years ago, we established our nationalist movement, its first aim was political—independence from colonialism. Within this nationalist movement, and very much a part of it, one of our objectives was to help the growth of a trade-union movement.

We have an officer in the organization whose special duty it was to stimulate and help the growth of trade unionism. Once firmly established, the trade-union movement was, and is, part and parcel of the whole nationalist movement. In the early days, when a trade union went on strike, for instance, and its members were in direct need of funds to keep them going, we saw no doctrine that would be abrogated by our giving financial support from the political wing to the industrial wing of the same nationalist movement.

It was simply a case of the right hand helping the left hand, or vice versa. It would clearly have been ridiculous to preach an imported doctrine of independence of the Tanganyika Federation of Labour from political control, and so to deny them the assistance they needed from the Tanganyika African Nationalist Union.

NATIONALISM AND PAN-AFRICANISM*

You have asked me to speak on African unity. I am an advocate of African unity. I believe firmly that, just as unity was necessary for the achievement of independence in Tanganyika or any other nation, unity is equally necessary to consolidate and maintain the independence which we are now achieving in different parts of Africa.

I believe that, left to ourselves, we can achieve unity on the African continent. But I don't believe that we are going to be left to ourselves! I believe that the phase through which we are emerging successfully is the phase of the first scramble for Africa—and Africa's reaction to it. We are now entering a new phase. It is the phase of the second scramble for Africa. And just as in the first one tribe was divided against another tribe to make the division of Africa easier, in the second the technique will be to try

* Excerpts from a speech delivered by Nyerere to the Second Pan-African Seminar, World Assembly of Youth. Reprinted, by permission, from *WAY Forum*, No. 40 (September, 1961).

to divide one nation against another nation, to make it easier to control Africa by making her weak and divided against herself.

It is for this reason, therefore, that before we can talk complacently about "African unity," we should examine carefully the external ideas that are likely to be imposed upon us, imposed not for the purpose of uniting us, but for the purpose of dividing us!

Two Blocs

Today the world is divided into two blocs—what one might call the "capitalist bloc" and the "socialist bloc," but generally referred to as the "Western bloc" and the "Eastern bloc." I have said "capitalist" and "socialist" for a good reason—it makes it easier to understand the forces behind these divisions.

What is wrong with capitalism? To my mind, capitalism went wrong when it divorced wealth from its true purpose. The true purpose of wealth is to satisfy very simple needs: the need for food, the need for shelter, the need for education, and so on. In other words, the end of wealth is the banishment of poverty—and wealth is to poverty what light is to darkness.

There is enough wealth in every state for every individual to satisfy these simple needs. But the moment individuals in any single state begin to use wealth not for the satisfaction of those needs, not for the banishment of poverty, but for the purpose of acquiring power and prestige—then there is no longer enough. Then wealth tolerates poverty; then wealth is no longer to poverty what light is to darkness. For there is not enough wealth in any nation to satisfy the desire for power and the prestige of every individual.

So what happens? There is then ruthless competition between individuals—not to get wealth to feed themselves, or to clothe themselves, or to house themselves, but to seize enough wealth to give themselves more power, more prestige than their fellows, i.e., wealth that exceeds their real needs and will enable them to dominate other individuals. When that stage is reached, one millionaire is prepared to spend millions simply in order to destroy another millionaire.

I believe that the purpose of socialism was to remove this sin of capitalism and to return wealth to its original use—the satisfaction of simple human needs, the banishment of poverty. I think it would be hypocrisy on the part of the capitalist countries—not to recognize the fact that this is happening in the socialist countries; that, within those countries, personal wealth is not a symbol of power or prestige, and wealth is used to banish poverty.

But I believe that the socialist countries themselves, considered as individuals in the larger society of nations, are now committing the same crime that was committed by capitalists before. I believe that, on the international level, they are now beginning to use wealth for the purpose of acquiring power and prestige! It would be equally hypocritical on the part of the socialist countries to deny this. Internationally, they are now engaged in using wealth in exactly the same way as the capitalist countries—for power and prestige.

And socialist countries, no less than capitalist countries, are prepared to behave like the millionaire—to use millions to destroy another millionaire; and it need not necessarily be a capitalist millionaire—it is just as likely to be a socialist millionaire. In other words, socialist wealth now tolerates poverty—which is an even more unforgivable crime!

Lure of Slogans

I believe that no underdeveloped country can afford to be anything but socialist. I think, therefore, that we in Africa are bound to organize ourselves on a socialist pattern. But let us at least provide another corrective to socialism, and prevent the wealth we are beginning to build in our own countries from being used for the purpose of acquiring national power or prestige. Let us make sure that it is used solely for raising the standards of our people. Let us not allow the wealth that we are creating to live side by side with poverty, and tolerate that poverty.

. . . I have said already that socialism arose to remedy the mistakes capitalism had made. Karl Marx felt there was an inevitable clash between the rich of one society and the poor of that society. In that, I believe, Karl Marx was right. But today it is the international scene which is going to have a greater impact on the lives of individuals than what is happening within Tanganyika or within Uganda. And when you look at the international scene, you must admit that the world is still divided between the "haves" and the "have-nots." This division is not a division between capitalists and socialists, or between capitalists and Communists; this is a division between the poor countries of the world and the rich countries of the world.

The poor countries of the world should be very careful not to allow themselves to be used as the "tools" of any of the rich countries of the world, however much the rich countries may seek to fool them that they are on their side! And don't forget that the rich countries of the world today may be found on either side of the division between capitalist and socialist countries.

I have said all this as a rather long introduction to what I am going to say about African unity. I believe the danger to African unity is going to come from these external forces and slogans which bear no relation to the facts of the world today; from the fact that today the rich countries of the world—both capitalist and socialist—are using their wealth to dominate the poor countries. And they are ready to try to weaken and divide the poor countries for that purpose of domination. That is why I said at the beginning that if we in Africa were left on our own, we would achieve unity on our continent—but that I do not believe we are going to be left alone. And I have explained why I think we are not going to be left alone.

But there is no need for fear. All we need to do is to use our intellect, to know what is good for us. We need to listen to the outside world, to accept from them what we believe is in the best interests of Africa and of African unity, and to reject—and reject in no uncertain terms—what we believe is not in the best interests of Africa and of African unity. And that includes all those attractive but misleading slogans about "democracy" and "socialism" which are too often used to cloak the real designs of the power-hungry. These old slogans bear no relation at all to what Africa is doing, and they are generally used for the purpose of dividing Africa into camps.

Artificial Nations

At the beginning, I used the phrase "the second scramble for Africa." It may sound farfetched, in the context of the Africa of the 1960's. . . . But anybody who thinks this is farfetched has been completely blind to what is happening on the African continent. Take, for example, the Congo: There were obvious weaknesses in the Congo situation, but those weaknesses were deliberately used in a scramble for the control of the Congo.

There are obvious weaknesses on the African continent. We have artificial "nations" carved out at the Berlin Conference;* we are struggling to build these nations into stable units of human society. And these weaknesses, too, are being exploited. We are being reminded daily of these weaknesses. We are told that tribalism will not allow us to build nations. But when we try to take measures to deal with tribalism, we are accused of dictatorship.

Whenever we try to talk in terms of larger units on the African continent, we are told that it can't be done; we are told that the units we would so create would be "artificial." As if they could be any more artificial than the "national" units on which we are now building! Some of the people who say this are genuinely pointing to a difficulty; but I believe many of them are deliberately emphasizing the difficulties on our continent for the express purpose of maintaining them and sabotaging any move to unite Africa.

The technique is very simple. One power bloc labels a move for unity a "Communist plot"—not because it is Communist, but because they don't like it. Another power bloc labels another move for unity an "imperialist plot"—not because it is so, but because they don't like it. What annoys me is not the use of these slogans by power-hungry nations, for this is something we do expect; but what does infuriate me is that they should expect us to allow ourselves to be treated as if we were a bunch of idiots!

So I believe that the second scramble for Africa has begun in real earnest. And it is going to be a much more dangerous scramble than the first one. For what happened in the first scramble? One imperialist power fought another imperialist power for the booty. What do you think is going to happen in the second scramble? No imperialist power is going to fight another imperialist power for the control of Africa; that would be too crude a method in the context of the 1960's. No. This time, one imperialist power is going to arm one African nation, and another imperialist power is going to arm another African nation, and African brother is going to slaughter African brother—not in the interests of Africa, but in the interests of the imperialists both old and new!

That is why I have often thought we must try and find a method which will enable us, in Africa, to avoid the weaknesses of the "national" state. We have the example of Europe before us, where

* The Berlin Conference of 1884–85 agreed on the partition of Africa among the European colonial powers.—ED.

one national state arms itself against another national state. In the world as it is today, nobody could seriously suggest that an African state can arm itself, or be armed, in order to defend itself against one of the great powers of the world. If an African state is armed realistically, it can only be armed against another African state. I think we should be very careful about this. We must not find ourselves committing the same mistakes committed by the nation-states of other continents; arming ourselves against ourselves, destroying our chances not only of raising the standards of living of our people—which is what we are here for—but also destroying forever the chances of African unity.

African Command

That is why, during the difficulties in the Congo, when the idea of an African Command was first proposed, I was very taken with it. I do think we in Africa should think very seriously of a method by which that idea could be put into practice. All that we need within our national boundaries are sufficient police forces for the purpose of maintaining law and order within those boundaries. As far as large military commitments are concerned, these should be on an African basis.

If such a thing could be done, it would achieve two objectives at least. First, it removes the danger I have already referred to— the danger of arming ourselves against ourselves, and thus depriving ourselves of the chance of achieving African unity, as well as of the materials for raising our people's standards of living. And secondly, it provides a real force for the defense of Africa against external aggression. Once again, I know, people have said that this is impossible, that it can't be done; but I believe it can be done.

What can be the role of the young people of Africa in all this? First, I would like to say that Africa is a young continent in two respects. Internationally, its nations are young nations. But Africa is also young in another sense—it is governed by young people. I think one of the troubles in the modern world is that nuclear power is being handled by people who were born in the nineteenth century and educated in the nineteenth century—people with a Victorian turn of mind who have been overtaken by the achievement of science and by modern ideas about human society.

They have not been able to adjust themselves; and while they repeat some of the slogans which sound very "modern" (and I have already said that many of the ones they shout are not modern at all), their actions are the actions of the past. They talk "unity" —and they divide. One advantage of youth is that it doesn't have this dichotomy. The young have had an education which is a present-day education; their ideas are present-day ideas. Youth, freed from the prejudices of the past, should be able to put into action the ideas which modern society demands—but to which the slogan-shouters do little more than pay lip service. Young leaders everywhere in the world find they are having to fight that Victorian attitude, and you can help them.

I believe that you, the youth of Africa, can understand that the role of African nationalism is different—or should be different—from the nationalism of the past; that the African national state is an instrument for the unification of Africa, and not for dividing Africa; that African nationalism is meaningless, is dangerous, is anachronistic, if it is not at the same time Pan-Africanism.

17. *Nnamdi Azikiwe*

Nnamdi Azikiwe was born in northern Nigeria in 1904 and was educated in mission schools and at Lagos, the capital. In 1925, he went to the United States and studied at Lincoln University, Howard University (where he received his B.A. degree), Columbia University, and the University of Pennsylvania (where he received graduate degrees in both arts and science). In 1938, he returned to Nigeria, where he established the newspaper West African Pilot *and became active in Nigerian politics. In 1944, he founded the National Council of Nigeria and the Cameroons, now one of the governing parties in Nigeria. In 1948, he was elected to the Legislative Council of Nigeria. From 1954 to 1959, Azikiwe served as Prime Minister of the Eastern Region of Nigeria, and in January, 1960, he was elected President of the Nigerian Senate. When Nigeria became independent, in November, 1960, he became Governor-General of the Federation of Nigeria. It was in this capacity, as Nigerian head of state, that he delivered an address (ex-*

cerpts reprinted below) to the Lagos Conference of African nations. In Azikiwe's earlier speeches (reprinted below), he defends party government and an organized opposition as essential components of democracy.

PARLIAMENT AND PARTIES*

The Party System

Thanks to the growth of political consciousness in this country, our people are becoming acquainted with the practice of parliamentary democracy. This has been used as a criterion to determine the political maturity of any people under the rule of others, and we can be no exception. As a matter of fact, it is a declared policy of Britain that no colony can be considered ready for self-government until it has made parliamentary democracy a political reality. In plain words, Britain is unwilling to confer the honor of self-government on any of its colonial territories until there is a full-fledged two-party system in operation. Our meeting today can be rightly regarded as a test of the efficacy of parliamentary democracy in Nigeria, because the items on the agenda indicate that we are due for serious heart-searching so far as the workings of the party system are concerned.

I must remind you that the party system of government is based on the control of public opinion. It is a systematic attempt by an interested group to control the political attitude of people through the use of suggestions and consequently to control their actions. Naturally, this arises from interested motives which have the primary purpose of obtaining public support for a particular idea or course of action. This makes it quite clear that the party system is a political medium to control the behavior of the public through diverse means of propaganda. The machinery of such an institution works smoothly on the basis of majority rule. In the words of John Locke: "A state is established through the agreement of a number of persons who unite themselves to live together in peace

* Excerpts from a speech delivered by Azikiwe on October 3, 1952; reprinted, by permission, from *Zik: A Selection from Speeches of Nnamdi Azikiwe* (New York: Cambridge University Press, 1961).

and to protect themselves in common against others, and who, for this purpose, subject themselves to the will of the majority. That was—and only that could have been—the beginning of every legally constituted government."

You will remember that on the eve of the Macpherson Constitution, we decided to constitute ourselves into a political party in order to persuade the majority of voters that our policy is the best suited for the political advancement of this country. We carried out propaganda and gained a considerable following which has enabled us to crystallize into an autonomous government in the Eastern Region, and an opposition party in the Western Region. We have now to take stock of our stewardship and chart our bearings on the boisterous sea of Nigerian politics. In doing so, we should attempt to detect the flaws in our party machinery, repair them, rebuild the machinery, and give it a new lease of life; but we must not destroy it.

Unless we are not conscious of our obligations to our various electorates, it is patent that none can denounce the system of party government in our country today without betraying the public trust. That being the case, I propose to make a résumé of the rationale of party politics in our country. As you are aware, a political party is an organization of voters freely and voluntarily formed, for the attainment of common ends. There is, however, an irresistible tendency actually to control the reins of government, and in so doing, there is a concentration of power in the hands of the few people who are willing and have the time and ability to practice those arts by means of which executive control is obtained and exercised. Since there must be conflict of views and clash of opinions among human beings, on a range of issues, it is but rational that those who hold substantially similar views upon any subject should draw together into cooperative effort in order to attain these ends; hence Edmund Burke defined a political party as "a body of men united for promoting by their joint endeavors the national interest, upon some particular principle in which they all are agreed."

It is universally accepted that the party system is the only effective *modus operandi* of parliamentary democracy. It is the result of the experience of sovereign nations through the ages, and no better substitute has been devised. The nature of its functions is variegated, but these run a gamut in almost all the ramifications of political activities, to wit:

1. Disseminating political propaganda and doctrines of the party.

2. Formulating positive policies which find expression in party platforms or manifestoes and other official pronouncements of party leaders.

3. Nominating candidates for public office and pledging the vote of the party to its candidates.

4. Conducting election campaigns involving the use of every conceivable device for convincing and persuading the electorate that the policies which its candidates represent are preferable to those of their rivals.

5. Controlling, after elections, the policy-forming organs of government so as to materialize the principles embodied in the party platform.

Thus it can be broadly stated that political parties function in order to make representative democracy workable, especially over large areas, through elections, referendums, and crystallization of public opinion. They facilitate decisions on vital issues by becoming an avenue through which the electorate may subordinate lesser differences of opinion for the good of the country. They also serve as a unifying force by controlling the various organs of government, and thereby secure harmonious and consistent policy and administration. There can be no doubt that party control is essential to an effective practicalization of democracy. As a former President of the United States said: "This is a government by parties, and there should be a party responsibility. When a policy has been pledged, the party should carry it out, and the leader who leads his party to performance is to be commended."

Since our party has been entrusted with the sacred responsibility of directly and indirectly guiding the destiny of two regions of the country, we have an obligation to make the party system of government a constructive force in our national life. We can do this by becoming consistent in our policy. Any party member who deviates from the norm of party policy must be seriously censured, since his behavior will stultify the ideal of party system of government. Therefore, we cannot accept party politics on the one hand, and then reject it on the other. We are either party-conscious, or we are not. If we belong to the former category, then we must be loyal to the party without qualification. By this I do not intend to imply the cultivation of servility or clannishness, which generate friction of an acrimonious nature, but within the bounds of reason, one can be a party man without necessarily being regarded as chauvinistic or unpatriotic. To think otherwise is either advertising ignorance of the party system of government or indicating distrust of it.

PARLIAMENTARY DEMOCRACY*

The domestic policy of Nigeria will be framed on the assumption that Nigeria shall continue to be a parliamentary democracy. The government of Nigeria shall exercise power so long as it retains the confidence of the legislature. It will express its belief in parliamentary democracy as government by discussion, based on the consent of the governed, whose will is collectively expressed by the majority of the duly accredited representatives of an electorate that is based on a universal adult suffrage and votes by secret ballot at periodic elections.

The expression of such belief in parliamentary democracy should take the following forms:

First, the government should recognize the existence of an opposition as an essential ingredient of democracy, and vote a salary in its budget for payment to the leader of the opposition; this salary should not be diminished during the tenure of office of such government.

Secondly, the government should express publicly its adherence to the rule of law and respect for human dignity, and should scrupulously act accordingly.

Thirdly, the government should at all times be prepared to support and not hesitate to enforce the fundamental human rights in order to ensure particularly freedom of speech, freedom of the press, freedom of peaceful assembly, freedom of association, and freedom of movement.

Fourthly, the government should protect the property of the citizen by ensuring and enforcing the right of the individual to

* Excerpts from a speech delivered on July 31, 1959; reprinted, by permission, from *Zik*.

enjoy his private property, and to be justly and adequately compensated if he is compulsorily deprived of the same.

Lastly, the government should act energetically and proclaim its belief in the right of the people of Nigeria to live in a society which respects free enterprise and which provides social security for its inhabitants.

Unless an opposition exists—as a "shadow cabinet" capable of replacing the government—democracy becomes a sham. We should not hesitate to put our stewardship as a government through the crucible of organized public opinion. We should be tolerant and allow our official actions to be thoroughly scrutinized no matter how it hurts. Failure to tolerate the existence of an opposition party would be disastrous to the existence of democracy. It is the easiest invitation to dictatorship, and we should eschew autocracy in any form. We should not give the impression that we have extinguished British colonial rule only to enthrone in its stead its Nigerian counterpart.

By adhering to the rule of law, we shall protect Nigerians from the forms of arbitrariness which are a specialty of power-drunk politicians. We shall ensure the independence of the judiciary and insulate the civil service, the police, and the armed forces from being subverted for political ends. All Nigerians should be equal before the law, and justice should be done without fear or favor. Discrimination should not be practiced on account of race, tribe, creed, or station in life. A Nigerian should be free to enjoy citizenship rights and privileges anywhere in Nigeria without molestation.

AFRICAN UNITY*

The main reason for convening this conference is to exchange views among African leaders at the highest possible level for the unity of the political entities comprising the continent of Africa. There have been conferences of this nature in the past, but this particular conference is very significant because it is the first time in African history that so many heads of state and governments

* Excerpts from a speech delivered by Azikiwe to the Lagos Conference of Heads of African States on January 25, 1962.

have assembled to confer among themselves for the future security and stability of African countries.

The importance of this continent to the world cannot be over-stressed. Africa is regarded by authorities as the birthplace of the human race. Africa is also regarded by them as the cradle of human civilization. In fact, we have at this conference the Emperor of Ethiopia, whose empire dates back to antiquity and was contemporaneous with Egypt, Nubia, Assyria, and Phoenicia. Thus, as a hub of human culture and treasury of natural resources, Africa became a magnet that attracted Greek intellectuals, Roman adventurers, European and American explorers, missionaries, empire-builders, storytellers, and soldiers of fortune.

Up to the period of the great discoveries made by European explorers, several empires and kingdoms flourished in Africa at all points of the compass. These nations compared most favorably with their contemporaries in Europe and Asia. Then came the revival of learning and the invention of gunpowder as a weapon of warfare and as an instrument of political control. These African empires and kingdoms disintegrated partly as a result of disunity created by fratricidal struggles for power and partly because of the slave trade.

Napata and Meroe are now ruins of an ancient civilization. Ghana, Mali, Mellestine, Mossi, Songhay, and Bornu are now relics of a medieval civilization. The Ashanti, Yoruba, Dahomey, Benin, and Hausa kingdoms are now objects of historical research. Zimbabwe, Monomotapa, Zulu, and the other kingdoms of East and Central Africa are now revered reminders of a historic past. Brother fought against brother, and the slave trade depopulated the realms ruled by both. And Africa became a "dark continent."

In this process of acculturation through the centuries, this continent was pillaged, and its inhabitants were pilloried under a most brutal and ruthless form of oppression, ranging from slavery to colonialism. By the middle of the twentieth century, a social revolution pervaded the continent, and this has brought in its train periodical tornadoes of change which are sweeping away the cobwebs and grime of the past to make room for the present political rebirth in Africa.

The era of the degradation of Africa lingered until the end of World War II, when only four African countries were sovereign states. Five years ago, there were only eight. But today, there are twenty-nine sovereign states in Africa, to be increased to thirty when Uganda becomes independent on October 9, 1962.

This brief excursion into the remote and immediate past of Africa is necessary in order for us to appreciate the political *risorgimento* taking place in contemporary Africa. It is also a lamp to guide our steps into the future, so that we may realize the value of unity and cooperation as factors in the evolution of nations in any continent.

Unlike Vienna, this conference has not been summoned for us to conspire to arrest the development of democratic institutions or the rule of law in Africa. Unlike Berlin, we have not congregated to partition any continent and gratify our territorial and expansionist ambitions to build colonial empires. Unlike Versailles, we have not met as victors to exact indemnity from the vanquished and divide the spoils of war. Rather, we have gathered in Lagos in a most solemn atmosphere to find practical approaches to the solution of problems of coexistence among independent states in Africa, on the basis of certain fundamental principles of international relations.

As members of the United Nations, all the states represented here agree with its purposes and principles: namely, "to maintain international peace and security . . . to develop friendly relations among nations, based on respect for the principle of equal rights and self-determination of peoples . . . to achieve international cooperation in solving international problems of an economic, social, cultural, or humanitarian character . . . to be a center for harmonizing the actions of nations in the attainment of these common ends."

The Lagos Conference looks at the continent of Africa as a miniature United Nations and seeks to adapt to Africa the tried and tested principles which guide the conduct of the member states of that international organization. If we succeed in this task, we shall have established the authority of the African states and shall command respect for the African peoples. This is very vital today, when the magnets of economic imperialism and neocolonialism are drawing the Western and Eastern blocs of the Cold War to intensify their struggle for hegemony in Africa.

At Monrovia, in May, 1961, the participants of this conference evolved a *modus vivendi* for African states, to enable them and their inhabitants not to live under the shadow of fear and insecurity to life and property. The principles enunciated in Monrovia include the following: the right of African states to equality of sovereignty, irrespective of size, area, or density of population; the right of African states to federate or confederate with any other state or states; the right of African states to respect for the principle of noninterference in their internal affairs; the right of African states to territorial integrity and inviolability by any other state.

The above principles are generally accepted and respected as a basis of relations among states in accordance with the law and custom governing the conduct of sovereign states. We in Nigeria feel that the acceptance of the above principles would, in the language of an African elder statesman, President Tubman, achieve greater understanding and a more positive attitude of cooperation among African states.

The experts who represented the Monrovia African states met at Dakar and recommended, among other things, the promotion of trade among African countries—through a regional customs union, the introduction of a common external tariff, harmonized policies of economic development, the establishment of a network of roads and other communications linking contiguous African countries, the exchange of economic information, and the founding of an African development bank.

We should take cognizance of the absence of certain African states, whose presence at this Conference is very much desired but whose absence is quite understandable. Six African states met at Casablanca on January 3–7, 1961, at the invitation of the late King Mohammed V of Morocco, to discuss the Congo situation. At the conclusion of the Casablanca Conference, the conferees reaffirmed their faith in the previous conferences of independent African states held in Accra in 1958 and in Addis Ababa in 1960; and they appealed to all African states to associate themselves with their common action for the consolidation of liberty in Africa and the building up of its unity and security. Then, they unanimously reaffirmed their unshakable adherence to the United Nations Charter and to the declarations of the Afro-Asian Conference held in Bandung, with the aim of promoting cooperation among all the peoples of the world and of consolidating international peace.

Having decided to form an African consultative assembly, the Casablanca states urged the creation of an African political committee, an African economic committee, an African cultural committee, and a joint African high command. At Conakry, the experts of these states recommended the establishment of a common market, the ending of customs barriers between their countries over five years (from January 1, 1962), the ending of quota systems and preferential treatment (from the same date), the creation of a council of African economic unity, the establishment of an African economic development bank, and, possibly the formation of a joint air and shipping company.

It should be noted that the Monrovia Conference was originally sponsored by six African states: Cameroon, Guinea, Liberia, Ivory Coast, Mali, and Nigeria. It was thought that these countries would be fully representative of the shades of political alignment in Africa at that time—namely, the Brazzaville states, the Casablanca states, and states which, then as now, were uncommitted. A few days before the Monrovia Conference, the foreign ministers of the Casablanca states met at Accra and decided that no Casablanca state should attend the Monrovia Conference. Consequently, Guinea and Mali, which had previously cosponsored the conference, reneged.

We have witnessed the same tactics recently, on the eve of the Lagos Conference. A meeting of foreign ministers of the Casablanca states met at Accra, last week, and by the weekend, they announced their decision not to attend the Lagos Conference. This means that of the twenty-eight African states (with a total population of 193.3 million) invited to attend this conference, twenty-one states (with a population of 135.1 million) have accepted the invitation to attend, while five Casablanca states (with a population of 53.1 million) have declined the invitation, and two states, Tunisia and Libya (whose total population is 5.1 million) declined to attend because the Provisional Government of Algeria was not invited. I have not included the Republic of South Africa, because it was not invited.

From general observation, it would appear that there is not much to choose between the accord reached by the member states of the Casablanca Conference and those of the Monrovia Conference. This is true to an extent, if the economic, cultural, educational, scientific, and technical programs of the two conferences are analyzed. But there is one basic difference of an ideological nature between the two groups which should attract the serious attention of all who sincerely advocate African unity. It is the conspicuous absence of specific declaration, on the part of the

Casablanca states, of their inflexible belief in the fundamental principles enunciated at Monrovia regarding the inalienable right of African states, as presently constituted, to legal equality, irrespective of their area and population; the right of African states to self-determination; the right of African states to safety from interference in their internal affairs through subversive activities engineered by supposedly friendly states; the right of African states to be secure in the inviolability of their territories from external aggression.

While the Charter of the United Nations provides for these safeguards in general terms, it is very material to the subject of African unity that its votaries should declare publicly and recapitulate their faith and firm belief by adhering specifically to the principles made famous at the Monrovia Conference. Otherwise, it can be a matter for speculation whether these principles are capable of becoming specters to haunt the conscience of those who would rather pay lip service to the Charter of the United Nations, while secretly nursing expansionist ambitions against their smaller and perhaps weaker neighbors.

We believe in the good intentions of the Casablanca states, but in the higher interest of African unity it is now a categorical imperative that all African states should declare publicly their adherence to the policy of nonintervention in the internal affairs of each other and their unscrupulous respect for the right of all African states, large or small, to coexist in accordance with the established principles and practice of the law of nations and the customs and usages of international intercourse.

The Lagos Conference, as an appanage of the Monrovia Conference, should tackle the problems of African unity with realism. At Monrovia, we agreed on a *modus vivendi*, and our experts met at Dakar to suggest specific means of attaining economic, cultural, educational, scientific, and technical cooperation which should lead to any political *rapprochement* that would be practicable. Our task at this conference is to unravel the *modus operandi* that would establish the effective unity that is so highly desirable in Africa. . . .

The unity this conference seeks is not one that is based on regimented uniformity. Total unity in Africa is impossible, as it is in all the other continents of the earth, but we can develop unity in diversity and channel diversity in unity, as the successful experience of Nigeria has shown. In the common search for unity in Africa, our diversity as densely populated and sparsely populated states can be a source of inspiration. So too, the smallness and largeness in sizes of our territories. The fact that some African states are members of the French Community, while some are members of the Commonwealth, and some are members of the Casablanca bloc should be a tower of strength to show how heterogeneous groups can be welded to become homogeneous in any field of human endeavor through prudent statesmanship.

Our identification with the United Nations is strategic because our numerical strength is now between one-fourth and one-third of its membership. With wisdom and restraint, coupled with adroit diplomacy, African states can be instrumental in building a hate-free, greed-free, and fear-free world, where man's inhumanity to man will either molder or wither or disappear.

The cause of African unity speeds on. The African states can be as separate as fingers in their domestic matters, but can be as united as the fist in matters of external and general concern. African states should be independent in all things that matter for human progress, but should be neutral in nothing which affects the destiny of this historic continent. The general aim of African states should be to build in Africa a democratic society, where there shall be peace and plenty and where no man is oppressed. Through mutual cooperation and respect for the fundamental rights of man and nations, we shall yet succeed in forging unity of purpose and identity of interest among the diverse peoples of Africa. . . .

Let us get on with the job of statesmanship to forge unity in this great continent. Our success would be a shining example to the other continents, which had their chance, but failed humanity at many crucial periods of history. History smiles on us today, and we have a great opportunity to revive the stature of man in the world and restore the dignity of man in Africa.

With faith in the ultimate success of our honest endeavors to safeguard human liberty, let us build a new Africa for a new world, where man no longer shall be a wolf to man.

18. Obafemi Awolowo

Obafemi Awolowo was born in 1909 in a small village in western Nigeria. He worked his way through primary school, graduating at the age of sixteen. He then became a teacher, won a scholarship to secondary school in Ibadan, and went to the University of London, where he earned degrees in commerce and law. On his return to Nigeria, he entered the field of journalism and politics. In 1951, he broke with Nnamdi Azikiwe to form his own political party, the Action Group, which won control in the Western Region of Nigeria, of which he became Premier in 1954. Since 1960, he has headed the Action Group opposition in the federal House of Representatives, although a financial scandal and political difficulties in the Western Region have recently undermined his position in Nigerian politics. He is generally regarded as more vigorously anti-Communist than many African leaders, and his party's electoral position leads him to oppose the one-party state as it has developed in African theory and practice.

A CRITIQUE OF ONE-PARTY SYSTEMS*

Apart from the united resolve of Nigerian leaders to keep the country together, there are two important factors which, if fully employed, will make for the permanent and harmonious unity of Nigeria. The first is the acceptance and the practical unfoldment of federalism, with all its implications, as the only suitable form of constitution for Nigeria. . . . The second is the pursuit and the

* Reprinted, by permission, from *Awo: The Autobiography of Chief Obafemi Awolowo* (New York: Cambridge University Press, 1961).

preservation of a democratic way of life in the conduct of our governmental affairs. Any departure or continued falling short at any level from this form of government might gravely threaten the unity of Nigeria and weaken her influence in the comity of nations. In view of what I have said before, any deterioration in the corporate existence of the country would be bound to provoke a countermovement, the form and extent of which I would not now dare to predict. Government by dictatorship is maintainable only by the use of force and by various acts of repression and oppression against those who disagree with or are critical of the dictator. One of the lessons which history has repeatedly taught, however, is that, however repressed it may be, mankind cannot permanently attune itself to the base and inhuman conditions of a dictatorship. Sooner or later (and in these modern times it is now sooner than later), those who have been repressed make an adamant and irrepressible bid for their liberation. The degree of the intensity of this counteraction would, to a large extent, depend on the degree of the depravity of the situation which it is sought to remedy. Russian Communism, with its diminishing human degradation, is a logical sequel to the gross and infernal excesses of Czarism. In all its long history, Russia has never known democracy. And it will be long after those generations which knew the Czarist days have died off before liberal democracy could ever have a chance of rearing its head among the Russians. The point must be stressed, however, that Russia is not a good example for aspiring dictators. Nor is Nigeria, on independence, likely to provide a fertile soil for more than a very limited period for the flourishing of autocracy at the federal, regional, or local level. In our case, we are fortunate that on the eve of independence, Britain has, at our demand and with our active cooperation, planted in our soil the sturdy plant of democracy. Those who have contributed to the achievement of this end will, I am sure, not relax their vigilance and efforts in the proper nurture of this new and glorious plant.

After independence, Britain will have no right to interfere in our affairs. Whatever association or cooperation there is between Nigeria and Britain would have to be voluntary. But it will not do for Britain and her friends in the Western democracies to say anything which would harmfully affect the activities of those who have dedicated themselves to the sacred task of guarding the existence and fostering the sturdier growth of our young plant of democracy. Similarly, it would be an act of bad faith for her to encourage, by tacit or other means, any group of people who might wish to contrive the destruction or sterilization of that plant, on the pretext that a nondescript plant of African origin and of better efficacy is more suited to Nigerian soil. I make these points because there is a newfangled theory now being propounded with erudition and gusto in the countries of the so-called Western democracies. The proponents of this theory hold the view that it is inappropriate and hardly fair to expect a newly emergent African nation to practice democracy as it is known and practiced in the countries of Western Europe and the United States. Every mortal blow that is struck by an independent African nation at the vitals of democracy is rationalized by these theorists as the African's peculiar method of adapting democratic usages to his barbaric and primitive environment. The denial of fundamental human rights, the destruction of the rule of law, and the suppression of opposition have been brilliantly and felicitously rationalized. The outrageous declaration by an African leader that a one-party system is in accord with the democratic way of life has been ably defended by these spokesmen of the Western democracies.

Two things strike me forcibly in this strange and apologetic attitude of the Western democracies toward the debasement of the great ideal of democracy. The first is this: The nationals of these imperial powers, for a number of reasons which are well known, have always had a feeling of superiority toward the peoples of their former colonial territories. When these colonial peoples attain to freedom, though they are discharged from the bondage of political subjection and inferiority, they are regarded as nominally equal in status to their former masters—but only nominally. For it would appear that in their heart of hearts, the white peoples, especially those of the Western world, still regard an African society as a group of inferior races, notwithstanding that they are politically independent. In this connection, the British people are the worst offenders. They are never tired of expatiating, to the point of nausea, on the length of time—the number of centuries—it took them to evolve from feudalism to democracy. This is an indisputable historical fact, and British contributions to human civilization are acknowledged. But our British friends overdo the story when they try to make it appear that the height which they have now reached and keep to can only be effectively scaled by their fellow English-speaking peoples. One brilliant

English writer has said: "Politicians should never read history books, and should cultivate short memories. Many owe their downfall to misguided attempts to translate the lessons of the past into current policies." In one sense, this is cynical advice, and in another it is a wise admonition. We must read history books, and do more than merely read them: We must learn, mark, and inwardly digest what we have read. We must do all this if we would avoid a repetition of the costly mistakes of the past, and benefit from the accumulated wisdom of the ages. But we must not in the process allow the facts of our national history, however noble and peerless, to occupy our minds to the extent of making us feel superior to other peoples. Specifically, the British must stop imagining and propagating the erroneous view that their achievements in the art of democracy are beyond the reach of others, or that the slow and painful course of their evolution must in other cases be strictly followed. It must always be remembered that we are now living in an age in which all that is good and bad on our planet is indivisible. Under existing conditions, latecomers have the singular advantage of benefiting from the experiences and accomplishments of older nations.

The second is a deliberate, subconscious, or unwitting confusion between the ideal on the one hand, and the methods by which the ideal is realized in practice on the other. The ideal of democracy is not liable to modification or distortion, even though mankind has invented different methods for its realization. In a democracy, the government must rule with the consent of the governed. The governed are inalienably entitled at periodic intervals to give this consent to the same or a different set of people who form the government. The expression of such consent must be free and unfettered, and must on no account be stultified or rigged. Furthermore, the consent must never be obtained by duress, threat, or intimidation, by undue influence or fraud. These are the principles which underlie the ideal of democracy. Wherever these principles (or any of them) are tampered with or abrogated, the resulting situation is anything but democracy. We all know that while these principles are solemnly observed in India, Britain, and the United States, the methods of their application differ among these countries. So the methods could differ in any African nation. But it is an affront to the African peoples to suggest that they are incapable of applying these principles.

Democracy and a one-party system of government are, in my

opinion, mutually exclusive. Under a one-party system, the party in power arrogates to itself the right to be the only ruling party for all time. All other parties, therefore, which differ from or are in opposition to it are either suppressed or absorbed. At subsequent elections, if there are any, the consent of the people cannot be said to be genuinely sought and freely given, because there is only one choice open to the electorate. Human nature is not susceptible to mass regimentation. Wherever there are two or more persons, divergence of opinion is bound to exist. Besides, there is, more often than not, more than one side to every question of national importance. The people are entitled to be given the chance to examine all sides of the problems confronting them, before expressing their majority will at the polls. Such an examination, however, will be possible only where people who hold different shades of opinions are allowed to organize themselves into parties if they wish, and are also free to explain their respective points of view to the electorate, who are the final arbiters as to which of the contending parties should be given the mandate to govern for any ensuing statutory period.

In acting as the apologists for those who destroy and discredit democracy, the spokesmen of the Western democracies do grievous harm to that noble ideal which they profoundly cherish, and which they are prepared to defend with their lives (as they have done in the past) if its practice in their homelands is at any time threatened. Communism is by reason of its birth a revolutionary and aggressive tenet. It is a legitimate reaction of the extreme Left to the tyranny of narrow-minded and callous rulers of the extreme Right. For centuries, the masses of the people have groaned under the remorseless heel of a privileged few, and every attempt by them to assert their wishes has been mercilessly suppressed and punished. On the other hand, democracy by its very nature is not a militant doctrine which can be imposed on others by means of violence and subversion. Free and unfettered consent can only be obtained by persuasion. But this is no reason for allowing a counterfeit imitation or a complete reversion of a great ideal to circulate as genuine currency. Communists have laid down dogmatic methods for the practice of Communism. Any deviation from the methods thus promulgated, even where the ideal is still being faithfully pursued, is condemned and denounced as deviationism. There are no dogmas for the practice of democracy; and democrats cannot and must not censure any nation on the ground of deviationism. But they must at least have the courage and honesty to insist that a flagrant departure from the ideal of democracy is not an acceptable variant of the most beneficent and ennobling form of government that mankind in all its long and checkered history has evolved.

THE EAST-WEST STRUGGLE AND
AFRICAN NATIONALISM*

There are two distinct ideological camps in the world today: the Western democracies and the Communist bloc. For reasons I will presently give, my preference is unhesitatingly and unequivocally for the Western democracies. No nation in the world is absolutely good or absolutely evil. There is still a color bar in the Western democracies. Negroes in America are still being discriminated against and can still be lynched with impunity. For her part, Britain is still guilty as before—though in a decreasing order of magnitude—of injustice to the black peoples in East and Central Africa. But such evils as are committed in the countries of the Western democracies toward the weaker peoples of the world are not only fast diminishing, but are being constantly subjected to strong and sharp criticisms in those countries by their nationals, without any risk to their lives or personal freedom. If you did likewise behind the Iron Curtain, you would not live to fight another day.

The world in which we live is still very far from perfection. We have got to take it as we find it and, like conscientious and honest people, strive to contribute toward its peace, progress, and happiness. From time to time, things will happen which in his judgment one individual considers to be wrong. Whether the individual is right or wrong in his judgment, he has an inherent and inalienable right to entertain such an opinion and to express it. The question is where, as between the Western bloc and the Eastern bloc, can a man freely exercise his natural right to hold and express any opinion, subject to such restrictions as may be laid down by laws enacted by the freely elected parliament of the land? The answer is obvious: It is in the Western bloc. As has been abundantly

* Reprinted, by permission, from *Awo*.

shown, we in Nigeria have won our freedom mainly as a result of unrestrained organized public opinion against the continuance of British rule. In our struggles against British rule we have enjoyed the support of many Britons as well. Besides, in the Commonwealth of Nations, a member nation could hold and express any views it likes. But that is not the way it is done in the Communist community of nations.

In the present world context, when atheistic materialism is threatening to destroy or stifle all that is best and noblest in man, neutrality in international affairs—whether passive, positive, or independent—is an unmitigated disservice to humanity. My own analysis has led me to the conclusion that neutrality as the basis of the foreign policy of certain nations is no more and no less than the projection, conscious or unconscious, of the deep-seated prejudices which those nations have had toward some of the countries of the Western democracies. But I must urge that in our foreign relations, we must forget the past and work for the future—the great future of our land and of mankind. As between contending forces, we should have enough courage to make up our minds, independent of any outside influence, as to which side is relatively right and which side is relatively wrong. Having made up our minds, we should have the honesty to pronounce our view and stand. To pretend that neither of two diametrically opposed ideological camps is right or wrong, especially if we occupy an influential position in the assembly of nations, is to encourage evil-doing and to damp the ardor for well-doing. There is a divine injunction as well as an attendant sanction which nations, like individuals, must never ignore. God Almighty, speaking to us through one of his prophets in Revelations III, 15–16, says to the neutrals:

I know thy works, that thou art neither cold nor hot: I would thou wert cold or hot. So then because thou art lukewarm, and neither cold nor hot, I will spue thee out of my mouth.

There is a policy which appears to be in vogue among some of the developing countries of the world. In their quest for financial and technical assistance, they adopt the tactics of wooing the nations of the two blocs at the same time, in the hope that in the anxious bid for new supporters or converts, they (the developing countries) will get the best of two worlds. I consider these tactics to be both disreputable and dangerous. Disreputable, in the sense that it amounts in my view to diplomatic double-dealing. If we want help from more than one nation, by all means let us seek it. But it is immoral to play two opposing forces against each other in the process. It is this kind of diplomacy that has been responsible for the fall of many nations in the past, for the many wars and incalculable miseries which have afflicted mankind, and for the tormenting fears and the mortifying distrust among nations which the world is now witnessing. The tactics are dangerous because acts of double-dealing (whether diplomatic or otherwise) never pay in the end. There are times when even the greatest tactician in diplomatic cunning is outclassed in his own game. It is then that he discovers that all he thought he had gained is but loss, and what is left of national honor and dignity is but the shadow of an illustrious past that is gone forever or of a potentially great future that will never come.

Pan-Africanism

A good deal has been said and written about Pan-Africanism. No one has as yet precisely defined what it means. The phrase has been indiscriminately used to denote government of the whole of Africa—the United States of Africa, or an all-African nationalist movement. I am firmly of the opinion that it is visionary now, and for many years to come, to labor for the emergence of a United States of Africa, or even of economic cooperation (such as exists in Western Europe) among all the countries of Africa. It is unrealistic in the extreme to expect that African nations, which have only recently won their independence from foreign rule, would be willing to surrender or even diminish their sovereignty in the pursuit of what is quite plainly an *ignis fatuus*. Apart from the impracticability of the proposition, any serious attempt to bring about political union among the states of Africa is sure to engender suspicion, distrust, and disharmony among those states. Economic and cultural association among the states of Africa, such as has brought into being the European Common Market, is no less fanciful than political union. Such an association presupposes, by and large, common economic problems and a similarity of political institutions and of social and cultural patterns among the participating countries. While most of the countries of the western zone of Africa have many things in common, the same is not true of all the countries of Africa.

Two instances may be cited to illustrate the points which I have just made. The first instance is Egypt. It is true that, physically and geographically, Egypt is in Africa. But apart from the fact that her entire political heart is in the Arab world, she has never regarded herself as having any social and cultural affinity with the black races of Africa. The United Arab Republic, the pet creature of Nasser, which has one foot in Africa and another in the Middle East, is the very antithesis of a workable African community. In view of his undisguised totalitarianism, and his territorial ambitions in Africa and the Moslem world, effective cooperation with Nasser—in any field at all—would be possible only if the black races of Africa were prepared to remain satellites in Egypt's orbit, as Syria now is.* Besides, there is no similarity between the economic and social problems of Egypt and ours. The second instance is South Africa, together with other such countries in Africa. In South Africa, the Central African Federation, and Algeria, the white settlers are in the minority, but they insist on dominating the indigenous African majorities. It is farfetched to imagine that there is any real community of interests between the black races of Africa and these domineeering white settlers.

As an all-African nationalist movement, Pan-Africanism can be a most potent organization if its membership is confined to black Africans and to those nationals of Africa, whatever the color of their skin, who believe in the absolute equality of all races. In this sense, Pan-Africanism should aim at giving active support to all dependent African peoples in their struggles for liberation. It should by constitutional means do all in its power to exterminate from the face of Africa the practice of racial discrimination and superiority, such as exists in South Africa, the Central African Federation, and East Africa. If the aims and objects of Pan-Africanism are limited in this way, and are not extended to the pursuit of a Pan-African government, the movement is decidedly on the right path, and Nigeria should give to it her fullest possible backing.

* This was written before Syria withdrew from the United Arab Republic in late 1961.—Ed.

19. Mamadou Dia

Mamadou Dia, who is Prime Minister of Senegal, was born in Khombole, Senegal, in 1910. He was educated in Senegal and taught in secondary schools there until after World War II, when he became active in the politics of French-speaking Africa. In 1948, he was elected to the Council of the Republic, the upper house of the French Parliament under the Fourth Republic. He represented Senegal in the French National Assembly from 1956 to 1958, returning to Senegal when the new constitution of the Fifth Republic hastened its evolution to full independence. Dia became Premier of Senegal and Vice Premier of the short-lived Federation of Mali (before its breakup in August, 1960). An economist by training, he has written a number of books about economic problems in French-speaking Africa. In the following selection— taken from the English translation of his book Nations Africaines et Solidarité Mondiale, *published in France in 1960—Dia is critical of Soviet aid and of certain types of African neutralism.*

INDEPENDENCE AND
NEOCOLONIALISM*

It would be a fatal error for the nations of the *Tiers-Monde,* especially those just recovering their freedom, to think that the struggle ends with the proclamation of independence. This admittedly is an important phase of the struggle, but it is only a first step that allows us to face up to basic tasks and crucial questions, and to apply bold solutions. A number of recently liberated states

* Excerpts from Mamadou Dia, *The African Nations and World Solidarity,* translated by Mercer Cook (New York: Frederick A. Praeger, 1961); reprinted by permission.

have understood fully that sovereignty in this world is real only when justified technically and economically. This is true of Israel, whose creative dynamism is constructing an imposing personality in a Middle East where most of its neighbors are not friendly. This is also true of Tunisia, where the realism of the leaders and, quite simply, of the Tunisian nation is starting the country along the road to development. This is the example that we are trying to follow in Mali.* One cannot warn too strongly against the illusions of nominal independence that would encourage a kind of internal immobility in so far as the old structures are concerned, and a close dependence on relations with the industrialized world.

To imagine subjects for political agitation is always easy. We know that one of the resources of leaders struggling with domestic difficulties is to invent a foreign scapegoat. It would be a mistake to exaggerate the possibilities of this "psychological action" that has become a method of governing.

We cannot indefinitely divert the attention of the masses from their condition, and postpone *sine die* the moment of reckoning. We will watch especially for a radical transformation of the economic relations with developed countries, a necessary condition for real development and consequently for real independence. On this point as well, we must view the situation clearly. The task will be difficult, for in the shadow of newly acquired independence a veritable strategy of dependence is cleverly contrived, heralding the advent of a neocolonialism.

The Soviet offensive in the underdeveloped countries, the threat of the Cold War that weighs on African states, eloquently illustrate this new evolution toward economic colonialism. It has been estimated that during the second quarter of 1957, nearly 2,300 [Soviet] technicians worked in nineteen countries for an average of a month and a half. During the same year, Soviet universities and enterprises received about 2,000 technicians from the underdeveloped countries for training. In so far as technical aid offers the possibility of ideological conquest, we must measure all the dangers—not in order to reject it, but to take the indispensable precautions. Furthermore, the countries of the East have devised a formula for aid, replacing gifts by a policy of credits with favor-

* This was written prior to August 19, 1960, while Senegal and the Sudan still formed the short-lived Mali Federation.—ED.

able repayment terms and interest (sometimes lower than the international rate of 1.5 per cent). But it is known that this form of assistance subjects the countries that receive it to an intolerable dependence, by depriving them of their freedom to buy wherever they please and forcing them to supply themselves from the lending countries almost exclusively.

It will be noted, moreover, that often there is a clause requiring reimbursement in capital goods, and finally, in the case of the U.S.S.R., the prices of goods delivered under contract are fixed unilaterally. The amount of this aid from the East to the underdeveloped countries has roughly equaled, until recently, the total volume of credits granted by the World Bank to more than twenty countries: about $2 billion, of which $378 million is for military aid, and the balance, $1.6 billion, for economic aid. In the battle between the ruble and the dollar, the latter has triumphed, for the United States has furnished $5 billion, the Soviet Union $1.5 billion.* But the kind of assistance provided by the Eastern bloc and the emphasis on technical aid confer, indisputably, a clear propaganda advantage upon the East.

Under the pretext of positive neutralism, the temptation for the underdeveloped countries is to surrender to the highest bidder. This would mean agreeing to make development a matter for bargaining; it would mean agreeing to transform our countries into a vast arena for sordid rivalries and to expose them to tragic consequences at the very moment when they thought themselves free. Positive neutralism—truly neutral and really positive—ought to adopt as its policy a real independence with regard to the new strategies of domination, by requiring from the opposing blocs respect for the free development of emergent nations, and a radical revision of economic and especially of commercial relations, on a truly cooperative basis. . . .

Independence appears as a major advantage, if not a precondition, for helping to achieve national development. We need not stop to list its virtues. Its psychological merits, with all the potential of energy that they imply, are not the least important. We prefer to stress the dangers of an attitude of euphoria that tends to make one accept a means as an end, thus paving the way for a rude awakening. We must not forget that independence is a

* As of 1960, when this was written.—ED.

means—a potent means—to enable proletarian nations to assure their rapid development by integrating modern economies into a world economy on the basis of equitable cooperation.

Let us add immediately that no development will confer real independence from powerful economies—socialist or capitalist—that tend to strengthen their domination, unless we can achieve vast communities transcending traditional territorial limits, reversing habits of thought, and destroying old myths that narrow nationalisms try to preserve. The economies of the Middle East, of the people's democracies in the East, and of North Africa would enjoy greater progress if their development could be assured in larger groupings.

This lesson is valid for West African economies, which are perhaps exposed to even greater risks because of the Balkanized condition in which they are attaining independence. The new market that they form, at a time when East-West rivalry is so keen, makes them easy prey for a new kind of colonization. It is vain to hope that positive neutralism will assure the development of African economies. The Indian example would be misleading because India practices neutralism within an organized whole. On the contrary, the example of the neutralist policies of the Middle East, which lack the support of a coherent economic ensemble, must make us reflect upon the consequences of an attitude that may prove to be more disastrous than clever.

In the final analysis, neutralism means freedom for any imperialism to implant itself in Africa. In view of the discreteness of African economies, it means freedom to stake out the continent with outposts and various zones of influence. We realize that neutralism, which is doubtless tenable on the scale of a great African nation not yet formed, is reduced to dangerous opportunism when practiced by small nations or dwarf states subject to the temptation of outbidding each other instead of presenting a united front to resist the new strategies of domination. Narrow nationalisms reflect a lack of historical perspective and are surely ill-advised when they hope to guarantee the development of the economies they want to liberate by suddenly reversing their policies, by skillful maneuvering, or by changing partners. The road to real African independence, constructed on a solid rock of a strong economy, lies not so much in neutralism as in large regroupings that permit the concentration of poles, centers, and axes of development.

That is why Mali will be an open nation that must expand to fulfill its role.

Secondly, let us remember that to become a reality, decolonization must be accompanied by a transformation of structures, particularly economic ones. It is not enough to have a national state, a national government, a national superstructure; it is necessary to promote a progressive national policy for the entire collectivity. In the examples discussed, we have proved that growth is not development, in either the human or the collective sense of the word. There is really no development—that is to say, collective creation, in the service of the community—unless the production techniques employed, no matter how perfect, have succeeded in integrating the most important sectors of the nation within the economic system. There is really no development if the raising of production and consumption levels is restricted to a few privileged individuals, even if these be citizens. Properly speaking, there is no development of an independent economy—in so far as that can exist—without a network of economic, financial, and technical facilities, and above all, without a total reconversion of relationships between evolved economies and younger economies, of whichever camp, of whichever ideology. We now know that neither the examples taken from the socialist camp nor those from the capitalist camp can serve as models without serious modification or thorough and profound readaptation. We know that even industrialization, so necessary for the modernization of the economy, is not a sufficient guarantee against the effects of domination when it proceeds by complementary investments or when it only creates factories for raw materials, poorly linked to the country. We know that despite the socialist brotherhood repeatedly proclaimed, the rules governing trade still rest on the principle of the greatest profit for the dominant economy.

But we are no less convinced of the weaknesses of the capitalist camp, the impotence of its methods, the senility of its institutions. Its solutions cannot satisfy us. We realize the necessity for proceeding on the ruins of colonialism to a "creative destruction" that must precede the birth of a national mass economy. Otherwise, we condemn ourselves to perpetuate domestic imbalance and to maintain underdevelopment, despite political changes and the appearance of economic prosperity, if only the prosperity of the capitalist sector. Decolonization in its economic aspect is the replacement of old relationships, based on force and on ruses that are again trying to gain headway, with a fruitful dialogue between economies that share a common solidarity. This is why the doctrine of an emergent nation such as ours cannot be one of exclusive, unilateral development, but rather—to quote François Perroux—one of "mutual development." In other words, economic problems can no longer be envisaged through the lenses of the politicians, but from the viewpoint of world solidarity.

With the discovery of the *Tiers-Monde*, the science of development has made considerable progress these last few years. One of the most enriching aspects of the revolution in this domain is the discovery of the specific economic vocation of each of the various civilizations. Hitherto, many had insisted and still insist, with some justification, on the influence of foreign civilizations on the economic structures of the dominated societies, and the resulting repercussions on social structures. Henceforth, attention will be focused on the role of the economy as a criterion of civilization, thus offering the economist a new perspective that snatches him from cold scientific orthodoxy to make of him what he really is: a humanist. The reference to the universality of the basic laws of economics remains valid in large measure, but more and more it seems that economic analysis gains from being practiced by diverse civilizations that do not of necessity share the same type of organization. On the contrary, all that we know of *Tiers-Monde* civilizations indicates their rejection of the economic symbolism of the West.

A few examples will illustrate this elementary truth. Among Indian and African civilizations, which are essentially spiritualistic, the idea of economic utility is appreciated otherwise than in the old or young materialistic civilizations, or civilizations issuing from formative processes where, in spite of spiritual factors, the materialistic element dominates. This is true of Western civilizations, which resemble one another in this respect, whatever ideological divergences—as profound as Christianity and atheism—may oppose them. There, no doubt, is where we must seek an explanation for the apparently paradoxical fact that Soviet Russia feels herself to be the daughter of the same mother as Catholic France: The concept of utility is interpreted in the same way by Western countries so different in political, economic, and social regimes. Despite the differences that split them today into two distinct, antagonistic worlds, economic utility arouses in both of them the same psychological complex and is inscribed in a uniform context of values. It is understandable that the reactions it provokes on both sides are similar and that its analysis can be deduced from the same principles. By the same token, it is understandable that the reception of this "concept" is more or less identical in Asian or African societies, despite the progress of Westernism caused by the interpenetration of civilizations.

Utility for an African or Asian is determined less by rational, concrete elements than by a kind of intuitive fear, with individual interests dissolving in the totality of group interests. It is necessary to start from this ontological conception of utility to understand why it is so difficult for African or Asian civilizations—especially the former—disturbed by Western influences, to accept the monetary symbolism of the West and the fetishism of money that is the great tyranny of civilizations considered advanced. Born to affirm a system of values unrelated to the value of money, the non-Western civilizations of Africa and Asia could only produce relationships in which monetary considerations always remain secondary.

Since economy is essentially based on human and social relations, since it is in essence socialistic, in the broadest sense of the term, the rule of the accumulation of money—the foundation of capitalism—cannot be the law that will determine the formation of structures in such civilizations. The economist who wishes to do a scientific job, to make an analysis that goes to the heart of reality, can no longer be content with established schemata, fixed norms, prefabricated models. Trying to discover the intimate nature of things, to grasp facts in all their complexity, he will formulate valid rules, deduce specific laws that will explain the elaboration of the economies studied and enable them to establish the conditions of their growth. We know today, thanks to the laborious investigations of the historical school, that economic development must be considered as a long, patient advance down through the ages, a tortuous historical process involving different forms of economies that are only ephemeral.

20. *Léopold Sédar Senghor*

Léopold Sédar Senghor, President of Senegal, was born in 1907. He was educated at Catholic schools in Senegal, and at the Lycée Louis-le-Grand and the Sorbonne in Paris. Senghor was the first African to receive the prized agrégation degree. In World War II, he served with the French infantry and was imprisoned for four years by the Germans. After the war, he became active in French African politics, was elected four times as a Senegalese representative in the French National Assembly, and held cabinet posts in French governments. In 1951, he organized the Bloc Démocratique Sénégalais, which received a majority of the seats in the 1957 internal elections for a representative assembly in Senegal. In 1958, his party joined with the Senegalese Socialists under Lamine Gueyé to form the Union Progressiste Sénégalaise (UPS). The following year, Senegal joined French-speaking Sudan in the short-lived Federation of Mali, which broke apart in 1960.

The first selection below—detailing Senghor's program for a humanistic, democratic "African socialism"—is taken from an abridged English translation of Senghor's report to a party congress in Dakar (then the capital of the Mali Federation) on July 1, 1959. (The full French text is available under the title Nation et Voie Africaine du Socialisme *[Paris: Présence Africaine, 1961].)*

Senghor has also published four volumes of poetry, as well as an anthology of African poets. He is one of the leading spokesmen for the cultural revival associated with the concept of Negritude, and writes for the publication of the Society for African Culture, Présence Africaine. *The selection on this subject is taken from a speech Senghor delivered at Oxford University in October, 1961.*

AFRICAN SOCIALISM*

In the respective programs of our former parties, all of us used to proclaim our attachment to socialism. This was a good thing, but it was not enough. Most of the time, we were satisfied with stereotyped formulas and vague aspirations, which we called scientific socialism—as if socialism did not mean a return to original sources. Above all, we need to make an effort to rethink the basic texts in the light of Negro African realities.

The antifederalists† have accused us of being atheists, Marxists, and of outlawing religion. Though this smacks of propaganda, it poses a fundamental question. Can we integrate Negro African cultural values, especially religious values, into socialism? We must answer that question once and for all with an unequivocal "Yes."

We are not "Marxists" in the sense given the word today, in so far as Marxism is presented as atheistic metaphysics, a total and totalitarian view of the world, a *Weltanschauung*. In this sense, Marx himself once said: "As for me, I am not a Marxist." We are socialists. In other words, we shall exclude neither Marx nor Engels from our sources; we shall start from their works as from those of the "utopian socialists," and we shall add to these sources the works of their successors and commentators. But we shall retain only the method and the ideas: the method, which can help us to analyze our situation; the ideas, which can help us to solve our problems.

We shall start from Marx and Engels. Whatever their limitations, their inadequacies, or their errors, they, more than all others, revolutionized political and economic thought of the nineteenth century. . . .

We may wonder, first of all, whether the socialism, the economics of Marx, is really "scientific." Yes and no. No, if one means by science the exact knowledge and formulation of economic facts in laws which permit one to foresee and to organize a balanced econ-

---

* Excerpts from Léopold Sédar Senghor, *African Socialism*, translated by Mercer Cook (New York: American Society of African Culture, 1959); reprinted by permission.
† Those opposed to the Federation of Mali (now defunct).—ED.

omy. *Yes*, if science is defined as comprehension of the real, if it
consists of deciphering the complexities basic to economic facts,
especially man's reactions to these facts, and if its aim is to unveil
"the economic law of motion of modern society."

So we must not seek in Marx—not even in *Capital*—an exposé
of economic laws. Considering them more or less as contingent
"appearances," Marx was not interested in them. Moreover, he
went so far as to predict changes that have not occurred.

In *Conflit du Siècle*, Fritz Sternberg has analyzed almost all
the changes that have taken place in economic, social, and political reality since the publication of *Capital*. They are impressive
and have been listed by other writers. In our résumé of Marx's
theories, we have skipped over most of them, and we shall now
mention only a few, while noting the recent studies made in
France by the Autonomous Socialist Party:

1. The class struggle is much more complex than Marx thought.
In fact, the working class is not a simple reality. Moreover, it is
diminishing while the several categories of salaried workers with
dissimilar interests are increasing.

2. The peasants, whom Marx considered more or less impervious to revolutionary ferment and dedicated "to the stupidity of
rural life," have belied his judgment in underdeveloped countries.

3. The theory of capitalist concentration has not been verified
by the facts. On the contrary, the number of small and medium-
sized businesses continues to grow in Western European countries.

4. Though periodic economic crises have not ceased, they are
becoming rarer, and we cannot reasonably foresee a general cata-
clysm ending the capitalist system, which is adjusting to economic
and social evolution.

5. "Socialism" has not triumphed, as Marx predicted, in the
industrial nations of Western Europe, but in the underdeveloped
nations of Eastern Europe and Asia.

By excessive simplification of the theory of class struggle—a
more precise translation of *Klassenkampf* would be a "class war"—
Marx overestimated the role of the determinism of things and
underestimated man's freedom and the organizing power of the
capitalist state. In fact, thanks to trade-union activity and a more
enlightened middle class, the capitalistic state, by a policy of in-

tervention and rational organization, has been able progressively
to reduce the surplus value. This surplus value, reduced by more
equitable taxation, has permitted the productive investments of
the postwar era and the institution of social security. Marx advocated social legislation; in his opinion, it would lead to increased
unemployment, bitter class antagonism, and, finally, to the revolution. However, social reforms have produced quite the opposite
effects.

We may also observe, in passing, that he did not pay enough
attention to the role of cooperatives, as preached by the utopian
socialists. We know that these have proved their worth in the
Scandinavian socialist democracies. Thus, a will to reform has replaced—in Western labor unions—the will to revolt. In the Communist countries, the "dictatorship of the proletariat," contrary to
the teachings of Marx, has made the state an omnipotent, soulless
monster, has stifled the natural freedoms of the human being, and
has dried up the sources of art, without which life is not worth
living.

One final word on this point. In Marx's day, colonialism was just
beginning. He could not foresee its universal development during
the second half of the nineteenth century. He spoke, of course,
about "the modern theory of colonization,"* but merely in the
etymological sense of the word. He had in mind only European
colonization of the United States. Moreover, his macroeconomic
theory, his almost blind confidence in proletarian generosity and
conscience prevented him from anticipating the opposition that
would develop between colonizing and colonized countries, between the well fed and the famished. It is a fact, now commonplace, that the standard of living of the European masses has been
able to rise only at the expense of the standard of living of the
masses in Asia and Africa. The economy of European nations consists fundamentally of selling manufactured products to underdeveloped countries at high prices and buying raw materials from
them at the lowest possible cost. And I am not talking about the
United States. The problem is different in France, but if the prices
paid for raw materials in African countries are supported, it is no
less true that French prices are generally the highest in Western
Europe. This compensates for that. In a word, the European prole-

* *Capital*, IV, 314–28.

tariat has profited from the colonial system; therefore, it has never really—I mean effectively—opposed it.

There we have a series of facts that we must think about, we men from underdeveloped countries, we men inspired by socialism. We must not consider Marx as an economist like Keynes, but as a sociologist, a philosopher. This is something that would have astonished the founder of "scientific socialism," since he refrained from "philosophizing." And yet his thought remains that of a philosopher. Beyond the economic "appearances," it dives into the human reality that causes them. For the *factual* view of things, Marx substitutes a profound insight into human needs. His is a new humanism, new because it is *incarnate*.

Humanism, *philosophy of humanism*, rather than economics—this is the basic character, the positive contribution of Marxian thought. As we said earlier, Marx does not formulate economic facts; he defines "the economic law of motion of modern society," which is a social "tendency" rather than a law. In his analysis, he advances by *postulates* and theories which explain the facts. . . .

For an African Type of Socialism

Let us recapitulate Marx's positive contributions. They are: the philosophy of humanism, economic theory, dialectical method. To these we may add trade unionism, planning, and also federalism and cooperation, which come to us from the French idealistic socialists: Saint Simon, Proudhon, and Fourier—to name only the outstanding ones.

Thus, we are not Communists. Does this mean that we shall practice anti-Communism? Certainly not. Anti-Communism, the "witch hunt," can have but one result: increased tension between East and West and a continuation of the Cold War at the obvious risk of unleashing a third global conflict, from which humanity would not recover. We are not Communists for a theoretical reason. Lenin's definition of matter proceeds from a one-sided concept, from a purely materialistic and deterministic postulate. At the beginning of *Anarchy and Socialism*, Stalin goes even further: "Marxism is not only a theory of socialism, it is a definitive view of the world, a philosophical system."

We are not Communists for a practical reason. The anxiety for human dignity, the need for freedom—man's freedom, the freedoms of collectivities—which animate Marx's thought and provide its revolutionary ferment—this anxiety and this need are unknown to Communism, whose major deviation is Stalinism. The "dictatorship of the proletariat," which was to be only temporary, becomes the dictatorship of the party and state by perpetuating itself. "The Soviet Union," said Mamadou Dia on his return from Moscow, "has succeeded in building socialism, but at the sacrifice of religion, of the soul."

The paradox of socialistic construction in Communist countries—in the Soviet Union at least—is that it increasingly resembles capitalistic construction in the United States, the American way of life, with high salaries, refrigerators, washing machines, and television sets. And it has less art and freedom of thought. Nevertheless, we shall not be won over by a regime of liberal capitalism and free enterprise. We cannot close our eyes to segregation, although the government combats it; nor can we accept the elevation of material success to a way of life.

We stand for a middle course, for a *democratic socialism* which goes so far as to integrate spiritual values, a socialism which ties in with the old ethical current of the French socialists. Historically and culturally, we belong to the current. Besides, the French socialists—from Saint Simon to the Léon Blum of *A l'Echelle humaine*—are not so utopian as they are reputed to be. In so far as they are idealists, they fulfill the requirements of the Negro African soul, the requirements of men of all races and countries. *Not by Bread Alone*—this is the title of a novel by Dudintsev, a citizen of the Soviet Union, and the Russians read this book avidly. Khrushchev was not mistaken: "De-Stalinization was imposed by the people by the thirst for freedom, the hunger for spiritual nourishment."

Concluding his report on the German Democratic Republic [East Germany], Michel Bosquet writes: "But when I ask him [the head of a labor union] what the workers demand, he replies: 'Today they want TV sets and motorcycles. When they get them, they will demand a shorter work week. And then? . . . I can only answer for myself. What I would like, what I miss, is more good literature.' "* This fact is not unrelated to a phenomenon observed in America: the appeal of the contemplative life, as a reaction against the surrounding machinism. Among American Cath-

* *L'Express*, June 4, 1959, p. 24.

olics, the proportion of priests to laity is one of the highest in the world.

This thirst for freedom, this hunger for spiritual nourishment, strengthened by the moral tradition of French socialism, explains why numerous French Marxists in recent years have shunned Stalinism and even Communism: Henri Lefebvre, Pierre Fougeyrollas, and Edgar Morin, among others, who have stated their reasons lately in sorrowful but lucid volumes.* The major reason, common to all of them, is that the Party has come to submerge the individual under the collectivity, the person under the class, to hide reality behind the screen of ideology. If we reflect about these cases, we shall discover that not only Marxism but Marx himself is "called to question"—except perhaps by Lefebvre. For, if the person is submerged, it is because Marx did not pay sufficient attention to the "natural determination"—namely, the *nation*—that is not effaced by class.

Marx underestimated political and national idealism, which, born in France upon the ruins of provincial fatherlands with the Revolution of 1789, won over the world. "Justice," Marx writes, "humanity, liberty, equality, fraternity, independence . . . these relatively moral categories which sound so nice, but which, in historical and political questions, prove absolutely nothing." I repeat: independence. If the creator of scientific sociology returned to this earth, he would perceive with amazement that these "chimeras," as he called them, and above all the concept of *nation*, are living realities in the twentieth century.

What is left of the 1789 Revolution? A political doctrine and technique, accepted nowadays even by the devout. . . . From Marxism there will surely remain an economic doctrine and technique, inasmuch as they do not contradict the teachings of Christianity and Islam—far from it.

But a third revolution is taking place, as a reaction against capitalistic and Communistic materialism—one that will integrate moral, if not religious, values with the political and economic contributions of the two great revolutions. In this revolution, the colored peoples, including the Negro African, must play their part; they must bring their contribution to the construction of the new planetary civilization. As Aimé Césaire says: "They will not

* Cf. Lefebvre, *La Somme et le reste* (La Nef de Paris); Fougeyrollas, *Le Marxisme en question* (Editions du Seuil); Morin, *Autocritique* (Julliard).

come empty-handed to the rendezvous of give-and-take." Between the two world wars, Paul Morand observed: "The Negroes have rendered an enormous service to America. But for them, one might have thought that men could not live without a bank account and a bathtub."

For a Strong Federal Democracy

Our democracy will be *federal*. . . . We do not need to remind you that local diversities, with their complementary qualities, will enrich the federation. Conversely, the federation will preserve those diversities. The decentralized federal structure will be extended, within the framework of the federal state, to regional and communal collectivities, even into economic and social areas. The Yugoslavian structures, adapted to our realities, will, in this instance, serve as a model.

Thus we shall fill the dangerous void now existing between the federal state and the village. Our leaders are bored with their freedom from responsibility. Even when they fill this void by the political formation of militants, they tend to devote their activity to contention over slogans. Regional and communal assemblies, among others, would give them a practical opportunity to exercise their responsibilities. A revolution remains ideological, therefore ineffective, so long as it is not translated into concrete action which, by transforming the structure, raises the standard of living and culture of the citizens. . . .

A federal democracy, yes . . . but a strong democracy. As the Secretary General suggests in his report, it is a question of avoiding two dangers: on the one hand, fascist dictatorship, which one observes in the antifederalist states; on the other hand, governmental instability, which was common in France during the Third and Fourth Republics. Both deviations are signs of weakness; in the long run, they provoke the revolt of the people and the disintegration of the state.

The Federation of Mali, like the federated states, will be a democracy.* The electoral law will continue to be impartial . . . not a law of circumstance, cut to the measure of the government or the majority party. Freedom of opinion, speech, press, assembly,

* In August, 1960, after this report was made, the Federation of Mali separated into its component parts, Senegal and the Sudan (which took the name of the Republic of Mali).—Ed.

and association is guaranteed by the constitutions of Mali and the federated states—in the antifederalist states also. But, with us, these freedoms do not exist only on paper; they are effectively enjoyed and will continue to be so. Above all, the right of *free settlement* of the citizens will be assured, whether or not they were born in Mali. A democratic policy pays dividends; in addition, it conforms to our humanitarian ideal. Already, public opinion in black Africa and France is grateful to us. This is excellent propaganda for Mali.

The rights of the minority, of the opposition, will therefore be respected in Mali. They will find their natural and legal limits in the rights of the majority, the popular will, which is sovereign; in other words, in the rights of the nation-state. For we are a quasi nation, as François Perroux says.

The stability of the executive is guaranteed by our constitutions. We need to assure it in actual political practice. It is necessary that governments govern, that they, along with the legislative assemblies, take the initiative of making laws within the framework of the doctrine and program of the majority party. Governments must apply the law firmly, and legislative assemblies must check on the action of the government. It is necessary that the party (congress, executive committee, and officers) have the final word in matters of control. Yet, to be effective, the various controls will be general and *a posteriori*. Meddling and harassing controls would not work. Here again, we shall avoid two dangers: granting government action a blank check, and taking away the executive power. The controls must be political, not technical.

Let us return to the rights of the opposition. Their role, certainly, is to criticize. But "criticism" means critical spirit, not spirit of criticism, systematic carping. In a democracy, criticism must be constructive and serve the general, not factional, interest. At any rate, one cannot grant the opposition more rights than the majority enjoys. The law also applies to the opposition, which is likewise required to observe it. Under the control of the majority party, the governments will take all necessary steps to curb demagogic opposition. They will not tolerate violations of the law, appeals to illegality or to violence, whether the pretexts be religious or racial. This is the democratic sense that we attach to the "dictatorship of the proletariat."

WHAT IS "NEGRITUDE"?*

Paradoxically, it was the French who first forced us to seek its essence, and who then showed us where it lay . . . when they enforced their policy of assimilation and thus deepened our despair. . . . Earlier, we had become aware within ourselves that assimilation was a failure; we could assimilate mathematics or the French language, but we could never strip off our black skins or root out black souls. And so we set out on a fervent quest for the "holy grail": our collective soul. And we came upon it.

It was not revealed to us by the "official France" of the politicians who, out of self-interest and political conviction, defended the policy of assimilation. Its whereabouts was pointed out to us by that handful of free-lance thinkers—writers, artists, ethnologists, and prehistorians—who bring about cultural revolutions in France. It was, to be quite precise, our teachers of ethnology who introduced us to the considerable body of work already achieved in the understanding of Africa, by the University of Oxford.

What did we learn from all those writers, artists, and teachers? That the early years of colonization and especially, even before colonization, the slave trade had ravaged black Africa like a bush fire, wiping out images and values in one vast carnage. That Negroid civilization had flourished in the Upper Paleolithic Age, and that the Neolithic revolution could not be explained without them. That their roots retained their vigor and would one day produce new grass and green branches . . .

Negritude is the *whole complex of civilized values—cultural, economic, social, and political—which characterize the black peoples,* or, more precisely, the Negro-African world. All these values are essentially informed by intuitive reason, because this sentient reason, the reason which comes to grips, expresses itself emotionally, through that self-surrender, that coalescence of subject and object; through myths, by which I mean the archetypal images of the collective soul; and, above all, through primordial rhythms, synchronized with those of the cosmos. In other words, the sense

* Excerpts from a speech delivered by Senghor at Oxford University in October, 1961; reprinted, by permission, from *West Africa,* November 4, 1961.

of communion, the gift of mythmaking, the gift of rhythm, such are the essential elements of Negritude, which you will find indelibly stamped on all the works and activities of the black man. . . .

In opposition to European racialism, of which the Nazis were the symbol, we set up an "antiracial racialism." The very excesses of Nazism, and the catastrophes it engendered, were soon to bring us to our senses. Such hatred, such violence, above all, such weeping and such shedding of blood produced a feeling of revulsion. It was so foreign to our continent's genius: our *need to love.* And then the anthropologists taught us that there is no such thing as a pure race: Scientifically speaking—races do not exist. They went one better and forecast that, with a mere 200 million people, we would in the end disappear as a "black race," through miscegenation. At the same time, they did offer us some consolation. "The focal points of human development," wrote Teilhard de Chardin in 1939, "always seem to coincide with the points of contact and anastomosis of several nerve paths"—that is, in the ordinary man's language, of several races. If, then, we were justified in fostering the values of Negritude and arousing the energy slumbering within us, it must be in order to pour them into the mainstream of cultural miscegenation (the biological process taking place spontaneously). They must flow toward the meeting point of all humanity; they must be our contribution to the civilization of the universal.

Biological miscegenation, then, takes place spontaneously, provoked by the very laws which govern life, and in the face of all policies of apartheid. It is a different matter in the realm of culture. Here, we remain wholly free to cooperate or not, to provoke or prevent the synthesis of cultures. This is an important point. For, as certain biologists point out, the psychological mutations brought about by education are incorporated in our genes and are then transmitted by heredity. Hence the major role played by culture.

Seen within this prospect of the civilization of the universal, the colonial policies of Great Britain and France have proved successful complements to each other, and black Africa has benefited. The policies of the former tended to reinforce the traditional native civilization. As for France's policy, although we have often reviled it in the past, it too ended with a credit balance, through forcing us actively to assimilate European civilization. This fertilized our sense of Negritude. Today, our Negritude no longer expresses itself as opposition to European values, but as a *complement* to them. Henceforth, its militants will be concerned, as I have often said, *not to be assimilated, but to assimilate*. They will use European values to arouse the slumbering values of Negritude, which they will bring as their contribution to the civilization of the universal.

Nevertheless, we still disagree with Europe: not with its values any longer (with the exception of capitalism), but with its theory of the civilization of the universal. . . . In the eyes of the Europeans, the "exotic civilizations" are static in character, being content to live by means of archetypal images, which they repeat indefinitely. The most serious criticism is that they have no idea of the *pre-eminent dignity of the human person*. My reply is this: Just as much as black Africa, Europe and its North American offspring live by means of archetypal images. For what are free enterprise, democracy, and Communism but *myths*, around which hundreds of millions of men and women organize their lives? Negritude itself is a myth (I am not using the word in any pejorative sense), but a living, dynamic one, which evolves with its circumstances into a form of humanism. Actually, our criticism of the [European] thesis is that it is monstrously antihumanist. For if European civilization were to be imposed, unmodified, on all peoples and continents, it could only be by force. That is its first disadvantage. A more serious one is that it would not be *humanistic*, for it would cut itself off from the complementary values of the greater part of humanity. As I have said elsewhere, it would be a universal civilization; it would not be the civilization of the universal.

Our revised Negritude is humanistic. I repeat, it welcomes the complementary values of Europe and the white man, and, indeed, of all other races and continents. But it welcomes them in order to fertilize and reinvigorate its own values, which it then offers for the construction of a civilization which shall embrace all mankind. The neohumanism of the twentieth century stands at the point where the paths of all nations, races, and continents cross, "where the four winds of the spirit blow."

PART IV

LATIN AMERICA

The Latin American experience is different from that of Asia, Africa, or the Middle East, yet the area faces many of the same problems of modernization and development. Although Latin America has been politically independent since the early nineteenth century, government has until recently been the monopoly of a small, European-oriented upper class, which wielded economic, political, and often military and ecclesiastical power. Ideological conflicts among the Latin American elite reflected the ideologies of Europe—with the positivism and anticlericalism of the European radicals, as well as the conservatism of the European landowning feudal classes.

In this century, radical and reformist ideologies have begun to involve the masses in political life. In some cases, European doctrines have been altered to fit the Latin American scene. (Christian Democratic, socialist, and Communist theories are represented in the selections by Eduardo Frei, Abel Latendorf, and in the December, 1961, speech of Fidel Castro.) In other cases, new formulations or combinations have been developed to deal with the special situation in Latin America (as, for example, the theories of Haya de la Torre and Betancourt). Even when the political leader has no systematic and integrated political theory (as, for example, Joscelino Kubitschek), he is still aware of the necessity to respond to the pressing problems of Latin America—the concentration of economic power in the hands of a few wealthy landowners, the lack of industrial development, and the preponderance of foreign (particularly American) influences in Latin American economic life.*

* It should be noted that there are considerable variations among the Latin American countries in the extent of industrialization and the seriousness of

Latin American leaders share the reforming zeal and anti-imperialist sentiments of those of Asia, Africa, and the Middle East. Until recently, however, there has been little awareness of a community of interest with other underdeveloped nations—partly because of cultural and linguistic barriers, partly because of the absence of the political links that the French and British colonial empires provided to bring the African and Asian nationalists into contact with one another. The Cuban revolution has considerably altered this situation. Certainly at its outset, and even today, the politically conscious elements in Asia, Africa, and the Middle East consider it a nationalistic, anticolonial revolution similar to their own. The Cuban role at the Belgrade Conference in September, 1961, was an indication of this attitude.

In addition to a desire for social reform and opposition to imperialism, other goals of modernizing nationalism are present in Latin American political thought. Economic development through planning and government action, industrialization at a rapid rate, and the expansion of literacy and educational opportunity are all objectives of the Latin American leaders. Although a multiparty system flourishes in such countries as Chile and Argentina, there is also a desire for strong government and an end to party strife. The single party has not been defended with the vigor with which the Africans defend it, but in the case of Mexico, an effective and democratic single-party system has been in operation for a number of years. In Brazil, an effort is being made to bring many of the parties together in a nationalist "front." Latin American nationalism has not led to a significant revival of interest in traditional culture, but Haya de la Torre of Peru has spoken of "Indo-America" as a distinctive cultural entity, and Eduardo Frei of Chile has called upon Latin America to make its distinctive contribution to world civilization. That a loosening of political ties with the United States also appeals to many Latin Americans was evident when Janio Quadros secured election as President of Brazil on a program that called for an "independent" foreign policy.

Counterbalancing the neutralist and anti-American tendencies are programs of political cooperation (through the Organization of American States), of military alliance (through the 1947

---

the economic and social problems. Thus Walt W. Rostow, in *The Stages of Economic Growth*, classes Argentina and Mexico as already in the "take-off" stage of economic development.

Treaty of Rio de Janeiro), and of economic assistance (through the Alliance for Progress, initiated in 1961). In addition, there is the vigorously anti-Communist attitude of many groups in Latin America—including the Catholic Church. It may thus be possible to attain the social and economic objectives of modernization without destroying the inter-American system, but the task will be among the most difficult ones confronted by United States policymakers in the years to come.

21. Fidel Castro

Fidel Castro was born in 1926, on a sugar farm owned by his father. He received his primary and secondary education in Catholic schools. At the University of Havana, where he studied law and was active in student politics, he was elected president of the student government. Castro joined an unsuccessful expeditionary force against General Trujillo of the Dominican Republic in 1947. A year later, he attended a student meeting in Bogotá, Colombia, and participated in the riots marking the meeting of the Organization of American States there. He received his law degree in 1950, and two years later sued unsuccessfully in the Constitutional Court of Havana for a decision that Batista's seizure of power had been unconstitutional. On July 26, 1953, after an attack on the Moncada barracks in Santiago de Cuba, he was captured, tried (his defense was later published as History Will Absolve Me), *and sentenced to fifteen years in prison on the Isle of Pines. Released in 1955 under an amnesty law, he went to Mexico, where he formed the 26th of July Movement. In November, 1956, he returned to Cuba and began the resistance movement in the hills of Sierra Maestre that was finally to come to power on January 1, 1959.* History Will Absolve Me *promised a return to the 1940 constitution, to agrarian reform, and to nationalization of the telephone and electricity "trusts." After coming to power, Castro did not hold elections (although this was implied by his promise to restore the 1940 constitution and by his references to the "popularly elected" government that would follow). In May, 1959, however, at the Economic Council of the Organization of American States in Buenos Aires, he spoke of elections as a check against oppression, and asked the United States to set up a $30 billion aid program for Latin America in the next ten years. At this time, he also repeatedly denied that he or his revolution was Communist. A year later, he* *asserted that because of "the intimate union and identification of the government with the people," elections were not necessary (see Castro's speech on "A Real Democracy"). In late 1959 and 1960, with the defection of many of the original revolutionaries on the grounds of increasing Communist control of Cuba, it became apparent that the Popular Socialist Party (PSP)—as the Cuban Communist Party was known—was becoming dominant in the group around Castro. This development was reinforced by Castro's increasingly close military and economic ties with the Soviet bloc, links that were strengthened after the United States cut off the Cuban sugar quota in mid-1960. Finally, in December, 1961, Castro announced his allegiance to Marxism-Leninism (although he did not say, as press reports first had it, that he had always been a Marxist-Leninist), and described the newly established Revolutionary Integrated Organizations as a preparatory step to the creation of an elite party, the United Revolutionary Socialist Party, under collective leadership along Leninist lines.*

HISTORY WILL ABSOLVE ME*

In the brief of this case there must be recorded the five revolutionary laws that would have been proclaimed immediately after the capture of the Moncada barracks and would have been broadcast to the nation by radio. It is possible that Colonel Chaviano may deliberately have destroyed these documents, but even if he has done so, I conserve them in my memory.

The First Revolutionary Law would have returned power to the people and proclaimed the Constitution of 1940 the supreme law of the land, until such time as the people should decide to modify or change it. And, in order to effect its implementation and punish those who had violated it—there being no organization for holding elections to accomplish this—the revolutionary movement, as the momentous incarnation of this sovereignty, the only source of legitimate power, would have assumed all the faculties inherent to it except that of modifying the Constitution itself. In

* Excerpts from Fidel Castro's defense statement at his trial (see biographical sketch) in 1953, later published as *History Will Absolve Me* (New York: Lyle Stuart, 1961); reprinted by permission.

other words, it would have assumed the legislative, executive, and judicial powers.

This approach could not be more crystal-clear or more free of vacillation and sterile charlatanry. A government acclaimed by the mass of rebel people would be vested with every power, everything necessary in order to proceed with the effective implementation of the popular will and true justice. From that moment, the judicial power, which since March 10 has placed itself *against* the Constitution and *outside* the Constitution, would cease to exist, and we would proceed to its immediate and total reform before it would again assume the power granted to it by the Supreme Law of the Republic. Without our first taking those measures, a return to legality—by putting the custody of the courts back into the hands that have crippled the system so dishonorably—would constitute a fraud, a deceit, and one more betrayal.

The Second Revolutionary Law would have granted property (not mortgageable and not transferable) to all planters, subplanters, lessees, partners, and squatters who hold parcels of five or less *caballerias** of land, and the state would indemnify the former owners on the basis of the rental they would have received for these parcels over a period of ten years.

The Third Revolutionary Law would have granted workers and employees the right to share 30 per cent of the profits of all the large industrial, mercantile, and mining enterprises, including the sugar mills. The strictly agricultural enterprises would be exempt, in consideration of other agrarian laws which would have been implemented.

The Fourth Revolutionary Law would have granted all planters the right to share 50 per cent of the sugar production and a minimum quota of 40,000 *arrobas*† for all small planters who had been established for three or more years.

The Fifth Revolutionary Law would have ordered the confiscation of all holdings and ill-gotten gains of those who had committed frauds during previous regimes, as well as the holdings and ill-gotten gains of all their legatees and heirs. To implement this, special courts with full powers would gain access to all records of all corporations registered or operating in this country, in order to investigate concealed funds of illegal origin, and to request

* A *caballeria* is a tract of land equivalent to about 33.3 acres.
† An *arroba* is equivalent to 25 pounds.

that foreign governments extradite persons and attach their holdings. Half of the property recovered would be used to subsidize
retirement funds for workers, and the other half would be used
for hospitals, asylums, and charitable organizations.

Furthermore, it was to be declared that the Cuban policy in the
Americas would be one of close solidarity with the democratic
people of this continent, and that those politically persecuted by
bloody tyrants oppressing our sister nations would find generous
asylum, brotherhood, and bread in the land of Martí—not the
persecution, hunger, and treason that they find today. Cuba should
be the bulwark of liberty and not a shameful link in the chain
of despotism.

These laws would have been proclaimed immediately, as soon
as the upheaval was ended and prior to a detailed and far-reaching
study. They would have been followed by another series of laws
and fundamental measures, such as agrarian reform, integral reform
of education, nationalization of the utilities trust and the telephone trust, refunds to the people of the illegal excessive rates this
company has charged, and payment to the treasury of all taxes
brazenly evaded in the past.

All these laws and others would be inspired in the exact fulfillment of two essential articles of our Constitution. One of these
orders the outlawing of feudal estates by indicating the maximum
area of land any person or entity can possess for each type of
agricultural enterprise, by adopting measures which would tend
to return the land to the Cubans. The other categorically orders
the state to use all means at its disposal to provide employment
for all those who lack it and to ensure a decent livelihood for
each manual laborer or intellectual.

None of these articles may be called unconstitutional. The first
popularly elected government would have to respect these laws,
not only because of moral obligation to the nation, but because
when people achieve something they have yearned for throughout
generations, no force in the world is capable of taking it away
again.

The problems concerning land, industrialization, housing, unemployment, education, and the health of the people—these are
the six problems we would take immediate steps to resolve, along
with the restoration of public liberties and political democracy....

It is not by statesmen such as Carlos Saladrigas*—whose statesmanship consists of preserving the *status quo* and mouthing
phrases like the "absolute freedom of enterprise," "guarantees to
investment capital," and "the law of supply and demand"—that
we will solve these problems. Those ministers can chat gaily in
a mansion on Fifth Avenue† until there remains not even the
dust of the bones of those whose problems required immediate
solution. In this present-day world, social problems are not solved
by spontaneous generation.

A revolutionary government with the backing of the people and
the respect of the nation, after purging the various institutions
of all venal and corrupt officials, would proceed immediately to
industrialize the country, mobilizing all inactive capital (currently
estimated at about $500 million) through the National Bank and
the Agricultural, Industrial, and Development Bank and sub-
mitting this mammoth task to experts and men of absolute competence, completely removed from all political machinations, for
study, direction, planning, and realization.

After establishing the 100,000 small farmers as owners on land
they had previously rented, a revolutionary government would proceed immediately to settle the land problem. First, as the Constitution orders, we would establish the maximum amount of land to
be held by each type of agricultural enterprise and would acquire
the excess acres by expropriation: recovery of the lands stolen
from the state, improvement of swampland, planting of large
nurseries, and reserving of zones for reforestation. Secondly, we
would distribute the remaining land among peasant families (with
priority given to the larger ones) and would promote agricultural
cooperatives *for the common use of expensive equipment,*‡ with a
single technical, professional direction of farming and cattle raising. Finally, we would provide resources, equipment, protection,
and useful guidance to the peasants.

A revolutionary government would solve the housing problem by
cutting all rents in half, by providing tax exemptions on homes
inhabited by the owners, by tripling taxes on rented homes, by

---

* Batista's presidential candidate in 1944 elections, Saladrigas was defeated. He became an influential member of Batista's government after 1952.—
ED.

† Located in the Miramar residential district in Havana.—ED.

‡ Italicized words omitted in the translation from which this excerpt is
taken.—ED.

tearing down hovels and replacing them with modern multiple-dwelling buildings, and by financing housing all over the island on a scale heretofore unheard of, with the criterion that, just as each rural family should possess its own tract of land, each city family should own its home or apartment. There is plenty of building material and more than enough manpower to make a decent home for every Cuban. But if we continue to wait for the miracle of the golden calf, a thousand years will have gone by and the problem will still be the same. On the other hand, today there are greater possibilities than ever of bringing electricity to the remotest corner of the island. The use of nuclear energy in this field is now a reality and will greatly reduce the cost of producing electricity.

With these three projects and reforms, the problem of unemployment would automatically disappear, and the work to improve public health and to fight against disease would be made much less difficult.

Finally, a revolutionary government would undertake the integral reform of the educational system, bringing it in line with the foregoing projects, with the idea of educating those generations who will have the privilege of living in a happy land. Do not forget the words of the Apostle:* "A serious error is being made in Latin America: Where the inhabitants depend almost exclusively on the products of the soil for their livelihood, the educational stress is on urban rather than farm life." "The happiest people are the ones whose children are well educated and instructed in philosophy; whose sentiments are directed into noble channels." "A well-educated people will always be strong and free."

The spirit of education lies, however, in the teacher himself, and in Cuba the teaching profession is miserably underpaid. Despite this, no one is more dedicated than the Cuban teacher. Who among us has not learned his ABC's in the little public schoolhouse? It is time we stopped paying pittances to these young men and women who are entrusted with the sacred task of teaching the young. No teacher should earn less than $200, no secondary professor should get less than $350, if they are to devote themselves exclusively to their high calling without suffering want. Moreover, all rural teachers should have free use of the various systems of

* "The Apostle" refers to Jose Martí.—ED.

transportation, and, at least every five years, all teachers should enjoy a sabbatical leave of six months with pay so they may attend special refresher courses at home and abroad to keep abreast of the latest developments in their field. In this way, the curriculum and the teaching system may be constantly improved.

Where will the money be found for all this? When there is an end to rife embezzlement of government funds, when public officials stop taking graft from the large companies that owe taxes to the state, when the enormous resources of the country are brought into full use, when we no longer buy tanks, bombers, and guns for this country (which has no frontiers to defend, and where these instruments of war, now being purchased, are used against the people), when there is more interest in educating the people than in killing them—then there will be more than enough money.

Cuba could easily provide for a population three times as great as it now has, so there is no excuse for the abject poverty of a single one of its present inhabitants. The markets should be overflowing with produce, pantries should be full, all hands should be working. This is not an inconceivable thought. What is inconceivable is that anyone should go to bed hungry, that children should die for lack of medical attention; what is inconceivable is that 30 per cent of our farm people cannot write their names and that 99 per cent of them know nothing of Cuba's history. What is inconceivable is that the majority of our rural people are now living in worse circumstances than the Indians Columbus discovered living in the fairest land that human eyes had ever seen.

To those who would call me a dreamer, I quote the words of Martí: "A true man does not seek the path where advantage lies, but rather, the path where duty lies, and this is the only practical man, whose dream of today will be the law of tomorrow, because he who has looked back on the upheavals of history and has seen civilizations going up in flames, crying out in bloody struggle, throughout the centuries, knows that the future well-being of man, without exception, lies on the side of duty."

THE ACCUSATION OF COMMUNISM*

I do not know whether the calumny against the Revolution—that it is Communist and infiltrated by Communism—is due solely to the fact that we do not persecute the Communists and do not shoot them. I do not know how the ideas of the Revolution can be defined in such a way that there will be no more intrigues or lies than there are at present, and that the infamous attacks against our Revolution will finally cease. Is it perhaps because we have a firm conviction of the freedom of mankind and the rights of man, and of equity and human equality, that we cannot conceive that anyone would desire to have rights that he keeps from others? Is it because we have pledged to discuss our ideas in conditions of equality with all others? Is it because we have pledged to carry out our ideals, not by force, but by reason and justice? On the contrary, if the theory is accepted that someone has a right to suppress others' rights, the easiest thing for the Revolution would be to suppress the right of everyone except those who are members of the revolutionary government to speak. But that would not be democratic, nor is it our philosophy, for clearly the right to think and speak belongs to all equally. Is it because we think this way, because this is our political philosophy, that the fear of Communists is being aroused, in order to incite division in the country and bring together the enemies in other countries against us? Can our Revolution be accused of being Communist? Can the ideals of our Revolution be confused? Have we not spoken with sufficient clarity on the doctrine of the 26th of July Movement? Are our purposes not clearly defined? Then why are these fears and fantasies pursued? Are they not trying to create obstacles for the path of our Revolution? If our ideas are very clear, if the majority of the people are behind those ideas, and we are all at the command of that movement and that Revolution, do the people not trust us? Can someone perhaps maintain that we have ever lied to the people? Can anyone think that we have lacked courage to

* Excerpts from a speech delivered by Castro in the Plaza Civica, Havana, on May 8, 1959; translated by the Editor from the text in *Guia del Pensamiento Político Económico de Fidel* (Havana: Diario Libre, 1959).

speak to the people? Can anyone think that we lack the necessary sincerity to speak what we think to the people? Can anyone perhaps think that we are hypocrites or cowards? Then why do we say that our Revolution is not Communist? Why, when we prove that our ideals are different from Communist doctrine, that the Revolution is not Communist or capitalist, that it is a revolution of its own . . . that it has its own ideology—entirely its own—which has a Cuban basis and is entirely Cuban, entirely Latin American, why then, do they start to accuse our Revolution of being something it is not? It is necessary to explain for once that if our ideas were Communist, we would say so here, and if our ideas were capitalist, we would say so here. We do not give anyone the right to decide for our conscience what we are and what we have a right to be. . . .

PLAN FOR THE ADVANCEMENT OF LATIN AMERICA*

Democracy and Dictatorship

How is it possible for democracy to be preserved under these conditions? We have declared the democratic ideal to be the ideal of the peoples of this hemisphere. We have declared that the democratic ideal is the ideal that can best satisfy the dreams of the peoples of this continent. Nevertheless, the economic and social conditions of Latin America make it impossible for our countries to attain their ideal of democracy. Be it a dictatorship of the Left or a dictatorship of the Right, a dictatorship is a dictatorship, and those in power completely deny the principles toward which the peoples of Latin America aspire. . . . The Pan-American ideal is true democracy with absolute respect for the dignity of man, a true democracy in which all the liberties prevail, a true democracy in a regime of social justice. The peoples of Latin America want neither bread without liberty nor liberty without bread. . . .

* Excerpts from a speech delivered by Castro in Buenos Aires, on May 21, 1959, at the Sixth Plenary Economic Council of the Organization of American States, reprinted from *Plan for the Advancement of Latin America* (Havana, 1959).

We have said that underdevelopment is an insidious enemy of constitutional governments—governments that find themselves so strangled by conditions of poverty that they are pushed into the grip of armed minorities. We made this statement precisely because we have known two kinds of governments. We have been subjected to strong-arm governments that suppress all liberties—freedom of press, of assembly, of association, of election—and use fire and sword to maintain the so-called peace and order about which they brag so much. Under these strong-arm governments, resentment grows, poverty worsens, suffering increases.

Thus, as soon as the people can overcome the restrictions imposed upon them, they put constitutional governments into effect. Full of dreams, and with their hopes high, they begin to exercise the rights that the new regime guarantees them. They begin trying to satisfy all their needs as quickly as possible. Then, since the tremendous problem is precisely that there are not enough resources to satisfy their needs, since the resources available do not reach far enough, all kinds of conflicts arise. These conflicts are forthwith called disorder or anarchy by the enemies of democracy—by those who are waiting for the opportunity to seize power again by force.

Democratic governments cannot solve these problems which are becoming more and more acute—with theories, or arguments, or reasoning. The theory is advanced that if investments are to be attracted, there must be complete peace and order. The theory is advanced that in order to attract investments, there should be no strikes. In other words, these are the requisites often cited for the economic development of a country. But what is never explained is just how such conditions can be achieved by the use of democratic procedures and without placing further restrictions on the people, without further depriving the people. What democratic government can stay in office after placing restrictions on the people, after depriving the people further in order to comply with the conditions demanded as a requisite for capital investment—sacrificing thereby its popular support at the very time that armed minorities are waiting for the democratic government's vulnerable moment in order to seize power? . . .

No system of government is more corrupt than a dictatorship. It is true that some constitutional governments are also corrupt, but the constitutional governments must be careful because they have to submit to elections; and if there is true democracy, if the citizens really vote, the governments can lose these elections. Furthermore, in a democracy, public protest serves as a check on corruption. In a democracy, freedom of expression serves as a check. In a democracy, the electoral process serves as a check, and this electoral process is repeated every few years. . . .

Sources of Development Capital

There are three ways to obtain capital—by saving, by obtaining financing of our own, or by private investments. I understand that until now, the economists have discovered no other way. Saving would be a solution, if we could freely sell all we produce. If the United States and Canada should remove all the protective tariffs that affect our basic products, if they should remove the subsidies on those articles, then we could sell to them everything that we produce and thereby obtain the gold and dollar reserves necessary for our industrialization. If Cuba, for example, could sell 8 million tons of sugar, we would be able to obtain the capital needed for our industrial development. But such changes would imply a change in the economic structure of the United States, and I am not going to be utopian because our experience has taught us the difficulties that, as a result of certain well-established interests, are always to be encountered when an attempt is made to eliminate some of those restrictions. . . .

The second way to obtain capital is by private investment. This is the formula that has been proposed lately as a solution, but it is no solution. On other occasions, when the possibilities for our economic development have been studied, it has been insinuated and more or less implied that private investment could provide the capital for industrialization, but that certain previous conditions were required for private investments. To begin with a "climate": What is meant by a "climate"? In the midst of 700,000 unemployed, can there be a "climate"? . . . A "climate" cannot be achieved in the midst of conflicts that stem from hunger, poverty, and unsatisfied need. . . . Private capital would go to those countries with the best conditions, those countries which are in the best economic situation and in which for that very reason the social conflicts are less. Private capital would not go to the countries in which the greatest social conflicts appear. Then large areas of the continent would remain neglected and abandoned to their

FIDEL CASTRO 265

own fate. Private investment would not solve the problem in these areas.

Furthermore, there are investments that do not interest private capital—for example, hydroelectric plants, which require $200 million or $300 million as initial investment. Private capital prefers to exploit petroleum resources. That is a sure investment. Private capital is not interested in certain kinds of investment that do not produce big profits. These investments have to be financed by loans rather than by private investments.

We are not opposed to private investment. But in our industrialization program, the private investments we should encourage are those that can be made by private sources of capital within our respective countries. Funds should be made available to them by government credit institutions, mobilizing resources provided through international credit institutions. We believe in the usefulness, the experience, and the enthusiasm of private investors. But we should hope for the private investments to be made by firms within our respective countries. Does this mean that we will exclude international investors? No. Companies with international investments will have the same guarantees and the same rights as the national firms. . . .

The third type of investment, the one that is made through public finance, remains. Why not agree that under the present conditions the best way to cooperate in a program of economic development is through a program of public financing? . . . The financial consultants of the Cuban delegation estimate that a ten-year loan of $30 billion is needed to carry out the economic development of Latin America. . . . I declare that what we need we can obtain only from the United States and through public financing. We understand, furthermore, that this is the easiest way for the United States to help Latin America; experience in recent years shows us that any other procedure—such as that of eliminating trade tariffs —would be politically more difficult. Furthermore, the large-scale loan is the foreign-aid program that the United States has used in Europe and the Near East. Why ignore in Latin America the program that was considered best for other places and would benefit both Latin America and the United States? . . . The important thing is that we should be convinced that the solutions I have discussed are the true solutions and that the assistance that Latin America needs should be made available in the amount needed really to solve the problem of underdevelopment—not to solve it halfway, but to solve it completely, so that we can build a lasting foundation for a democratic family of nations in this hemisphere.

A REAL DEMOCRACY*

You who produce things, you who work, who sacrifice yourselves, who have been missing the pleasant things of life, you always were, are now, and will be tomorrow, members of the majority of the people.

And yet, you did not run things; you were the majority, and others used to run things for you. You were managed, you were governed by others who not only did what you were supposed to do, but as a rule did it to the detriment of your interests. They ruled in your place and against you.

They invented a democracy for you, a strange, peculiar democracy in which you, who represented the majority, had nothing whatever to say about anything; in which you, peasant, and you, workman, you fellows who produce most of what is worth anything and who, combining efforts with the white-collar workers, produce all our wealth, all our income—you, who produced everything, did not even have the chance to learn how to read or write, often not even to sign your name.

They invented a very peculiar democracy for you who were the majority and yet were practically nonexistent as a political element of our society. They spoke to you about rights and privileges of the citizen, and all those rights and privileges only meant that your child had to starve to death before the closed eyes of an indolent government, that your other child had to go through life without learning his ABC's, that you yourself had to sell your hard work for whatever they condescended to pay for it—if you were lucky enough to find someone who would buy it.

They spoke to you about rights that never existed as far as you were concerned. Your children were not sure of even the right to a country school, or the right to medical attention, or

* Excerpts from Castro's May Day, 1960, speech; reprinted, by permission, from *Monthly Review*, XII, No. 5 (September, 1960).

the right to a piece of bread; and you yourself were not sure of even the right to work!

They invented a democracy in which you, who represented the majority, did not mean anything. And thus, despite your tremendous strength, regardless of your colossal might, in spite of your sacrifice and your endless toil for others as a mere cog in our national life, you, who were the majority all the time, neither governed anything nor could even manage your own affairs!

A democracy is that form of government in which the majority runs things, where the majority means something, and the interests of that majority are protected; a democracy is that in which a man is assured of all his rights, not only the right to think freely, but also the right to know how to think, the right to know how to write what he thinks, the right to know how to read what others think and say. Also the right to eat, to work, to become educated, and to mean something within your society. That is why this is real democracy, the democracy brought to you by the Cuban Revolution, by our Revolution.

A real democracy is one in which you, peasant, get the land we have been recovering for you, after wresting it from foreign hands! A true democracy is one in which you, sugar-cane plantation worker, receive nearly 3 million acres of planted land so that you will no longer have to live as an outcast! A true democracy is one in which you, workman, are assured of your right to work, and know that nobody can kick you out into the gutter to starve to death! A real democracy is that in which you, poor student, have just the same opportunity to get a university degree, if you are talented enough, as the son of any rich man. A true democracy is one in which you who are the son of a laborer, or of a poor peasant, or of any poor family have a schoolteacher and a decent school to educate you. A real democracy is one in which you, old man, will not live in want when you no longer can earn enough for your own support! A true democracy is one in which Cuban Negroes have the right to work and do not have to be afraid of seeing anybody take it away from them because of stupid racial prejudices! A bona fide democracy is one in which you, woman, are recognized as an equal of all other citizens, and even have the right to take up arms to defend your country, next to your man! A pure democracy is one in which the government transforms fortresses into schools and is trying to build a house for every family, so that every Cuban father will have a roof for his children!

A real democracy is one in which whoever falls sick has a physician to treat him. A true democracy is one that does not go around recruiting peasants to convert them into soldiers (who, after being thoroughly corrupted, are converted into enemies of the workman and of their own peasant brothers), but changes that peasant soldier, not into a protector of the privileged, of the heartless landlords, but into a defender of his brothers, the peasants and the workers of his country. A real democracy is this, your democracy, which does not divide the people and does not play brothers against brothers; whose government discovers the strength of the people and combines its various elements, makes the people stronger by uniting them, hands a gun to the peasant, to the workman, to the student, and the women, and the Negroes —hands a gun to the poor man and to whoever is willing to fight for a just cause.

A real democracy is this, our and your democracy, in which not only the majority's rights prevail, but loaded weapons are handed to that majority! That, my friends, can be done only by a really democratic government, ruled and managed by the majority. This is the sort of thing that could never be done in any of those phony democracies.

I would like to know what would happen if a loaded rifle were delivered to each of those Negroes of the South in the United States, where so many of them have been lynched, abused, humiliated, and robbed for centuries!

What an oligarchy of despoilers or a military caste of plunderers and tyrants can never do, what no minority government will ever dare to do is to hand a gun to each worker and to each student, to each young man and each poor citizen—to each one of those who make up the majority of the people!

Of course, that does not mean that the rights of the others should not be considered. The rights of the other people are worth considering in the same measure as the interests of the majority, to the same extent that the rights of the majority are considered. However, the truth is that the rights and interests of the majority are the ones that should prevail over the rights and interests of the minority, and not vice versa.

And that real democracy, that pure, bona fide democracy, that true and honest democracy, is the kind of democracy we have in this country now, the kind of democracy we have had since January 1, 1959.

That democracy has asserted itself directly in the intimate union and identification of the government with the people, in this direct dealing, in this determination to do things and strive for the good of the great majority, in the interest of the great majority of the country. That direct type of democracy has been exercised here more purely, a thousand times more purely, than that false democracy, that phony democracy that resorts to sly methods, predicated on corruption and fraud, to distort and falsify the true will of the peoples.

And this democracy of ours has operated in that direct way because we are going through a revolutionary process. Tomorrow it will be as the people say, as the people decide, as may be demanded by the needs of the people, by the aspirations, hopes, and desires of the people. Today we have here a direct interdependence between the people and the government. Someday, when this revolutionary process will have advanced far enough, when the people freely decide (and the revolutionary government will immediately interpret and obey the will of the people) that we should adopt new policies and procedures; once the most important tasks have been completed and the most fundamental goals of the Revolution (among which is, in the first place today, the defense of our Revolution and of the country) have been reached, then the people and the government will adopt the procedure considered most fitting to the circumstances and characteristics of a revolution already consolidated and victorious in every way—a procedure chosen by you and us, the people and the government!

Nobody holds a public office for sport or personal gain; we are only fulfilling our duty, all of us; we are all willing and ready to sacrifice everything, to work until sheer exhaustion overcomes us; we are all intent on reaching a single goal, a single purpose, and that purpose is to serve our cause and to carry it to final victory! . . .

I AM A MARXIST-LENINIST*

The Revolution and Socialism

This was the method the Revolution had to follow, the method of anti-imperialist struggle and of socialism—that is, the nationalization of all the large industries and businesses, the nationalization and social ownership of the basic means of production, and the planned development of our whole economy at the pace permitted by our resources and by the aid we have been receiving from outside. This is something else very favorable to our Revolution: the fact that we can count on aid and solidarity, which enable us to carry our Revolution forward without the enormous sacrifices that other countries are required to make.

We have had to carry out an anti-imperialist and socialist revolution. The anti-imperialist and socialist revolution had to be a single revolution because there is only one revolution. This is the great dialectic truth of humanity: imperialism, and, opposed to imperialism—socialism. The result of this opposition is the triumph of socialism, the supremacy of the epoch of socialism, the overcoming of the stage of capitalism and imperialism, the establishment of the era of socialism and, after that, the era of Communism.

If there are still any anti-Communists here, they need not be afraid. We will not have Communism in less than thirty years. This is the way it is with Marxism. One cannot simply leap over a historical stage. Perhaps the historical stage that some underdeveloped countries can omit today is the construction of capitalism —that is, they can begin the development of the economy of the country by way of planning and socialism. What cannot be skipped is socialism. The Soviet Union itself, after forty years, is beginning to construct Communism and hopes to have advanced considerably in this direction at the end of twenty years.

Thus we are in a stage of construction of socialism. What is this socialism we should apply? Is it utopian socialism? Clearly, we must apply scientific socialism. On this subject I had to begin by saying with complete frankness that we believe in Marxism,

* Excerpts from a speech delivered by Castro on December 1, 1961; translated by the editor from the text printed in *Revolución*, December 2, 1961.

that we believe it is the most correct, most scientific theory, the only true theory, the only true revolutionary theory. I say this here with complete satisfaction and confidence. I am a Marxist-Leninist, and I will be a Marxist-Leninist until the last day of my life.

Past Attitude toward Communists

And how am I a Marxist-Leninist? Am I one halfway? We revolutionaries do not know how to be anything halfway. We can only be something 100 per cent. And we will devote our energy entirely to this. Besides, it is a great satisfaction to have been an illiterate at eighteen years of age and to be a revolutionary, which I feel I am, at thirty and a "little." The "little" I believe is thirty and six. At eighteen, I had learned something, but there was much that I did not know. And we say this with all frankness to the people, with loyalty and clarity, as we have always spoken to the people—I have always spoken with complete frankness.

Did I have prejudices? I believe it is good to speak of this. Did I have prejudices with regard to Communists? Yes. Was I at times influenced by the propaganda of imperialism and by the reaction against the Communists? Yes. What did I believe regarding the Communists? Did I believe they were thieves? No, never. I always considered the Communists both in the university and elsewhere to be honorable people, honest and all that. But this has no special merit, because nearly everybody recognizes this. Did I have the idea that they were sectarian? Yes. Why did I have these opinions about the Communists? I am absolutely convinced that the ideas I had concerning the Communists (not with regard to Marxism, but with regard to the Communist Party) were like the ideas of many people, the product of propaganda and prejudices inculcated practically since childhood, almost since school days—in the universities, in the movies, and everywhere. Do I consider they could be wrong? Yes, I feel that they could be wrong. Marx, Engels, and Lenin are themselves the first to admit that they could be wrong, that they could make mistakes, because they did not consider themselves infallible.

What was my opinion of the militants of the Communist Party? Was it the opinion they really merited? If for a long time they were ignored, attacked, excluded, left out because they were considered a kind of plague, we should also recognize that it took great courage to be a Communist. Not today—no, we are going to see to it that it is rewarded from now on, of course!

It took courage to be a Communist at that time. Felix Torres has told me how they took him out of the prison of Santa Clara and made him go to Yaguajay on foot—on foot to Yaguajay! And this was the way it was, an infinity of sacrifices and efforts. The merit in being Communists when they were persecuted, when all doors were closed to them, when all presses, newspapers, and opportunities were shut off—we should recognize that merit. Much more, of course, than to be one today. Today, conditions are different. On that point, I have said that we must make efforts that the socialists and Marxists are real Marxists in the complete meaning of the word, that they are prepared for all contingencies.

But I wanted to say that I had prejudices against the [Popular] Socialist Party, prejudices that originated in the electoral campaigns. I confess it with the complete honesty with which I should confess all things. I am not going to ask anything from the Socialists. I say this when we are completely united and are all comrades, all socialists.

At certain moments at the beginning of the Revolution, we had some friction which arose out of differing conceptions on some points, but, fundamentally, because we were not talking to one another. I ought to say that there are people here who were victims of the intrigues of the first days, when, each time something happened, it was said that a group of Communists was creating a problem and instigating a riot. I must say myself that at one time I thought it was the Communists that were creating a riot in one place where a group of people had taken action with clubs against a citizen. . . . Afterward, I discovered that it was not Communists who had created the riot, but divisionist elements. . . .

This is the way it was at the first stage—the conflict between two things, in reality between prejudices, between a series of things. If a Communist was working on anything, his Communism had to be clandestine. But immediately there were the UPI, AP, and all the American newspapers crying out "ten, twelve, fifteen Communists." It was curious in those days that they called all the comrades Communists, and there were a number of comrades who were not members of the Communist Party but members of the 26th of July Movement. They called them that already, and published their Communist antecedents to all the world. They began a campaign that had, in many areas, a response influenced by the propaganda of anti-Communism and imperialism. Fortunately for all our efforts, these stages have passed.

I think that one of the bad aspects of those first days was the lack of greater interchange among the various organizations. Each of us was going somewhat on his own. It was the same revolutionary struggle which should have been more and more in contact, in discussion, and in interchange, to promote more and more unification.

I should mention one of the things in our terrible experience. Someday, when historians write about this stage and want to describe some characteristic of this revolution, they may say that we were establishing a socialist revolution without socialists. At that time, there was so much anti-Communist prejudice that when a Communist functionary was assigned to the smallest matter, a wave of protest arose, followed by numerous intrigues on the subject. At that time, our methods were socialist—a collective farm, a cooperative, a nationalized industry—those were all socialist institutions. We had good comrades for those jobs—wonderful comrades of the revolutionary movement of the 26th of July—but they did not succeed. If those men did not succeed, how were we going to succeed?

One of the most difficult things, then, was to carry out a socialist revolution without socialists. Later, when the process of unification of the revolutionary forces and the revolutionary organizations had begun, when anti-Communism was being defeated and destroyed, a stage came in which it was easier for a number of the members of the Socialist Party to carry out numerous functions without so much intrigue and divisionism.

The Integrated Revolutionary Organizations (ORI)

What was the meaning of this union? What was the significance of this moment in which the unification of all the revolutionary organizations took place? It meant—among other things—hundreds, thousands of cadres, of trained people, of people who had passed through sacrifices, through hard and difficult tests, and had a political education. On this point, I remember that some people came to me and said, "When are we going to carry out the program of the 26th?" And I said, "What program of the 26th are we going to carry out? Why not a Marxist-Leninist program?" And, "Why are we going to carry out two Marxist-Leninist programs?" This is reality. Anything else is a figment of the imagination.

Therefore, it meant the addition of thousands of trained leaders, who were indispensable, fundamental, and necessary for the creation of socialism. It signified the addition of all the cadres of the Revolutionary Directorate. They did not have the number of experienced leaders that the Socialist Party had, because there were people who said that no, they would rather do this or they would rather do that. You have to be a complete ignoramus with regard to the facts of revolution to think that a revolutionary can choose to do this or that. What we know about all revolutions is that work is divided today among all, and it is so great that it cannot be carried out; that many comrades, if they are in the army, would prefer to go to a military academy; if they are civil servants, they would prefer to go for something like a vacation to a school of revolutionary instruction. That is, the revolutionary considers it a rest—compared to the work which he must do—to be a pupil in the school.

The revolution today can count on all the cadres of all the revolutionary organizations. The important addition of the [Popular] Socialist Party has brought the cadres of the old militants educated in socialism by the Socialist Party. The addition of the Directorate has brought young people. The 26th of July Movement could not bring older, politically educated people, but has brought many young persons who were enthusiasts and revolutionists by vocation. It has also added all the experience acquired in the seizure of power. That is, we all have brought something, one way or another, and we represent the basic forces.

These forces were asked to unite in one single organization, and they have, therefore, joined together in the ORI. It was not easy. It took a long time, and at the end they joined together into the Integrated Revolutionary Organizations (ORI).

The manifestations of sectarianism have been disappearing in the same way that exclusiveness is going to disappear, in the same way that the practice of excluding people because they are Socialists is going to disappear, naturally, and so will sectarianism and these manifestations.* Certain manifestations of extremism are also going to disappear. Often extremism is a type of disease

* On March 26, 1962, Castro criticized a number of leaders of the Popular Socialist (Communist) Party for their "sectarianism" and attempt to dominate the ORI. Other groups in the ORI include the Union of Pioneers, the Cuban Women's Federation, the Young Rebels (recently changed to Young Communists), and the Committees for the Defense of the Revolution.—ED.

that should not be confused, of course, with revolutionary firm-ness. Extremism is also a manifestation of a petty-bourgeois spirit in the revolutionary movement, and we must struggle against extremism just as much as against sectarianism.

There are many things that our people have had time to learn. They have had time to get rid of widespread prejudices picturing socialism as something terrible, inhuman, and hard—as a type of slavery—which is precisely the description that imperialism tries to impute to socialism. . . .

The Party of the Vanguard

We have all contributed to this unity, and we feel satisfied that we have contributed to it. We are all of us struggling to organize and create a strong, disciplined, and firm political organization of the vanguard of the working class and of the Cuban Revolution. How are we trying to do this? In the same way that the traditional parties do it—by inviting everyone, by opening up one's gates wide, so that all can come into the party? No.

What did the bourgeois parties, when in power, do? They opened their gates wide and invited everyone. Whatever party came to power immediately had a million members—all of a sud-den. When we were naïve and did not know anything about politics, we accepted what the newspapers said—"As proof of what the Soviet Union is, the Communist Party does not have more than 5 million members in a population of 200 million"— as evidence, by capitalism and imperialism, that a minority ruled! In this way, they tried to make us see a Marxist revolutionary party from the standpoint of a bourgeois party. With a bourgeois party, the more people, the more boasting. The bourgeois party does not have ideology: It is a gang of politicians, a group of indi-viduals who stick together and defend class interests. When more people belong, then there are more jobs and more boasting. They are not in the least concerned with the thinking of the members of the party. Hence, they try to conceal very carefully the fact that a Marxist revolutionary party is a party of the vanguard, a party that gives direction, and an elite party—that if the Soviet Union attempted to enlist Party members, there would be tens of mil-lions of them. They conceal the fact that . . . a revolutionary party is an elite party, which directs and works fundamentally through mass organizations, through trade unions, through the youth, through women's federations, through committees for defense (an invention of the Cuban Revolution and a phenomenal mass organization), the peasant associations, the cooperatives (the collective farms are already in the trade unions). That is, the party gives direction and orientation through all the mass organizations.

Thus, the standard which the political organization of the Cuban Revolution should have is, in the first place, that of selection and quality. It will not be a quantitative organization; it will be a qualitative organization. . . .

And since, besides, we are conscious of the great enthusiasm of the masses, and of their revolutionary spirit, a party that is developing and becoming articulate in these conditions has all favorable conditions to select the best elements and the most positive and valuable people from the masses, and, to make them members of this organization. It is fundamental that these be precisely the best people, the best of the mass organizations—those who attain the honorable function of being members of the United Party of the Socialist Revolution (PURS).

The more that this is the case, the more every worker, peasant, intellectual, and citizen will realize that it means that every citizen can be a member of the United Party of the Socialist Revolution apart from whether he is a worker or not. That is, the gates are open for every true revolutionary who builds the revolution and is disposed to carry out his assignments and accept the program of the United Party of the Socialist Revolution fully and with complete conviction. . . .

Thus, I think that the ideal system, the most perfect encountered by man for governing a country (a system that does not aspire to be eternal but simply transitory, as are the stages which the history of a country is destined to realize) is a system of government with a revolutionary, democratically organized party under collective leadership. This means that this party ought to exercise the functions of leadership.

This is the best system if democratic standards function, if the standards of collective leadership function. If democratic standards do not function, if the standards of collective leadership do not function, then the system can be very bad, like any other system. But if the fundamental principles of internal democracy maintain a collective leadership, this is without any doubt the most perfect method of government, especially for a country in a stage of revolutionary transition.

What does this mean? In the first place, if this party is not a party that amasses membership but a party that selects them, the best citizens of the country will enter this party, on the basis of their conditions and merits. They will enter into revolutionary cells. There will be a long-term process of learning, direct experience, and the fulfillment of duty.

Little by little, because of his merit, a citizen can go on assuming responsibilities that continually grow greater. This citizen can arrive at membership of the regional directorate, of the central directorate, of the national directorate. He can hold these positions according to his merit. This is not the case of the king who passes on his power to his idiot son. It is not the case of a military leader who happens to be successful, because there can be men who are excellent war-makers and, as war-makers, acquire fame and prestige and, as rulers, are perfectly stupid. This is not a question of demagogues, or of clowns, or of theatrical personalities. In a party where the standards of discipline, principle, selection, internal democracy, and collective leadership predominate, a stupid person cannot advance—an idiot cannot become head of state. The lucky adventurer cannot do so. This school will be a school in which men are proving themselves, where they are learning and where they are acquiring proficiency. . . .

So what can the party of this revolutionary people do? This party will be the great instrument of merit, the instrument of revolutionary calling and revolutionary intelligence. This party should be above individuals, because it is the party that is going to include not the value of one intelligence, but the value of tens of thousands, of hundreds of thousands of intelligences; not the value of one hero, but the value of the heroism of all; not the value of one spirit of sacrifice, but the value of the spirit of hundreds of thousands of citizens and the spirit of combat, of love of the revolution. This is what the United Party of the Cuban Socialist Revolution must be.

22. Abel Alexis Latendorf

*Abel Alexis Latendorf was born in Buenos Aires in 1928. He was
an officer of the Federación Universitaria de Argentina (Argentine
National Union of Students) from 1945 to 1949, and represented it
abroad during the Peronist period, when it was forced underground. From 1957 to 1959, he was Secretary-General of the Central Committee of Socialist Youth, and in 1959 was elected a member of the Executive Board of the National Committee of the
Socialist Party. (The Argentine Socialist Party is the oldest and
strongest of the Latin American socialist parties.)*

*The selection below is taken from a collection of interviews
with Argentine leaders of the parties of the Left. Latendorf's responses are typical of orthodox Latin American socialism—in his
intense hostility to American imperialism, his insistence that only
the working class can carry out the anticapitalist revolution, and
his opposition to Soviet suppression of East European socialism.*

A SOCIALIST ANSWER TO LATIN
AMERICAN PROBLEMS*

The Left is the movement or political idea that calls for a change
in the capitalist social structure and the substitution of a classless society based on common ownership of the means of production and exchange. The Left proceeds from the Marxist proposition of the class struggle to develop a program that aims at the
liberation of the proletariat by its own effort, through a worker
party. Consequently, this proposal must relate the country in which

* Excerpts from an interview by Carlos Strasser, in *Las Izquierdas en el
Proceso Político Argentino* (Buenos Aires: Editorial Palestra, 1959); translated
by the editor.

it is made to the other countries in the historical space and time in which these relationships take place. It is not sufficient that there be a class feeling and a revolutionary group feeling or an idea to which one adheres. Especially in the underdeveloped areas, there must also be a strong anti-imperialist effort and solidarity with the struggle carried out by the masses in the nation as a whole. The Left is anticapitalist, anti-imperialist, anticlerical, antimilitarist, revolutionary without concession, and disposed to understand the country as it is and not as it would like it to be. . . .

U.S. Imperialism

The cases of Cuba, Venezuela, and Guatemala . . . should be all too instructive as to the possibility that handing over a national economy to Yankee imperialism can bring any benefit. Only revolutionary programs will solve the Latin American problem—solutions that will be carried out against the wishes of the United States and in spite of its imperialism. North American imperialism, at the height of its development, exports machinery (often technically obsolete), capital, and, on a much smaller scale, manufactured products. This is a new step in the development of imperialism. English imperialism exported finished products and capital for the public services. The new type of imperialism arises from the crisis in North America and its overproduction of machinery. Did English imperialism benefit Argentina? Does imperialism develop for the benefit of the countries it dominates? Are there examples in the history of the modern world of beneficent imperialisms? Argentina needs to develop its heavy industry, and North American imperialism has no interest in its development. . . .

The Popular Parties

There is no such thing as a bourgeois democratic revolution in Latin America. The proposals of the APRA and of Acción Démocratica, as well as that of the MNR, have evidently failed in practice and are on the way to collapse.* The attempt at this approach (which is valid for European countries in different historical and

* Alianza Popular Revolucionaria Americana (APRA) is the party of Haya de la Torre in Peru; Acción Démocratica is Romulo Betancourt's party in Venezuela; Movimiento Nacional Revolucionaria is the reformist party in Bolivia.—Ed.

economic conditions) explains the limits placed on the popular movements which were destroying political and economic structures and arousing the support of the peasant, mining, and factory-working majorities. . . . Each of the popular national movements of the Latin American Left is a clear and dramatic demonstration of the incapacity of the bourgeoisie for revolution. The revolutionary and distinctive creative force for the future of our people is in the working classes with a class-consciousness and class purposes. . . .

The Communist Countries

The case of China is distinct from that of the U.S.S.R. Yugoslavia and its national Communism should also be considered apart. There, economic and political development was carried out by the Communist Party and the guerrillas, not by Russian soldiers. The countries that are called "popular democracies" by the Soviets and "satellite peoples" by the Yankees should be treated separately from Poland, where true socialists work within Communism for the realization of a national way.

The Thirty-first Congress of the Uruguayan Socialist Party has clearly summarized the socialist interpretation of the political development in the Communist countries:

The Soviet Union has undergone a profound crisis. The Soviet bureaucracy which holds dictatorial power has deformed Marxism and profited from a special type of crude exploitation exercised over the countries of the frontier (which implies the existence of a real system), but it has been assaulted by a powerful mass movement which demands the cessation of its brutal oppression, free participation in the determination of its own destiny, and a better standard of living. There have been definite political indications of a readiness to make irreversible concessions, but there has not been a profound change in the structure of Soviet (governmental) organization. The most eloquent example of this process has been the Twentieth Congress of the Communist Party of the U.S.S.R. . . .

The crisis of Communism has had a special effect in those regions of Asia and Eastern Europe where popular revolutions or the power of the Soviet Army has created the so-called "popular democracies." These peoples learned a bitter lesson as to the subordination of their national destinies to the interests of the Soviet Union. Their economies have been subjected to the development and requirements of the Russian economy. The results have been pronounced

agricultural disorganization, acute distortion of industrial development, and, naturally, a sharp decline in the standard of living of
the people. It has also led to a brutal restriction of liberties, rights,
and profound cultural expression.

This complex of factors led to the revolutions in Hungary and
Poland, as well as the marked differentiation of the historic conduct
undertaken by China. These facts are eloquent indications of the
crisis of dissolution which is affecting the Soviet world and adds to
the process initiated by Yugoslavia, eloquent proof that the peoples
—especially the working class—repudiate the exploitation and re-
visionist heterodoxy of Soviet doctrine and maintain a lasting hope
in a socialist future. It is especially instructive that these popular
revolutions, wherever they took place, did not intend to restore the
old capitalist regime, but rather struggled to establish a true socialist democracy, overthrowing the bureaucratic system, and creating worker councils and, for a lamentably brief but well-known
period, liberation from political oppression.

The Anticolonial Revolution

Perhaps we can consider the revolutionary effort of the despised
masses of the colonial, semicolonial, and dependent countries as
the most important event of this century. In some countries—
in Burma, for instance—it was the socialists themselves who led
the popular struggle against imperialism. Socialism ought to support liberation movements of Asia and Africa, even when they
do not share all its principles, for they constitute an inevitable
stage toward a new internationalist, proletarian world. As in Asia
and Africa, especially in Latin America, the function of socialism
should be to act as the vanguard of the masses in the struggle for
the integration of our Balkanized countries against imperialist
pressure. However, it is necessary that the socialist worker van-
guards breathe class methods and purposes into these mass national movements. Only in this way can these great mass movements avoid becoming victims of their limitations and doctrinal
errors. . . .

European Socialism

The English Labour Party and the European Social Democratic
parties in general have very different conceptions from that which
is valid for the underdeveloped countries. They can be criticized
for not having worked with the proletariat in the ardent effort

to prevent the outbreak of two world wars. In general, we must admit that European social democracy is appropriate to social conditions that are different from those of the underdeveloped countries, where conditions are becoming more acute. Consequently, revolution is more likely in the countries on the periphery than in those of Europe. English labor has been influenced by these conditions to work for access to Parliament and to the comfort that can come from an increase in the standard of living of its population at the cost of the living standards of the workers of the exploited world.

23. *Victor Raúl Haya de la Torre*

Victor Raúl Haya de la Torre was born in Trujillo, Peru, in 1895, and educated both in that country and in England. He began political activity as a student and, after leading a protest movement against the government, was jailed and expelled from the country. While in exile in Mexico, in 1924, he formed the Alianza Popular Revolucionaria Americana (usually referred to as the APRA, or Aprista Party). Its program called for the involvement of the Indian in political life, Latin American unity, and opposition to foreign imperialism. In 1931, he returned to Peru from exile to run for the Presidency. He probably won the election, but the government imprisoned him and killed many of his followers. He was released in 1933, but went underground to avoid being arrested again. In 1945, he came out of hiding, and his party, supporting the election of a Conservative President, won a considerable electoral victory. In 1948, however, dictatorship returned to Peru, and Haya de la Torre took refuge in the Colombian Embassy, where he remained until 1954, when he was given a guarantee of safe conduct to leave the country. After the overthrow of the dictatorship in 1957, he returned to Peru.

Now once again active in national politics, Haya de la Torre was a Presidential candidate in June, 1962. He received the largest number of votes, but the elections were nullified by a military coup d'état. *His political writings are characterized by an effort to develop a distinctively Latin American (he would say Indo-American) political formula which does not imitate European or American models. He is anti-Communist and anti-imperialist, but believes that an alliance of the workers, the peasants, and the middle classes can control and utilize foreign investment (for "imperialism is the first stage of capitalism in underdeveloped countries"), establish rural cooperatives, and develop the countries of Latin America under a "directed" economy which also allows private enterprise and initiative. The works from which the following selections are taken were published two decades apart. In his more recent writing, as is evident here, Haya de la Torre has somewhat softened the dogmatism of his original theory, particularly with regard to nationalization and relations with the United States.*

INDO-AMERICA*

In my opinion, the term "Spanish America" corresponds to the colonial epoch, the term "Latin America" corresponds to the republican period, and the term "Pan-America" is an expression of Yankee imperialism. "Indo-America" is the expression of the new revolutionary conception of America which, having passed through the period of Spanish and Anglo-Saxon conquests, will create a definite political, economic, and social organization on the national base of its workers, who represent the tradition, and the race of the exploited indigenous masses who, throughout the economy of (Central and South) America (the unity of which is indestructible) have formed the basis of our productivity and the core of our collective life from the time of the period before Columbus.

It is true that the terms are used at the same time. Some say Pan-America, others Spanish America, some Latin America, and others Indo-America. But this coexistence has a social and economic significance. Up to the present day in (Latin) America, there has also been both a coexistence and an opposition between the various periods of historic evolution that followed after one an-

* Excerpts from Victor Raúl Haya de la Torre, *¿A Dónde Vá Indoamérica?* (Santiago de Chile: Biblioteca América, 1936); translated by the editor, by permission.

other in other continents. In (Central and South) America, we have, living together and at the same time in opposition, within the frontiers of our continent or even within the frontiers of each country, all forms of social organization and every level of economic development—savagery, barbarism, and civilization, communal primitive agriculture, feudalism, manufacturing, industrialism, and imperialism. Indians who have never known the use of a wheel as a means of locomotion see swift airplanes in the skies above their mountains. The young gentleman of Buenos Aires who plays golf and visits London has as compatriot and fellow citizen the half-naked Indian in the Chaco. The same thing is true in Peru and Mexico and Colombia and Central America.

This lack of definition, this contradiction, this historic juxtaposition, if the terms are appropriate, describes in great part the dialectic of our educational development. (Latin) America has been and is a land that has experienced invasions—as Europe once did. From the immigrations and transmigrations of the period before Columbus . . . from Asia, from Indo-America, from Oceania, from the North to the South and back, America has been the site of invasions and countless conquests. Three centuries of Spanish domination represent a long period in our history. It seems to us almost an eternity because it was so recent, but it is less in time than the eight centuries of Arab domination over Spain, for example. The Arabs gave Spain a great civilization and formed a southern racial mixture. They left behind 10 per cent of the word-roots in the language, according to the philologists. The Arabs would have the right to demand, as thanks from the Spaniards, that they call Spain Ibero-Arabia or something similar. But the Arab invasion was just that—an invasion—and historically it created a movement of independence in which many Hispano-Arabs fought to free themselves from the tutelage of their racial ancestors. The religious factor in this struggle corresponds to the period and is less clear than in the struggle of the natives [of Latin America] against Spain. Yet, in both conquests and "reconquests," we can see economic causes which are the basis of all great historic phenomena.

In (Central and South) America, after suffering the inroads of feudalism and mercantilism along with the conquest and Spanish colonization, we now have been suffering the invasion of industrialism or capitalism. . . . It may be that this new invasion will be less extensive in this period, when everything proceeds at a faster pace, but it *is* an invasion with its own particular characteristics, its own particular politics, and with formidable social effects. The question for the future is whether we will undergo further invasions. Underneath these conquering influences from outside, there persists one economic fact—the conqueror always seeks wealth. And the Indian or his descendants, in the great majority, work to create this wealth. It has been calculated by experts that there are more than 75 million Indians in (Latin) America. This means approximately 75 per cent of our total population.* Those Indians, with their own traditions, their own languages, their own suffering and aspirations, with their own great problem, constitute in their immense majority a work force, "productivity," the hand that creates the riches. This is the way it has been from the social point of view until now and, relatively speaking, always in (Latin) America. . . .

We in the vanguard, the Apristas, the anti-imperialists of (Latin) America, who are inclined to interpret history economically, have adopted the term Indo-America as a fundamental expression. The invasions of the Anglo-Saxon, Spanish, and Negro races have come to us, are coming to us, and will come to us; they have contributed and continue to contribute to the context of a new (Latin) America. Yet there survives underneath all these the force of the labor of the Indian. If in Cuba he has been wiped out and in Argentina and Costa Rica absorbed, the Indian continues to be the ethnic, social, and economic basis of (Latin) America. This is true both for those who live in the framework of modern civilization and for those who in great number are still grouped in primitive tribal organizations. Many other races are mixed with the Indian race, but this America of ours will find its identity and its course before those 75 million natives have disappeared. Every immigration, every conquest has partially modified the Indo-American race, but the ethnic basis of our people is still definitely native.

Those who live in this period struggle against the Yankee capitalist imperialism just as those who lived 100 years ago struggled against feudal Spanish, French, and Portuguese imperialism. Yankee domination, if it lasts, will also leave its profound traces on us, just as the Spanish domination did. The "Latin American" period, which historically replaced the "Spanish American" period,

* The present population of Latin America is nearly 200 million—double Haya de la Torre's 1936 estimate.—Ed.

can be succeeded also by a "Pan-American" stage. We are working against this, especially as regards its imperialist implications. After these three stages, which result from ethnic, political, economic, and spiritual invasions, will come the Indo-America which is to be established and defined. The new revolution in Latin America will be a revolution with an Indian base and orientation, with the native conscience and subconscious expressed in an economic and social renaissance. The Mexican revolution is a symptom of this great movement. The countries where the Indian does not predominate in Latin America cannot withdraw from his influence. . . .

Imperialism in Action

The first stage of industrial capitalism in Central America, as in the majority of our countries, begins with imperialism, which is "the last stage of capitalism" in the typical industrial countries. Capitalism arrives then in these agrarian countries at the height of its expansion, voracious, and developed, without any of the bourgeois virtues that emerged during the historic evolution of European societies in the period of transition from feudalism to industrialism. In Central America, as in most of the Latin American countries, capitalism arrives already imperialist, violent, and piratical, not to construct but only to exploit and withdraw all, leaving almost nothing behind. Vice, corruption, false views of life and of progress are raised up in consequence, and only sorrow and disillusionment are left, a grave danger for those people—their most complicated and serious political, economic, and social problem. . . .

The Struggle of the Two Imperialisms

There are two imperialisms struggling for Latin America, that of Europe and that of North America. But European imperialism is continually losing its influence, while North American imperialism is increasing. Business . . . is one of the aspects and manifestations of imperialism. The commercial struggle between Europe and the United States for Latin American markets is one of the most important consequences of the imperialist struggle between the United States and Europe, a struggle that has other manifestations in the battle for special concessions—linked to the tendencies for political domination of our countries of which

Pan-Americanism is an instrument—and to the subjection of the economic life of our countries to the investors. . . .

The Reform of Cordoba

After 1918, from one end to the other of the Latin American continent there arose a new awareness among the youth. From the old University of Cordoba there was the first outcry: "Until now, the universities have been a perennial haven of mediocrities, a source of profit for the ignorant, a secure shelter for the weak, and, what is still worse, a place where all forms of tyranny and stupidity find a source of inspiration. The universities have succeeded in being the faithful reflection of those decadent societies which present a sad spectacle of senile immobility. For this reason, knowledge passes silently by those mute and closed dwellings, or enters mutilated and grotesque into the service of bureaucracy. If in the name of order we are asked to follow along deceitful and docile, we proclaim aloud the sacred right of revolution. Henceforth, the only hope is the heroic destiny of the youth. Sacrifice is our greatest stimulus, the spiritual redemption of the youth of Latin America our only recompense, for we know that our ills are the ills of the entire continent." And the "sacred right of revolution" was exercised in Cordoba, in Buenos Aires, in La Plata, in Lima, in Montevideo, in Santiago de Chile, in Havana, in Bogotá, and in Mexico. The students of the old universities revolted against the past. In that tumultuous and lyrical movement against the old educational systems, there streamed a new spirit of youth which sought to free itself from everything that closed off the past from the future. Henceforth, there was only one (Latin) America. In its broad and fertile lands, a struggle has arisen that will be final. On the one side, the spirit of the past—reactionary and diminishing; on the other side, the revolutionary impulse of youth, which sees its destiny looming up before it. From 1918 to 1925, the conscience of the youth developed and became more precisely defined. At that time, it aimed at the renovation of the educational system and a spiritual confederation of Latin America. Today it seeks a more profound transformation. It struggles for the renovation of the social systems. It aspires to a political confederation of our twenty republics which are divided by artificial nationalism and menaced in common by the conquering imperialism of the United States and the North.

The spirit of (Latin) American youth continually advances to the future. Misunderstood by the old generations of our bourgeois classes, by our bureaucracies, by our oligarchies, it has in them a near and implacable enemy. Young blood, blood of the new liberators of America, has watered our soil. Graves for our new victims have been dug in our land each time that our youth has proclaimed "the sacred right of revolution." But our struggle has hardly begun. Our enemies are powerful and inexorable. They consist in the alliance of Latin American feudalism, the sad remnant of the conquering brutality of Spain, and powerful Yankee imperialism—animating spirit of our new bourgeois class, exalter of our provincialisms, inciter of our tyrannies, creator of our governments, and accomplice in our degenerate internal struggles. . . .

The Aprista Thesis

For the fulfillment of *Aprista* doctrine, a party has been created which, like the work it hopes to accomplish, is Latin American in character. The base of this party is in the producers, in alliance with the middle classes, also involved in the struggle against imperialism. The party attempts to form an "anti-imperialist consciousness" in the working classes—a consciousness that they are the ones who produce for imperialism, and they alone are those who can place conditions upon it and constitute a force of liberation—without hoping that the proletarians of Europe and the United States will destroy the capitalist system, the origin of imperialism. The alliance with the middle classes reinforces the action of the working classes, especially those which are specifically laborers—new in their role as controlling forces in the state, just as the (economic) system in Latin America which determines their existence as a class is new.

Aprismo already has opened the doors to the future because, following the economic independence of Latin America—an independence that will have to be based on equality in the exchange of raw materials and finished products and the investment of capital according to the principle of progressive nationalization of the sources of production under the control of the state—it will bring about the industrialization of our countries. As a result, a working class will be formed, and favorable conditions will be created for the rapid total direction of the economy and the abolition of the capitalist system. While this revolutionary process is being carried out, *Aprismo* will utilize the anti-imperialist forces of today, not excluding the middle classes, which are threatened with extinction by imperialism. It will seek to defend them through the anti-imperialist state which, by nationalization and progressive socialization of the sources of production, will be definitely oriented in the direction of state capitalism, preventing the middle classes from tending toward large private capitalism, which would mean a return to imperialism.

Aprismo thus presents a complete doctrine and a realistic method of realistic action—that is, an integral economic, social, and political program to secure the economic independence of Latin America.

THIRTY YEARS OF *APRISMO**

The Land of Reflection

Aprismo can demonstrate a particular origin that distinguishes it from the other movements and doctrines of the same type in Indo-America—not only because of its characteristic Bolivarian militancy (it is in Bolivar's glorious name that only the APRA demands the unification of the continent), but also because of the special quality of the numerous movements that preceded it. One can trace their beginning from the active youth movement that between 1918 and 1923 established and propagated the University Reform in all of our republics. From this movement, the founders of APRA have drawn two active inspirational ideals to be translated into moral slogans: to liberate our generation from the "mental colonialism" of Europe, and to unite the intellectual and manual workers to attain together the ambitious goal of a democratic civilization—to establish a confederation of all of our peoples and to attain for them economic justice, without impairment of their liberty. . . . Without these guidelines, it would have been unthinkable, unexpected, and perhaps heretical to conceive or attempt a judgment from *here* and not from *Europe* of our particular historical reality and our special sociological problems.

*Excerpts from Victor Raúl Haya de la Torre, *Treinta Años de Aprismo* (Mexico City: Fonda de Cultura Económica, 1956); translated by the editor, by permission.

This continent was still the "land of reflection," alluded to by Hegel. In its soil were the buds, offshoots, and seedlings—accidental in all cases—of all the ideas, philosophic sects, literary novelties, and partisan tendencies that could be of use to the Old World. And thus, just as we had countless spokesmen of the utilitarianism of Bentham and Mill, of Saint-Simonianism and of Comte's positivism, of materialism with all its varieties, and of idealism of various kinds, and as there was no lack of monarchists, Jacobins, anarchists, and others, all with their respective heterodoxies and oppositions, by the same process—to pass over a century and move to the world conflagration of the first great war and beyond—Marxism was developed and the Bolshevik echo of Marxism resounded and then there sprang up the totalitarians, the racists, and the perennial growth of jingoism. But one or the other, those for, and those against, always in imitation—inasmuch as it was obligatory not to go beyond the European models, and not to be separated from their pre-established patterns of thought. . . .

Aprismo *and Communism*

The total separation between *Aprismo* and Communism is obviously fundamental. They start out from divergent historical conceptions. For Communism, the pronouncements of Marx, conceived in one area and one given period (Europe in the nineteenth century), are unimpeachable truths of universal validity. For *Aprismo*, the Marxist conception is an important historical antecedent, but not unchangeable. It is limited and relative to the particular conditions of space and time that make it dialectically opposed to a reality that is different from that of Europe. Marx himself declares in the prologue of *Capital* that the basis of his observation was England—the England of the industrial capitalism of the middle of the nineteenth century—and that from the examination of the English reality, he deduced his "theoretical ideas" as "physics observes the physical phenomenon wherever it occurs." The "classic soil" of the capitalist system is England— that is, the country which, being in the forefront of industrial development at that time, was the prototype of all the others. From here, in a generalization of universal scope, the founder of scientific socialism goes on to say in the same prologue: "The country that is the most industrially developed alone shows the way of the less developed, the image of their own future."

That is the English model. And this was an unfulfilled *European* prediction of world economic development. In the "mirror" (as some translators have figuratively translated the idea of Marx's word "image"), there was hardly the reflection of the future of many countries, and none was reflected as an exact replica. The evolution of capitalism has taken unexpected directions in the last hundred years, and some non-European areas have prospered economically without in any way resembling the special English model. . . .

Then, distinct from the Communist transplantation to Indo-America of the "party of only one class" and of the European employer, *Aprismo* has put forward arguments that thus far have not been answered: among others, that of the lack of comparability of the proletarian class of the large capitalist countries in a state of advanced industrialization which *produce machinery*, to the producing class of the colonial and semicolonial countries whose infant industrialism, working with raw or half-finished materials, *does not produce machinery*—a fundamental distinction to which I shall return shortly; also the various types of class-consciousness which cannot be confused, that of the long-standing and highly trained proletariats at a high level of civilization, and that of those with a brief history and a much slower and lagging development. *Aprismo* emphasizes the different character—so often referred to by the *Aprista* thesis—of the urban and rural middle classes of Europe and those of Indo-America and the necessity of incorporating our middle classes in the single popular front of *Aprismo*. For these classes are the first ones affected by imperialistic expansion, and from this source have come excellent leaders and vigorous civic movements in defense of the economic emancipation of our peoples. . . .

Between the Communist anti-imperialism in the service of the Soviet empire, and *Aprista* anti-imperialism in defense of our countries, there is the firm separation between two economic and social scenes which cannot be compared—that of the Old World and that of the New World. They should not be confused, despite the way in which the imperialists and their agents and helpers have thoughtlessly claimed to involve us against our will with domestic Communism, which is clearly obedient to foreign ideologies and direction and which attacks us unscrupulously and ceaselessly. . . .

Latin America and the French Revolution

For the discontented colonials of Portuguese and Spanish America, the French Revolution was a great example. Despite the fact that the social and political content of the French movement corresponded to an economic and social stage much more advanced than that which historically was the case among the Indo-American peoples, we adopted the slogans, the precepts, and the formulas of Paris as an infallible recipe that could give us also "liberty, equality, and fraternity." While in France this signified the collapse of feudalism, in Indo-America it represented the affirmation and independence of the feudal colonial power. There the landowning aristocracy was crushed, while here the landholding native aristocrats liberated themselves by revolution from the empire of the mother country and captured the state as an instrument of their class domination.

In these circumstances, the same antifeudal ideology of the French bourgeoisie was used in a revolution of the feudal landowning Spanish- or Portuguese-American class against the economic and political yoke that the Spanish (and Portuguese) crown imposed on it. And from this paradox alone, the result was that, paradoxically, the revolutions of emancipation of Indo-America resulted in political regimes that were democratic in name and corresponded to a later economic and social stage of bourgeois capitalism, but in contradiction to the feudal organization of the dominant system of production in our lands—since independence did not destroy the large plantation but confirmed it. The ideas of the French liberals and radicals lost their subversive effect once the Indo-American republics were established. The slaves were not liberated at once, in spite of the democratic creed. Despite the initial cry of emancipation, the slavery of the Indian continued. Isolation, dear to the landowner, the single class that triumphed from the revolution of independence, brought about the division and subdivision of the ancient viceroyalties of Spain into many republics. All this took place because the economic basis on which society rested was feudal. . . .

Imperialism, the First Stage of Capitalism

Aprista theory recognizes that imperialism, the first stage of capitalism in our countries, brings with it industrialization, although this is unilaterally imposed, and it represents a period of evolution of the economy and of civilization superior to that of colonial feudalism. Modern imperialism, especially North American imperialism, which is so advanced and refined in its methods, only offers advantages and progress at its outset, and produces in our country a progressive movement of the working masses who pass from semislavery and servitude or from the elementary forms of free labor to its specifically proletarian type.

It should be said that as "the *first* stage of capitalism," imperialism brings about the emergence in our countries of the industrial proletarian class, although, for this particular type of industrialism, which is not metalworking, manufacturing, or heavy production, this proletariat is very far from displaying the same characteristics and having the same experience and same class-consciousness as the long-standing and highly trained proletariats of the imperialist countries of developed industrialism. Our industrial working classes in a semicolonial industry of raw materials have a different character.

Thus, imperialism as an economic phenomenon, as the first stage of capitalism in Indo-America—as a stage of ineluctable, progressive industrialization—is both dangerous and necessary. With it, we run the risk of subjection, but without it, there would be inevitable stagnation and retrogression.

Given the preceding propositions, we can conclude that the way for the Indo-American peoples to defy imperialism is to defend themselves from inundation, but without making the water disappear. With this advanced figurative comparison, we mark one of the fundamental *Aprista* declarations, different from those which serve as pretexts for the Communist theses on the phenomenon of imperialism. These tend to direct revolutionary action to stop up the very sources and foundations of the whole system of capitalist production, one of whose huge and widespread effects is imperialism. My book in 1928 has already explained with all exactness that industrial capitalism, which is imported into Indo-America with the imperialist stage, is incipient, young, and colonial or semicolonial in type; that it cannot be compared, as to both its origin and its method of production to the industrial capitalism of the regions of the world in which this economic system has developed. Consequently, this imperialist capitalism has created an industrial proletarian class that is also distinct from the old and organically established industrial proletarian class of Europe. Using their own Marxist teachings as a weapon of argument against the

Communist generalizations—according to which the capitalist system can be eliminated only by the revolutionary activity of the industrial proletariats of countries that are highly developed, where class-consciousness and organizational strength have made possible that transformation—my book concludes "that the radical abolition of the capitalist system cannot be accomplished except where capitalism has arrived at the climax of its development, namely in the large countries, which are in the vanguard of world industry. It does not then have to be in the colonial or semicolonial countries—which, recently, are experiencing the first capitalist stage or stages—that capitalism can be destroyed."*

On the other hand, the economic capacity of the United States does not permit us to assume that an impending collapse of its power is so near that it would signify our unexpected emancipation. Still, supposing the defeat of the United States in a military conflict with another imperialist power, would this bring liberty to Indo-America or reduce it to submission under a new master? . . .

The Mexican Revolution

This is the first instructive lesson of the agrarian revolution in Mexico upon which APRA draws. This movement and the University Reform are the two particular Latin American developments of this century that are precursors of *Aprismo*. From the latter comes the current of reform leading to our emancipation from mental colonialism through a new interpretation of Indo-American life; and from the former come numerous lessons in iron and steel given by a social revolution that is not socialist, but agrarian, antifeudal, and anti-imperialist.

In my book of 1928, I reiterated these concepts, which I had already published earlier, from 1924 on: The Mexican revolution is the first social movement of our century. It antedates the Russian Revolution and, obviously, that of China, although the imperialist element of the United States press calls it retroactively Bolshevik or Communist, in the same way in which subsequently until today every democratic social movement of the Left in Indo-America has been labeled. But it is not only an agrarian and antifeudal revolution, as it referred to itself in its adopted title, but something more. It is an anti-imperialist revolution and a heroic prelude of revolution. This double character of the Mexican revo-

* *El Anti-imperialismo y el APRA* (Mexico City, 1928), p. 22.

lution is, as I understand it, indivisible, and this explains many of the frustrations of that particular movement.

Aprismo recognized, then, in the Mexican revolution its particular social, nonsocialist character, although many Latin Americans repeated the European terminology in pompously calling it socialist, and I noted that, as far as that was concerned, "it is not indispensable to be Communist in order to be a revolutionary." But I noted as the principal cause of its "limitations and errors" the isolation of that cruel and heroic popular revolution, and with that assertion I confirmed one of the basic conclusions of our doctrine. No country of Indo-America can liquidate feudalism or emancipate itself economically from imperialism by itself. Both these tasks of general liberation go beyond our nationalist insularity and demand joint action by the countries of Indo-America. Feudalism and imperialism are economic and social systems that are continent-wide and exceed, in their organic field of activity and interdependence of interests, the frontiers of our twenty divided countries. . . .

Aprismo has maintained its premises: Capitalism, or the industrialization of Indo-America, begins in the form of imperialism. Our countries cannot destroy the capitalist system, whose roots and focal points are very far from us. The capitalist system, because of its economic capacity, does not allow us to assume its imminent downfall. Communism, with its dictatorship of the proletariat and its soviets, is unthinkable in Indo-America, whose socioeconomic reality is not Russian. Both Communism and fascism are specifically European phenomena. Our resistance to imperialism is in no form a doctrine of chauvinism against the people of the United States, because imperialism is an economic problem. Our anti-imperialist resistance supposes as the "first step" the political and economic unification of Latin America, and this union will bring us to the end of feudalism by progressive nationalization and cooperativist organization of agricultural production and of other types of wealth and the creation of a new type of state—the anti-imperialist and democratic state of the four powers: legislative, executive, judicial, and economic—based on economic and functional democracy. . . .

The Aprista State

The state proposed by APRA should be, first of all, a state of economic defense that is in opposition to the capitalist system, which generates imperialism—a distinct and special system that results in the abolition of the old oppressive regime. But the new state cannot be capitalist or bourgeois along the lines of France, England, or the United States (countries where capitalism has its origin and its base), nor can it be a feudal state. It is described as the "anti-imperialist state" because it should organize a new economic system, scientifically planned under the form of state capitalism—different from that attempted in Europe during the war, although aimed at directing the national economy and progressively bringing the production and circulation of wealth under state control. In my book of 1928, written more than four years before the election of Franklin D. Roosevelt as President of the United States, I could not use the North American New Deal as an example of that state control of the economy, but there was a clear reference to it as "cases of partial state control of the economy," as in Argentina with petroleum and in Uruguay with the reforms (so little studied in the other countries of Indo-America) introduced by the Colorado Party and its famous statesman Jose Batlle Ordónez. The new state, which would not be based on one class, but would be democratic and representative, involving the three major classes of our country—the peasant, the worker, and the middle class—would efficiently channel and coordinate the effort of the three classes represented in it, and would be the cornerstone of Indo-American unity and the effective emancipation of our peoples. . . .

Nationalization

The "progressive nationalization of wealth" can mean ownership, shared ownership, or control and supervision by the state (according to the situation) of certain sources of wealth—in particular, those which, since they are possessed by foreign businesses, end up in the hands of the governments of those nations of which the owners of the enterprises are citizens. *Aprista* nationalization is inclined to state control through development corporations, in accord with the mechanism of the democratic state of the four powers, and to the stimulation of agricultural and industrial cooperatives, but with respect and guarantees for private property, as in Mexico.

The program does not claim that nationalization without anything more is enough, since we place much emphasis on the scientific magnitude of the problem and the immediate necessity of studying it profoundly in order not to incur the very grave responsibility for having adopted under pressure a nominal and artificial nationalization that would lead to the failure of the business and the loss of the reform itself. In addition—and this ought to be clarified without equivocation—it is necessary to leave a wide field for private initiative, both national and foreign, in its constructive action to promote the ending of feudalism, and the industrialization which is indispensable for the progress of our people. There is a simultaneous, twofold task, to activate and to accelerate the evolution of the backward regions of our economy.

What, then, are those backward regions of the Indo-American economy that need to be activated and transformed in a new type of progress? I have said it already: They are fundamentally our feudal and semipatriarchal systems of primitive production; the reality and the spirit of the *latifundio*, which is still predominant in Indo-America. They are the feudal system that gives us the class of great semibarbarous lords of the lands and mines, slave-holders, masters of the country, and holders of power. They are the allies of imperialism who day by day become its agents and its subordinates. . . .

Relations with the United States

And this essential postulate (essential because on it *Aprismo* bases all its program of the relations between imperialist capital and our countries which require it) is expressed also in the concrete and repeated sentence which is the key to our conception of the problem of imperialism as an economic phenomenon: "The United States is as necessary for us as we are for her." On the basis of this premise, whose reiteration is always timely, the idea and program of the *Apristas* becomes more attainable.

But today, when the doctrine of the Good Neighbor Policy has begun to bear fruit with the detachment of political imperialism from economic imperialism, when North American capitalist investment in Indo-America has lost the unconditional protection of Washington, it is more feasible to demonstrate that imperialism, as the first and necessary stage of capitalism in the underdeveloped countries, has a constructive economic function and fulfills a historic mission of progress with respect to the systems of production which preceded it. Still more, it has also been possible for it to become evident that imperialism, freed from the patronage of the Department of State, could and can meet with the states of Indo-America in conditions of relative equality, and thus negotiate with them, and that this negotiation would bring mutual benefits, because it is based on a principle specifically established beforehand—that foreign capital which seeks areas of investment in our country is driven by an economic necessity as pressing as that which requires us to receive it. By such a reciprocity of interest, it is possible for our states to control investment by a planned and coordinated economy and through appropriate legislation, which guarantees just security to foreign capital. All this depends on us and not on the United States. . . .

Intervention

What is important is to begin by distinguishing good and licit intervention from bad and illicit intervention. . . . Collective intervention can be justified when it is a matter of defending the very existence of a democratic regime based on popular sovereignty —without which the state lacks the institutions of national sovereignty since the government cannot show the real mandate of the people when it has usurped it. It is this case of flagrant usurpation, the most frequent and demoralizing type of attack against democracy in our continent, which should bring about a collective intervention which is fully permissible. Nevertheless, the restrictive propositions of the Inter-American Treaty of Reciprocal Assistance of 1947, of the Charter of the Organization of American States, and of the Pact of Bogotá of 1948 refer exclusively to "external aggression," whether by force or not, of one state against another which can endanger the peace of America from within our hemisphere or outside it, and this is where the weakness of the so-called Inter-American system is evident, the principal objective of which is "to maintain the peace and security of the continent" and not to protect the integrity and security of the democratic order based on pure respect for human and civil rights. For, if indeed it is announced in the Charter of the Organization of American States that "the solidarity of the American states and the high purposes with which it is pursued require the political organization of these states on the basis of the effective exercise of representative democracy," and if they proclaim "the fundamental rights of the human person" and point out what this means for well-being, for work and culture, without any distinctions of any kind, all this is only so much poetry, as beautiful as it is elusive, in the majority of our republics. No democratic principles can be valid and lasting when the fulfillment and implementation of those precepts is confined to governments whose democratic values can be trampled underfoot by any general seizing power and supplanting popular sovereignty with the bayonet.

24. Romulo Betancourt

Romulo Betancourt, the son of a wholesale grocer, was born in 1908 in a village twenty-five miles from Caracas. Educated in Caracas, he began his political career in a movement against the Gomez dictatorship in 1928, when he was a third-year law student. He was imprisoned and then took refuge in Costa Rica, Colombia, and Peru. After the death of Gomez, he returned to Venezuela in 1936 and organized an underground revolutionary party. In 1939, he was expelled from Venezuela and went to Chile, where he headed a committee that organized the First Congress of Popular and Socialist Parties—a meeting of the democratic reform parties of Latin America. In 1941, he returned to Venezuela and established the Acción Democrática Party. In 1945, he headed a revolutionary junta that prepared the way for the election of Romulo Gallegos as President in 1947. Nine months after taking office, Gallegos was ousted by Perez Jimenez, a military dictator, and Betancourt again went into exile. When a popular uprising with military support overthrew Perez Jimenez in 1958, Betancourt was elected President.

The following selections indicate Betancourt's conception of the historical roots of Latin American social problems, and his party's program of democracy, economic planning, agrarian reform, and government regulation of foreign investment.

DEMOCRACY IN VENEZUELA*

When our country was discovered, the Spaniard found here not a people of advanced native culture, like the Aztec, but the people of a primitive pastoral economy. But here, as in the rest of Latin America, the work of the Spanish discoverer was that of conqueror rather than colonizer. It is interesting in this respect to note the observation of Hegel in his *Lectures on Universal History* regarding the fundamental difference between the practices of colonization in North America and in Latin America. In the northern part of our continent, the Anglo-Saxons arrived as people who were already living in an advanced stage of economic and social development in their motherland and had experienced the industrialization of a modern country. Latin America was conquered, but not colonized, by two of the most backward nations of Europe who were living in a state of feudalism and could not bring modern organizational methods to America, since those modern methods did not exist in their homelands.

The historic evolution of our country began with the despoiling of the indigenous masses. Land passed from the hands of its natural proprietors to the hands of the conquerors. José Vasconcelos has recorded the form in which landed property was established in our countries. Land was given to agents "as far as the eye can see." In this form, landed property originated in our countries on the basis of large plantations (*latifundios*)—on the basis of the concentration of great extensions of land in very few hands—and this is the way our economy, based on slave labor, was established. When there was not a sufficient number of Indians for the most difficult work, when it was necessary to have people in the mines who were physically stronger, Negroes were brought from the African jungle.

The colonial evolution created a distinctive Venezuelan social structure. A French traveler, François de Pons, who visited the eastern coast of the *terra firma*—as our country was called in the poetic geography of those times—noted that Venezuelan society

* Excerpts from Romulo Betancourt, *Trayectoria Democrática de una Revolución* (Caracas: Imprenta Nacional, 1948); translated by the Editor.

(substantially the same as today) was like an inverted pyramid: at
the summit, a privileged minority, and an extensive human base
made up of all varieties of the popular working classes going from
the Negro and the Indian to the quadroon and mulatto. Within
this pitiful mass there were many slaves. In the evolution of the
colonial period, there emerged a dominant class made up of the
descendants of the *conquistadores,* who fought with the authorities in Central America for political and economic reasons.
Economic reasons are noted by Bolivar in his magnificent letter
from Jamaica: the Spanish monopoly on foreign commerce, the
legal limitations established on the development of certain agricultural products, the heavy taxes necessary for Spain's maintenance
of a parasitic court in Europe.

In addition, the domestic nobility became a cultivated class
which, in the lecture rooms or in Spain, acquired a knowledge
of various matters. The contraband literature of the (French) en-
cyclopedists came to it. In 1810, this class revolted. The revolution of independence thus developed as a movement determined by specifically economic and social causes. But it would
be a fatalistic and mechanistic conception of history to say that
it was only for these reasons that the revolution of independence
took place. It was conditioned by previous historical facts and
phenomena, but it was carried out by the dynamism of men who
were no more than thirty years old, led by Simon Bolivar. . . .

But independence, which freed us politically from Spain, was
frustrated as a movement of social emancipation. Bolivar was in
fact expelled from Venezuela by the oligarchy, which did not want
an economic and social change. Bolivar had been the first to suggest the question of agrarian reform in Venezuela. In 1830, in place
of a division of the land, pieces of paper and military goods were
distributed. This enriched certain speculating businessmen and
some of the military leaders. . . .

Because of the great role which we played in the war of independence, because of the fact that the Liberator [Bolivar] was born
in Venezuela, there has always been a warlike sentiment in the
national subconscious and, together with this, permanent discontent among the people that they cannot enjoy the most elementary advantages of material and spiritual life. The popular
masses of Venezuela have always been ready to follow the first
military leader who launches a demagogic proclamation. This ex-

plains our constant civil wars and also why Venezuela has been a
land of successful military leaders.

Little by little, the economic and social realities have changed.
The discovery of oil—despite the very slight benefit the country received during the dictatorship of Gomez—permitted the state to
construct highways. Although it was hardly the intention of the
dictator, these highways, with all their imperfections, contributed
to bringing Venezuelans together and establishing links among
them. They basically undermined one of the negative factors in
our history, the interregional rivalries and struggles among the
states, which were based on the lack of contact and mutual ac-
quaintance among the various regions of a country like ours, with
a population that numbers less than 4 million inhabitants and is
dispersed throughout an immense geographical area of 625,000
square miles.

The evolution in military technique obliged the dictatorship to
create a military school. Since modern arms cannot be handled by
illiterates, it was necessary to have education. But culture is the
most vigorous enemy of autocratic governments. This military
school created by the dictatorship was dominated by the spirit
of that young, technically minded officialdom of our country,
which, together with the people, made possible the Revolution
of October 18, 1945.

Simultaneous with the creation of the petroleum industry,
the dissatisfied and class-conscious proletariat of that industry
appeared in various regions of the country. Beginning in 1936,
this alert and vigilant proletariat was one of the most resistant
and solid bulwarks of the democratic movement of the country.
In 1937, the popular candidates received 96 per cent of the votes
in the municipal elections, despite official repression and lack of
liberty. Our country has demonstrated its capacity for democracy,
and each time that there have been elections, notwithstanding the
skepticism which fear of fraud created, the electorate has responded by casting its votes in the voting booths. All this demonstrates that the pessimistic sociologists are wrong. Venezuela, like
Colombia, Brazil, Chile, Cuba, and all the other countries of
Latin America, is perfectly capable of organizing itself in an
economic, political, and social order. We are a people who can
be governed democratically and legally. We are resolved to follow
our own course, to make our own history. We do not wish to adopt

a contemplative attitude with regard to the past, burning incense before the portraits of our liberators and behaving like descendants unworthy of them. We are a people who are accomplishing something that will be the pride of the new America.

POSITION AND DOCTRINE OF ACCIÓN DEMOCRÁTICA*

Democratic Planning

The additional income that Venezuela can obtain from its petroleum and its iron ore must be distributed in an honest and rational fashion, but even with the greatest administrative honesty, if there is no system of priority of public investments, if the country is not convinced that there are basic problems whose solution is indispensable, we would not be responding to the challenge which is presented to all Venezuelans—the challenge of being a country which is paradoxically among the most wealthy in Latin America and the most overwhelmed with problems and calamities. The investment of public income cannot be carried out, in our opinion, without a system of planning, without a coherent plan. Indeed, there are two forms of planning—the authoritarian form, which is carried out in Russia, for example, by compulsory methods, and democratic planning, such as is taking place in India under Nehru and in Puerto Rico under Muñoz Marín. . . .

Democratic planning means the orientation of public investments in accord with a strict system of priorities and the creation of an atmosphere favorable to private activities that are productive of wealth. It does not mean a police state imposing on every business what must be produced and how much should be produced— but a system for the rational application of fiscal resources and the orientation of private capital in directions useful for the whole community. . . .

* Excerpts from Romulo Betancourt, *Posición y Doctrina* (Caracas: Edition Cordillera, 1959); translated by the editor.

Agrarian Reform

It is also necessary to carry out agrarian reform in Venezuela. This is a thorny question, but we must discuss it with direct frankness. Agrarian reform and the modification of the system of landholding and development is necessary in Venezuela for reasons of economic development and for social harmony. There is dangerous social discontent in Venezuela. Professor George Hill, who directs the faculty of sociology in the Central University of Venezuela, wrote thirteen years ago about the average peasant in our country. Now, coming back here, he has said publicly that he met in rural areas exactly the same problems he had seen more than a decade ago: the lack of land, of schools, and of sanitation for the peasants. In addition, today there is the difference that the vast, impoverished peasant masses compare their own backwardness and misery with the economic development of the city. . . .

Agrarian reform is possible, and we Venezuelans concerned about the national future will carry it out by normal and peaceful means, without violent conflict, through the application of reasonable laws. There is no question of expropriating the farmer or the plantation owner who cultivates his own land, since in this country, where there is a tendency to invest rather in urban development, whoever goes to the country to work on it ought to be actively encouraged. When a necessity arises to expropriate a certain piece of land, the logical course is to pay its owner partly in cash and partly in agrarian bonds issued by a financially solvent state such as Venezuela. There is no need for demagogy to arise in the country for us to proceed in accordance with the various differences of the different regions into which we are divided geographically and even culturally. In some places, we will have to establish a system of small landholding. In other areas, we will establish systems of cooperative production similar to those which were called "agrarian communities" in 1947. And in still other areas, there will be a system of industrialized agricultural enterprises. But in every case we must confront in a serious and responsible fashion the dramatic problem of Venezuela—that of the thousands of men without land and the thousands of acres of land without men. Any responsible government in Venezuela must confront this problem, and I am sure, because I have a rational optimism with regard to the level of maturity of this country, that this agrarian reform can be realized normally, as it was realized in Japan after the war under the government of a person who can hardly be called a revolutionary, General Douglas MacArthur. . . .

Regulation of the Oil Industry

What, then, can we do with the problem of the oil industry? There are two possible attitudes: that of the demagogue who says that the "bloodsuckers of Wall Street" and the "vultures of international finance capital" have a stranglehold on the country; or the other, the serious attitude of a responsible nationalist, that a government which has the support of the country because it has been chosen in free elections, and which acts on the basis of the reports of a National Petroleum Commission, on which all the political parties and all economic sectors and technical groups are represented, can suggest to the oil industry a change in the present situation.

Because I am not a demagogue, I have said more than once that this suggestion would have positive results. In 1945, when I had the honorable responsibility of presiding over the destinies of the republic, our government initiated new negotiations with the oil companies. We decreed the payment of a special tax on utilities in the years 1944–45 because we believed that those utilities had been excessive. In that form, the treasury obtained a supplementary income of 5 million bolivars. We established a 50-50 participation between the companies and the nation. For the first time, the Venezuelan state utilized the part of the oil that belonged to it as a royalty, as a matter of exchange, thus rectifying the absurd conception, accepted without question by previous administrations, that the government of our country could not receive commercial benefits from oil because the oil did not belong to it but to the companies.

Finally, the companies made contracts for the first time with the trade unions, and in three years this permitted an increase of nearly 200 per cent in the income of the workers' sector as well as increases in salaries and social assistance, with an evident favorable repercussion throughout the whole national economy—especially in the sectors of Zulia and the eastern states which produce petroleum, because the increased capacity for consumption of these areas evidently raised their purchasing power.

I have said that these negotiations can be carried out in the quiet manner of a commercial transaction, because it is not a question of making oil into an explosive political issue, but of acting like the proprietors of wealth who negotiate in businesslike fashion with those who wish to develop and exploit this wealth. I do not have the least doubt that a government elected by the people, representative, responsible, and made up of trained personnel with information regarding administrative problems, can secure a favorable readjustment in Venezuela concerning its principal and almost sole industry for the stabilization of the whole country. . . .

The Principles of Acción Democrática

We [Acción Democrática] are an organization which is democratic in philosophy, and, as a consequence of this, we affirm categorically that sovereignty resides in the people and that the people are the sole legitimate source of power. Only through the electoral process can the nation be governed legitimately.

We are a revolutionary organization—revolutionary in the sense that the word has in the contemporary political lexicon. That is to say, our organization is fundamentally interested in carrying out a structural change in the state and in Venezuelan society, but without resorting to violence—carrying out that change through normal and peaceful means of legal regulation. We do not conceive of democracy as simply a formal cover for an unjust social order. Hence, together with the guarantee of the exercise of civil liberties to all Venezuelans, we propose the redistribution of national income (which is very high in this country because of oil receipts) in a form that will make the economic misery of the majority of the people and social injustice disappear from the Venezuelan scene. Liberty, yes, but, together with it and complementing and stabilizing it, land and credits for the dispossessed peasant, the vigorous development of national industry (both that of manufacturing and that of agriculture and husbandry), and the radical termination of all administrative luxury expenses, to be replaced by expenditure on the basic problems of the nation—manufacturing which is really Venezuelan, education, sanitation; worker, peasant, and middle-class housing, highways and other communications, public services, and irrigation.

We are a nationalist and anti-imperialist party—nationalist because we think Venezuela should defend and strengthen its national character in the face of the risks to its particular way of life which threaten a small nation in a world in dispute among great powers. But our nationalism is neither backward nor chauvinistic. We believe that Venezuela cannot aspire to be an island outside the international community and, above all, outside the Latin American community. The mandate of history and the demands of today force the peoples of Latin America to move quickly toward forms of continental understanding and integration.

We are anti-imperialist because our party strongly rejects the idea that Venezuela should be the satellite of any other country. We labor for dignity on the international plane and only respect the multilateral pacts that are consented to freely. We do not admit the idea that foreign investors can treat a country as a colony. The natural riches of Venezuela should be exploited, preferably with resources and techniques of Venezuela, for the full profit of the country. The importation of foreign capital into areas where it is needed ought always to be allowed only if it comes by legal negotiation. We must reject definitively the conception held by sectors of international capitalism that when they invest in our country, they can consider it a zone of occupation.

We are primarily a party of the people. Workers, peasants, and members of the middle class form the wide base of our activists. The organic front of the exploited classes which are integrated in the AD coincides in its basic lines with the advance of other social classes. The industry, agriculture, and husbandry of our nation cannot help deriving benefits from the policy, put forward by the AD, of increasing the now subhuman level of income of the immense majority of Venezuelans.

We are a civilian party in the sense that we assign the function of directing and orienting public life to political parties formed of militants recruited in the streets and not in the barracks. But we have not been and are not antimilitary. We have always maintained—and we have confirmed this in government action—that Venezuela needs armed forces that are appropriate, sufficient, well organized and equipped, that enjoy the respect of the nation and are free of political influence. . . . We support the legitimate right of the Communist Party to function in Venezuela as a legal organization. When we are in power, we respect that right. We believe that "witch-hunts" in the twentieth century are contrary to the very essence of the democratic form of government, and everyone who supports an idea or purveys a doctrine has a perfectly legitimate right in a democracy to organize politically in favor of that idea and doctrine. But Acción Democrática—yesterday, today, or tomorrow—has not had, does not now have, nor will it have any ideological sympathy with the Communist Party. The Communist Party is organized in support of an international doctrine, and the doctrine of Acción Democrática has been forged to deal with a national reality. It is a doctrine with a definite, categoric, and irrevocably Venezuelan national character. . . .

We have said that we do not like the single [único] candidature, for as Monsignor Carrillo, Curate of St. Teresa's, has said, "God alone is unique." Whatever may be the arguments in favor of the single candidate, there is always a certain disagreeable plebiscitary air about it. The formula of the single candidate is understandable in countries where there is a single party, where there is a dictatorial governmental structure, whether of left or right. A single candidate can emerge in Russia or Spain, but not in a country where there is a free play of the parties.

25. Eduardo Frei

Eduardo Frei was born in Santiago in 1911. He took a law degree at the Catholic University of Chile in Santiago, where he was a prize-winning student and active in national and international student organizations. After finishing his studies, Frei went to edit a newspaper in Iquique (in the provinces), where he wrote his first book, Chile Desconocido (The Unknown Chile). In 1938, he was one of the group of young Catholic leaders who withdrew from the Conservative Party to form the National Falange, which stood for a reformist policy very different from that of its counterpart in Spain. Frei was President of the Falangist Party three times, and in 1945 he was named Minister of Roads and Public Works—a post he held for nine months until opposition to his reform proposals forced him to resign. In 1949, he was elected to the Chilean Senate, and in 1954 he was appointed by the United Nations Economic Commission for Latin America to head a committee to make recommendations for closer inter-American cooperation on development problems. In 1957, the Falangist Party changed its name to the Christian Democratic Party of Chile, and a year later the party nominated Frei as its candidate in the Chilean presidential elections.

In the following selection, Frei demonstrates the influence of the papal encyclical, Quadragesimo Anno (1931), on his thinking. He attacks the evils of Communism and capitalism and develops the Christian Democratic conception of a "middle way," which consists of the involvement of the worker in management and ownership, the promotion of intermediate groupings between the individual and the state, and state action to limit the power of large economic concentrations. While Frei admires the prosperity of the United States, he is critical of its failure to give Latin America adequate economic aid, particularly in view of the imbalance of the terms of trade which permits the U.S. to buy Latin American raw materials at abnormally low prices. The similarity of many of the practical conclusions of his theory (regarding planning, a mixed economy, and state control of foreign business) to those of reformists like Betancourt or Haya de la Torre is symptomatic of the increasing cooperation between the left-wing Christian Democrats and the reformist and popular parties, such as Acción Democrática in Venezuela.

CHRISTIAN DEMOCRACY IN THEORY AND PRACTICE*

Capitalism and Communism

If we compare the proposals of *Quadragesimo Anno* with the realities of the present, we can observe that they are still perfectly valid. The world of economics is still oscillating between the extremes of liberalism and collectivism, capitalism and Communism, free enterprise and statism. In the face of these, the encyclical proposed a system of moral ideas that can produce a different for-

* Excerpts from *Pensamiento y Acción* (Santiago de Chile; Editorial del Pacifico, 1958); translated by the editor, by permission.

mula. The task that was presented to Christians was precisely to construct this formula. Can we say that they have constructed it?

If we continue our observation, we can assert that the formulas presented at the two extremes are simple, effective, and, from their point of view, efficient. Are we able to offer a formula that is characterized by equal efficiency and clarity? This is the problem.

But the fact that these formulas are simple, effective, and efficient does not mean that they are appropriate—or, more precisely, that they give human meaning to the economy. We mean by this the subordination of economic goods not to the final purpose of the increase of wealth for profit or to a myth—the state—but to man, that he may attain his full development and his specific ends.

Slavery was a simple, efficient, and effective formula for centuries, and it still exists in many areas. Slavery is an institution that has always been present in the human species, has never disappeared, and today has appeared under more sinister guise, not based on the color of the skin as in the last centuries, but on the color of ideas, as has been fully demonstrated. Yet this does not justify it as a formula for economic organization.

Similarly, the advantage of these extreme positions, which consists in their real viability, does not justify them morally and ought not discourage us in our search for a new synthesis. It is a fact that the liberal economic system has produced the system of capitalism as the Pope described it. And here I would like to state a reservation and give an introductory explanation. I have come to think that the confusion of tongues at the Tower of Babel did not refer to the birth of the various languages, since that could have been resolved with translations, but to the fact that, in the same language, our words acquire a meaning so different that, according to who speaks them, they stand for concepts that are absolutely antagonistic. It would be useful to make a dictionary with the new and "Babelian" meaning of words.

The word that has been most corrupted by propaganda is "peace." When a Christian reads the word "peace" in the Gospel, he knows what it means, but if he reads Congress for Peace, he knows that it refers to a meeting convoked by the Communists to make propaganda for their doctrine, to attack the United States, and, in a way, to prepare for war.

There are a number of disturbing misunderstandings between the United States and Latin America, especially in economic and sociological terminology. "Liberal," for North America, means "progressive," while for South America it means an economic doctrine or party that supports the classical liberalism of Adam Smith, Locke, and other Europeans. The same thing is true of the word "capitalism," which for North America is synonymous with "democracy" and "free enterprise," rather than the regime and existence of monopolistic capital, the predominance of capital as an economic and social factor, as it was conceived and analyzed in *Quadragesimo Anno* and other documents.

There is something that we should understand. Capitalism as a system dehumanizes the economy, although, in its first stage, it meant an enormous expansion of economic development and the creation of wealth. Yet there is no doubt that it tended to concentrate economic power in a few hands, to allow the great monopolistic powers to control the market so that, by a fierce dialectical process within its own structure, it led to the disappearance of economic freedom. In the productive process, it separated labor from management and, more than that, from the concept of property and the exercise of that right.

With regard to [the evils of] capitalism, we note that there are two well-defined plans of action: the reformist and the revolutionary. The revolutionary aims at the destruction of the regime in a sudden, violent, and total manner. In fact [in revolutionary regimes], private capitalism has been replaced by that of the state, the property holder who controls capital by the bureaucrat who controls the power of the state, the business manager delegated by the stockholding property owner, by the managerial bureaucrat delegated by the government which administers the state, and the more and more concentrated powerful monopoly capitalists by the powerful supermonopoly of the state.

Basically, we could say of the two systems that Communism is a continuation of capitalism, drawing the latent tendencies in its structure to their logical conclusions. The two differ not in technique, but in purpose. Technically, there is no difference if the administrative group is made up of private stockholders or of bureaucrats representing state ownership. The difference is that the first is directed by various groups that exercise control for their own interests, and the second is directed by those who administer the state for the purpose of collective goals. This could be a greater justification of the second system, but if we analyze what has happened more profoundly, we will see that this advantageous result is more apparent than real.

On the theoretical level, this seems very clear, but at the practical level, it does not occur with the simplicity that the scheme appears to offer. When capitalism is a monopoly under the sole control of the state, there results as a consequence a concentration of power in the bureaucracy that is as merciless or more merciless in its operation than the private businessman. According to the classic example of the textbooks of sociology, a worker, representing labor, alone and isolated, appeared before the employer burdened by a triple inferiority—psychological, economic, and legal. But the condition of the worker who confronts the bureaucrat-employer suffers from the same inferiority and adds a fourth—political inferiority. The private employer wielded the weight of his economic power, while the state employer wields the weight of his economic and political power, since he also has behind him the purposes of the state. Hence, for the worker, his real juridical condition has not changed, only the name of his employer. . . .

But Christians refuse to accept the alternatives of capitalism or Communism, because they know how closely the two are linked in their basic development. It is curious that some have appropriated the idea of capital as if capital and capitalism were synonymous, although there is also a statist and Communist capitalism. Similarly, there are those who think that private initiative and personal liberty are synonymous with individualistic liberalism. The goals of liberty and initiative can only be conceived and realized in a new system of values. If they could be attained in the past century, in a limited class and social type, present historical conditions demand that they be indicated in a different social situation and with a different purpose and meaning. Freedom today depends on a decent standard of living, and initiative cannot be a matter of appetite and interest, but must be integrated into the collective common good.

It is a fact that capitalism and philosophic and social liberalism have not succeeded in giving expression to the desires of the common man. They have brought the world to an increasing proletarianization, which is the reverse of what is affirmed by some superficial arguments concerning the distribution of small property or corporation stocks. In economics, secondary facts are of no importance, and the terms are essentially relative. It is a question of power. Today someone who has a piece of land exercises his property right, but economic power resides in high finance, in the cartels, and in the concentrated holdings of the large corporations.

In this, everything is subject to change. A century ago, the one who dominated the textile industry controlled industrial power. Twenty years ago, a nation with a heavy steel industry led in economic and political domination. Today power resides in nuclear energy, and in time the possession of a steel industry will be no more important than the production of textile fabrics.

Production has become technically complex. It requires an immense effort of scientific creativity. It means the domination of vast markets, variable and delicate in their reactions, which are aimed at satisfying human necessities, but which do this by periodically destroying the man who produces the goods in order to serve the same man when he tries to satisfy himself as consumer. There is the latent danger of a machine system that is so fearful, moving at such a continually increasing velocity (it is enough to look at the production figures in the European countries which, seven years after being devastated by war, surpassed all the prewar levels, without citing the American figures, which can only be expressed in billions) that it can only be managed by concentrated and absolute power, because the uncontrolled expression of its demands cannot be resisted by a normal democratic state. On the other hand, to leave this machine system uncontrolled in a fundamentally weak state which does not have the active specific mission of defense of the common good would be even more fatal and impossible. The system of counterbalances of which Donoso Cortés spoke a century ago would be operative here: no internal control on man; propaganda that arouses an unlimited appetite for goods; economies that are incapable of satisfying the desire for these goods, arousing the multitude to desperation when it considers its misery. What is the only state which is able to discipline and contain this?

Thus it is that capitalism leads inevitably finally to Communism. Thus it is naïve to find the remedy in a system of partial improvement—a house and a salary. The problem of the economic system is much more profound and concerns the whole structure, the motivations, the fundamental conceptions of the economy and its purpose, and of man as a moral being.

A *Third Alternative*

But here there arises a new problem with regard to this productive mechanism whose technique dominates the world and whose moving force appears to subjugate it. The extremes present formulas that fasten on us like claws. Do we possess a way, a method, that offers something other than aspirations, intentions, or principles?

We cannot merely sketch an outline with a feeling of impending catastrophe, because this is not realistic and because there is no doubt that in many nations efforts are being made to develop a formula for the economy which has a human significance. These efforts correspond to the conditions of the natural life of man and to a historic evolution whose transforming movement takes place through a thousand actions and reactions; among which not the least is the influence which impels a revolutionary center toward the circumference, as was the case with the French Revolution and more recently with the Russian Revolution.

We can note, among these efforts, the developments in the Scandinavian countries, based on a cooperative socialism, as well as what is represented by the European Coal and Steel Community, and, in addition, the undoubted development in the conditions of North American capitalism—the laws for the control of monopoly, the worker organizations, the real spirit of social democracy, the progressive taxes on high income—so that it cannot be considered the same as the earlier individualistic form of capitalism. Nevertheless, this experience cannot be considered as entirely valid for us, for it occurs in very special conditions, because of both the immense wealth [of the United States] and the different character of its international trade and the profit it obtains from these exchanges, which permit it alone to enjoy the advantages of the system. There are also certain important experiences in Germany and Italy, and, still more important, the English experience of a great democratic nation trying to realize one of the greatest peaceful revolutions of recent times.

In all these experiences, we can say that they have tried to find a form of organization of the economy, not for money but in the interest of society. They have attempted to conceive the national economy as a whole in the service of the national community, to improve the conditions of work and elevate the standard of living, to find a way for the worker to participate in the very process of directing the economy, to assure for the state certain aspects of economic activity, especially the financial aspects, which, because of the power they exercise, cannot be in the hands of private persons.

Many of these experiments have constituted an undoubted success, and many a complete failure. No nation has demonstrated more valor and devotion in this attempt than Great Britain. The meetings of the Trades Union Congress are relevant in this matter. Maintaining a pronounced respect for individual liberty and personal property, and considering that private initiative and enterprise have controlled the whole economy and resources of the nation, keeping in mind the common interest of the nation, they have had the courage to progress and change whatever practical experience showed to be mistaken.

We are going to outline our position not only to those who accept Christian thought, but also to the groups called humanistic socialists, who have had practical experience with the program of Marxist socialism, but who also recognize the essential principles that have been maintained by Catholic philosophy on the sociological plane. The great task of Christians consists in being able to explain this method, which can be perceived only uncertainly and inexactly. Its principal elements have, as a matter of fact, been demonstrated to be valid.

The action of the state cannot be an absorbing and paralyzing intervention, but must respect intermediate organisms—the family, the city, the region, the trade union, the business enterprise. It must exert an effective authority for orientation, planning, and leadership. It ought to be strong enough to prevent the creation beyond its regulatory authority of economic powers which can oppress and control the market for products and for work. It cannot be the impotent witness of what goes on in the market, because it would mean the end of liberty if each citizen were left to act according to his interest and his influence.

For this purpose, it is necessary to have higher controls, to create new conditions and to coordinate but not to constrain them. It is necessary to have planning, because this represents the common good of the whole nation and because all isolated efforts represent only a part of the interest of the whole. We know today that the income of a nation is distributed among labor, capitalization, and profit. The state should know which part can be used for consumption and which should be utilized for capital, which proportion can go to the public sector and which to the private sector. It can and ought to maintain a monetary flow according to the volume of economic activity. No one today can believe that this must be subjected to a freedom that would be a fiction, destroying itself by the very mechanism of economic factors.

But this action for the common good can better develop and perhaps can only be developed when it is not thought that a progressive statism is being established when colossal bureaucratic powers are created, which, by their very ineffective existence, consume the resources they are administering so that the mechanism created by man destroys man rather than serving him.

We think, for example, that the government of the United States, when it created the Paley Mission to study raw-material resources, reserves, and conditions in the world, fulfills its task of watching over the destiny of the nation better than when an improvising government of ours thinks that it has made progress by its improvisation in creating new supervisory groups. . . . The same thing happened in Italy, where the government faced the problem of housing by establishing construction areas and factories for prefabricated materials, substituting for direct construction a national effort with the cooperation and initiative of all citizens. Thus the state served man better than by creating institutions which, whether for financial or technical reasons, have demonstrated themselves incapable of resolving this difficult problem. But this is hardly a mention of a fundamental theme whose concrete application must be worked out and defined. Nevertheless, there remains the fundamental question—namely, that of the economic structure itself, the functioning of the productive unit, and the harmonization of the factors that compose it. On this subject, it has been difficult to make progress. Some try communitarian forms, which are attractive without as yet having any experimental validity. The experiences of codetermination are thus far varied, but one cannot say that they are conclusive.

Today a new era is opening up. The business enterprise is composed of the investor who provides the capital, the manager, and the worker. If we could imagine a vast process of universal extension of property through the organized acquisition of shares by the worker, not in the limited context of the old worker-stockholder, but a planned and large-scale access of labor to capital, we could imagine a social organization in which man would participate in the economic process in two ways—as worker, by his salary, and as owner of capital, through profit. This process ought not to be thought of solely as limited to the enterprise in which the worker is employed, but applied to any enterprise, since the important thing would be to give the worker property and, more than that, to involve him in the process of capitalization, which is the foundation of the economic process, the condition of stability for the worker himself, and the sole form that offers the possibility of raising his standard of living.

This would require action that would make it easy for organized savings to go into investment, something that could not occur without a more equitable distribution, the present goal of the worker movement and of the employees. This type of investigation requires an effort of creative imagination, but it is an especially difficult problem that must be resolved, like all those which aim at transforming structures and institutions in which very diverse factors enter, which cannot be foreseen. Their difficulty cannot be appreciated except at the time when they are carried out, and no effort of logic is capable of anticipating it. It is for this purpose that I make these observations, to arouse others to the study of those possibilities which are open to reflection and action.

The publication of these investigations and studies also has another incalculable value. I would be bold enough to say that our good fortune of living together in a democracy (and I employ this word in its true sense and not in the extravagant abusive sense with which it is distorted and rendered vacuous) is linked to the effort to solve this problem. There is no doubt about the attraction of extremist formulas or, in South America particularly, about the failure of many attempts to realize social justice, not so much because of the resistance of "the interests" as the lack of a concrete vision and capacity for action on the part of those who feel and claim to interpret these desires. No one could affirm that the present type of economic organization has the consent of the working masses who support the productive process with their labor. Even among the managers and modern businessmen, dissatisfaction has penetrated deeply, but this lack of confidence is derived from the fact that those who have claimed to transform the system have not been able to offer anything else that is rationally clear, experimentally operative, and economically efficient. Progress has, in most cases, come down to an increase in the functions of the state and the dictation of a new law, but life has followed its old rhythm, and the conditions of work have remained the same, sometimes with the elimination of obsolete machinery, but without greater benefit either in the productive process or in social progress.

But this does not mean that this has brought peace or the conviction that it is not necessary to undertake reform. On the contrary, this has created more despair, bitterness, and skepticism, with the grave danger of directionless outbursts or the turning of the most active intellectual and proletarian elements toward the Communist doctrine as the form of organization of the state, the economy, and society.

The foundations of a humanistic economy should be the result of an encounter between our philosophy and the scientific experience that emerges from the economy—the vivid comprehension of the reality in which we live and the will for presence by the Christian as a constructive element in the society to which he belongs. . . .

The Economic Problems of Latin America

The Economic Commission for Latin America has done more to enable Latin America to discover itself, understand its problems, see its true situation, and penetrate to the basic causes that produce its poverty and its imbalance than all the unfounded oratory and excessive slogans without substantive basis. The economics faculties of the universities have developed in South America an understanding of the economic problem that has had two very important results. The first is that they know what they are talking about. This in itself is a revolution, since we know that very often the tragedy of some of the countries of South America is that they want to help themselves but they do not know how to do so or how to defend what they have. . . . The second fact, which I find as important as the first, is that this common language, supported by a scientific system of common ideas, reveals something of fundamental importance. Facts are neutral, and in all these countries whatever may be the governmental changes, the language of discourse is the same. It does not matter that a government of one orientation or another goes to conferences over the years, because in this area the foundation that supports their position is firm. They all point in the same direction, and consequently there is a common effort and, what is more important, a continuous effort, since the flush of oratory of one delegate at one time does not carry decisive weight. . . . From the speeches of the delegates of various countries, we can also draw certain specific conclusions from this conference:*

1. The inequity of the terms of trade.
2. The meaninglessness of the expression "private investment" because we have not had it, and because in general the system designed to attract it has not produced the results that were hoped for.
3. The unfair treatment involved in the world distribution of aid, of which only an insignificant percentage has gone to the southern continent.
4. The evident process of industrialization which Latin America has experienced and which in some countries has not meant any real progress except a progress at the expense of other activities, which has produced a serious internal disequilibrium that is revealed in a more or less accentuated inflationary process in which unfortunately we [Chileans] have gone the furthest.
5. Lastly, in relation to agricultural development, the nutritional situation is in need of fundamental reform. This is also a condition for any future policy of economic and social betterment. . . .

Cooperation with the United States

Today there are those who understand that (Latin) America can have a program for the future. Since nations cannot live solely for one day, they must develop hope and broad vision. The American continent does not have the glory—but neither does it have the tremendous burden—of the centuries-old traditions that prevent many nations from developing. America has youth and purity of intentions. This continent could be the synthesis of an authentic democratic process of which today we are only seeing the beginning. It could provide a program of hope for a world in torment.

The United States, thanks to its immense wealth, has developed a democracy which perhaps, with all its imperfections, is one of the most complete that has yet been witnessed. But it is a democracy built in part at the expense of a world economic disequilibrium.

If the United States would understand that it cannot have a continent behind it where distrust and hatred continue to in-

* The Conference of the Organization of American States, at Caracas, in 1954.—Ed.

crease, that it cannot get votes in conferences and formal agreements with governments which many times are imposed on countries and are not the result of their consent, that those among the
peoples of Latin America who defend the legitimate interests of
their nations are better friends for Pan-American cooperation, that
those who speak a clear language are much more capable of building a policy of solidarity in the future—then it would take a decisive step for American solidarity.

I think that no responsible person in Latin America can deny
the fact that cooperation with the United States is of fundamental
importance for this continent's economic development, its future
prosperity, and the well-being of its peasant, industrial, and mining
masses. If this cooperation does not exist, the masses of these
countries are going to experience long years of bitter suffering and
backwardness. Those who make use of hatred for strategic purposes are basically sacrificing their peoples. They are the counterpart of those who sell out (to the foreigner).

Those who really work for true friendship between Latin America and the United States are those who are proposing a policy of
justice, frankness, and cooperation, on the basis not of weakness
but of firmness in saying what is taking place. It is necessary to
convince the North American public that just as the workers of
the United States have succeeded by a bitter struggle in arriving at
a level of social justice without impeding progress, so also Latin
America must by bitter struggle arrive at full international justice
and real economic cooperation in defending its riches, in defending
its workers, and in defending its life.

26. Joscelino Kubitschek

*Joscelino Kubitschek was born in 1902. He received a medical de-
gree in 1927, and was then medical officer with various government
services before entering politics. He represented his home state of
Minas Geraes in the Brazilian National Assembly from 1934 to
1937 and again in 1946. From 1950 to 1954, he was Governor of
the state, and in 1956 was elected President of Brazil. In 1958, he*

wrote a letter to President Eisenhower proposing Operation Pan-America, a vast program of economic assistance to Latin America, similar to that finally adopted by the Kennedy Administration under the title Alliance for Progress. In the following selection, he discusses the prospects for democracy in Latin America.

OPERATION PAN-AMERICA*

Some of the factors that get in the way of stable democracy, to which I have alluded, are powerful in Brazil. It was with this in mind, and knowing the economic outlook in Latin America, that I wrote a letter to President Eisenhower on May 28, 1958, suggesting that all of us in this hemisphere examine our consciences about all of our shares in the destiny of Pan-Americanism. It was this letter that started the movement known as Operation Pan-America, which today has been changed—I do not know why—to Alliance for Progress.

The objectives of the Alliance for Progress cannot be based exclusively on stopgap assistance. It must aim fundamentally at two objectives: to help strengthen the economic structure of the Latin American nations, and to contribute toward the stabilization of commodity and raw-material prices. As proof of the instability of prices in my country, suffice it to say that in the first year of my administration, coffee exports produced $1.1 billion, whereas the same volume, in my last year, produced $700 million. The fluctuation of prices constitutes, no doubt, one of the most consistent threats to the economy of Latin America.

That we were right when we clamored for the urgent formulation of a new international policy I believe that by this time no one doubts. Events unhappily have proved us right. Now we see what we could have avoided if Operation Pan-America had found in this country enough receptivity for effective action at the right moment.

The thesis of Operation Pan-America—the need to develop for the survival of democracy—was not realized at the moment when it was proposed in the form of active cooperation and friendship implicit in the policies of your government and mine. I was

* Excerpts from a speech delivered by Kubitschek at Harvard University, on March 7, 1962.

frankly rather shocked when I saw that some United States policy-makers thought that democracy could survive among politically sensitized masses of people living in a state of privation and destitution.

When Operation Pan-America was proposed and defined, the potential crisis in all of Latin America had become widespread. However, the state of affairs in Cuba had not yet revealed itself. The trip made by your courageous ex-Vice President Richard Nixon was a surprise and a revelation for all of you. Operation Pan-America was timely and unpostponable. Later events caused your present chief of state to come around to giving greater and more favorable attention to the difficult and dramatic situation of our American family.

Operation Pan-America would have avoided many things, among which is the compound fracture in our continental relations manifest at the Conference of Punta del Este. I do not say this only now. When I was President of the Republic [of Brazil], I always advocated international unity in clear, definite terms. In a speech I made in 1960, one month before passing the keys of state to my successor, I said the following: "In spite of the insistent campaign of persuasion begun by Brazil, and other nations of our community, the great nations of the West have not taken into account the dramatic evidence of the facts, and continue to give only a minimum of attention to the problems of Latin America that are becoming more critical every day." I said further:

> In the face of an extensive worsening of social and economic conditions in Latin America, United States policy has been characterized up to now by a failure to face the deeper causes of unrest. We have no right to complain about the United States as a nation, but as friends and allies we do seek to examine the ministrations of the great republic of the north to a degree relative to the way she exerts leadership of a world cause with which we are solidly identified. I have no proxy to speak in the name of the other republics of the hemisphere. Each one of them knows best what to say. Nevertheless, in the name of democracy, I feel at liberty to say it is incomprehensible that the only natural allies upon whom the West can depend are looked upon with indifference by the highly developed nations. As I see it, proof of indifference to genuine hemispheric stability is the fact that no urgent attempt has been made to implement a coordinated program for the development of this hemisphere. Without a concerted economic effort, it will be impossible to im-

pede the disturbing forces that spread the Cold War over the continent. Latin America is on the brink of a dilemma. Either it industrializes, or it will give up on democracy. . . . Every day I am more convinced that the final and decisive fight for world domination will take place on this continent.

These words, addressed to all Brazilians on New Year's Eve, 1960, express my concern in clear terms.

Democracy is sustained by faith. The time is ripe to revive our faith and try to give it a new spirit. I have reason to affirm that today in our country there are fewer Communists than there were ten years ago. Nevertheless, it is important to recognize that the danger of Communism is greater now, because the Brazilian people—though they have always defended liberty . . . and, during the last war, were the only Latin American nation to send an expeditionary force to Europe to fight for democracy, without having had in itself any political or social outburst of a blood-letting character—are today determined to achieve economic development and obtain better living conditions at all costs.

Brazilians prefer to act peacefully, but if this way proves ineffective, rest assured that revolutionary methods will be adopted. I do not believe that a revolution would be started by the Communists, but they would be the winners in the end. Herein lies the real danger of Communism. The Latin American peoples may be forced to follow a revolutionary process in order to vanquish underdevelopment and misery, and those revolutions may end up Communist. Cuba is the living example of what might happen.

Latin America must be realistically considered as a battleground upon which we are engaged in a struggle to determine not only the fate of a region, but an entire way of life. Eradicate disease and stagnation in the different sections of our hemisphere, create wealth, nurture the well-being of the civilization we know—these shall be the all-redeeming acts.

May the United States hold on high the banner of the Alliance for Progress and be guided in its spirit. But that same banner had been unfurled in Latin America under the name of Operation Pan-America, whose prime motive was, in the defense of democracy, to consolidate for all time the freedom and unity of the American family. Let us, therefore, join hands and, with heart and mind ever fixed upon our common cause, resolutely press forward together, as indissoluble partners in democracy for peace and progress!

Selected Bibliography

Introduction

ALMOND, GABRIEL, and COLEMAN, JAMES S. *The Politics of the Developing Areas.* Princeton, N.J.: Princeton University Press, 1960.

DEAN, VERA MICHELES. *Builders of Emerging Nations.* New York: Holt, Rinehart and Winston, 1961.

——. *The Nature of the Non-Western World.* New York: New American Library of World Literature, 1957.

EMERSON, RUPERT. *From Empire to Nation.* Cambridge, Mass.: Harvard University Press, 1960.

KAUTSKY, JOHN H. (ed.). *Political Change in Underdeveloped Countries.* New York: John Wiley & Sons, 1962.

MILLIKAN, MAX F., and BLACKMER, DONALD L. M. (eds.). *The Emerging Nations.* Boston: Little, Brown & Co., 1961.

SETON-WATSON, HUGH. *Neither War nor Peace.* New York: Frederick A. Praeger, 1960. Revised paperback ed.; New York: Frederick A. Praeger, 1962.

WARD, BARBARA. *The Rich Nations and the Poor Nations.* New York: W. W. Norton & Company, 1962.

Part I: Asia

BRECHER, MICHAEL. *Nehru, A Political Biography.* London: Oxford University Press, 1959.

JACK, HOMER A. (ed.). *The Gandhi Reader.* Bloomington, Ind.: Indiana University Press, 1956.

MINTZ, JEANNE. *Indonesia, A Profile.* Princeton, N.J.: D. Van Nostrand Co., 1961.

TINKER, HUGH. *The Union of Burma.* (3rd ed.) London: Oxford University Press, 1961.

WARD, BARBARA. *India and the West.* New York: W. W. Norton & Company, 1961.

Part II: The Islamic World

CALLARD, KEITH. *Pakistan, A Political Study.* New York: The Macmillan Company, 1957.

FISHER, SIDNEY. *The Middle East, A History.* New York: Alfred A. Knopf, 1959.

LERNER, DANIEL. *The Passing of Traditional Society: Modernizing the Middle East.* Glencoe, Ill.: The Free Press, 1958.

VATIOKITIS, P. J. *The Egyptian Army in Politics.* Bloomington, Ind.: Indiana University Press, 1961.

WHEELOCK, KEITH. *Nasser's New Egypt.* New York: Frederick A. Praeger, 1960.

Part III: Africa

HEMPSTONE, SMITH. *Africa—Angry Young Giant.* New York: Frederick A. Praeger, 1961.

HODGKIN, THOMAS. *African Political Parties.* Baltimore, Md.: Penguin Books, 1961.

LEGUM, COLIN. *Pan-Africanism.* New York: Frederick A. Praeger, 1962.

SPIRO, HERBERT J. *Politics in Africa, Prospects South of the Sahara.* Englewood Cliffs, N.J.: Prentice-Hall, 1962.

WALLERSTEIN, IMMANUEL. *Africa, The Politics of Independence.* New York: Random House, 1961.

Part IV: Latin America

ADAMS, RICHARD N., *et al. Social Change in Latin America Today.* Council on Foreign Relations; New York: Harper & Brothers, 1960.

BLANKSTEN, GEORGE. "Political Groups in Latin America," *American Political Science Review,* LIII, No. 1 (March, 1959), 106–27; reprinted in Kautsky, John H., *Political Change in Underdeveloped Countries* (New York: John Wiley & Sons, 1962), pp. 140–66.

DAVIS, HAROLD E. *Latin American Social Thought Since Independence.* Washington, D.C.: University Press of Washington, D.C., 1961.

DRAPER, THEODORE. *Castro's Revolution: Myths and Realities.* New York: Frederick A. Praeger, 1962.

JOHNSON, JOHN J. *Political Change in Latin America: The Emergence of the Middle Sectors.* Stanford, Calif.: Stanford University Press, 1958.

MATTHEWS, HERBERT (ed.). *The United States and Latin America.* New York: The American Assembly, 1959.

MEYER, KARL E., and SZULC, TAD. *The Cuban Invasion.* New York: Frederick A. Praeger, 1962.

SILVERT, KALMAN. *The Conflict Society: Reaction and Revolution in Latin America.* New Orleans, La.: The Hauser Press, 1961.